Introduction to Educational Technology

Published by :
Lotus Press Publishers & Distributors

Introduction to Educational Technology

C.P. Singh

Lotus PRESS

4735/22, Prakash Deep Building
Ansari Road, Darya Ganj,
New Delhi - 110002

Lotus Press : Publishers & Distributors
Unit No. 220, 2nd Floor, 4735/22, Prakash Deep Building,
Ansari Road, Darya Ganj, New Delhi- 110002
Ph.: 41325510, 98118-38000
• E-mail : lotuspress1984@gmail.com
www.lotuspress.co.in

Introduction to Educational Technology

ISBN: 81-8382-024-7 (PB)

Printed & Published by : **Lotus Press Publishers & Distributors,** New Delhi-02

Preface

The book "Educational Technology" as a paper is being taught to B.Ed., M.Ed. and other E.T.T. students in Education courses syllabus in almost all the Indian Universities and Institutions. The various courses conducted by institutions at the Central and State level too have been considered in respect of their syllabus, course contents and requirements. The present book is designed to highlight the technology of Teaching and it will prove a dependable work of reference to teachers, teacher-trainers and teacher-trainees besides the researchers in the field.

Starting with Introduction to Educational Technology going on with teaching strategy; teaching methods; Micro teaching; presentation of lecture in class; Guiding principles :n Teaching; Developing interpersonal skill; Guiding and counselling Computer in Education Hardware and Softwere in teaching etc. have been dealt with keeping in view the requirements of the syllabus written in lucid and simple language; supported with examples from day to day life situation, the book comes out to renderfull help and proper guidance to the teacher trainees.

Publisher

CONTENT

❐

1

Introduction to Educational Technology

1. Introduction

Modern age is the age of science and technology. The world of today is very dynamic. The life of man in the primitive age was altogether different from his life in this sputnik age. There have been tremendous changes in the life style of human beings which may be attributed to the contribution of science and technology, science has extended the frontiers of our knowledge in various ways and directions. Science is considered to be a blessing to mankind. Nothing better has happened than the advent of science in man's life. The contribution of science and technology has been experienced in almost all the spheres of human life including education. The National Policy of Education 1986 has observed "Education Technology will be employed in the spread of useful information; the training and re-training of teachers, to improve the quality, sharpen awareness of art and culture, inclucate abiding values etc. both the formal and non-formal sections".

1.1 Meaning & Background

Before understanding the meaning of educational technology it is essential to know the meaning of technology. The word 'technology' has been taken from the Greek word (technikoes) which means an art and which is related with skill and dexterity. The term 'technology' implies the application of science to art. The concept of technology has developed during the last few years. It is a new area in the discipline of education. Educational technology is comprised of two words 'education' and 'technology'. When we apply the science of learning and communication to teaching we evolve a technology. There are three major factors that emphasize the linking of education with technology.

(i) Explosion of population.

(ii) Explosion of new knowledge.

(iii) Explosion of scientific and technological development.

Educational Technology is concerned with the development, application, and evaluation of system, techniques and aids to improve the process of human learning. It could be conceived as a science of techniques, methods and media by which educational goals could be realised. Generally the term "Technology" denotes the systematic application of the knowledge of science to practical tasks in industry. Hence, **"Educational Technology"** may be roughly defined as the systematic application of the knowledge of sciences to practical tasks in Education. It is not primarily concerned with the task of prescribing the goal although it does help in specifying the goals and translating them in behavioural terms. It is a communication process resulting from the adaptation of the scientific method to the behavioural science of teaching/ learning. Educational Technology widey accepted as the application of system approach in the systematic design of a learning system to bring about improvement in teaching-learning evaluation process.

Educational Technology not an end in itself but a means to accomplish some educational and instructional objectives already determined and clearly defined. It tries to make the whole teaching-learning process more and more meaningful for both the teachers and the learners. It modifies teacher's method of teaching and learner's behaviour for their own betterment and for the betterment of the mankind. It is not the same thing as instruction or education or learning but an aggressive invention which includes in itself every thing that helps in shaping personality of the learner.

Earlier the Concept of Educational Technology was used as a synonym to audio-visual aids like pictures, charts, maps, and models meant for direct teaching-learning. With the advent of physical science and electronic revolution there came an era of hardware and software like projectors, tape-recorders, radio and T.V. etc. Then came the age of mass media which led to massive communication revolution for instructional purposes. With the advent of programmed instruction and programmed learning, a new dimension of educational technology came into existence. It has individualized the process of education and introduced a system of self-learning in the form of self-instructional material and teaching machine. The concept of programmed learning added another dimensions to the meaning of educational technology when some new devices and approaches such as Micro-teaching.

In other words we can see one aspect of Educational Technology related to the use of specific techniques such as educational television, radio, programmed learning and other audio-visual aids. In another aspect, Education Technology is seen as the application of scientific and other organised knowledge to the practical problems of education. In the particular context of the developing countries, the emphasis is on the application of techinques and knowledge with a view to mobilising and optimising the available human as well as technological resources. Educational technology is seen both as a means as well as service to effect and facilitate better and more productive learning systems. It may be defined as a separate field in the theory of education dealing with the development and application of the use of educational resources.

Educational Technology should not be confused with teaching or instruction or education or learning or engineering but it should be taken as a sum total of all such aspects which go a long way in shaping the personality of the learner in a meaningful context.

It is neither technology in education nor technology of education but both and all pervasive which pervades the whole teaching-learning process to make it meaningful for the teacher who teaches and the learner who learns and modifies his behaviour for his own betterment and the betterment of mankind.

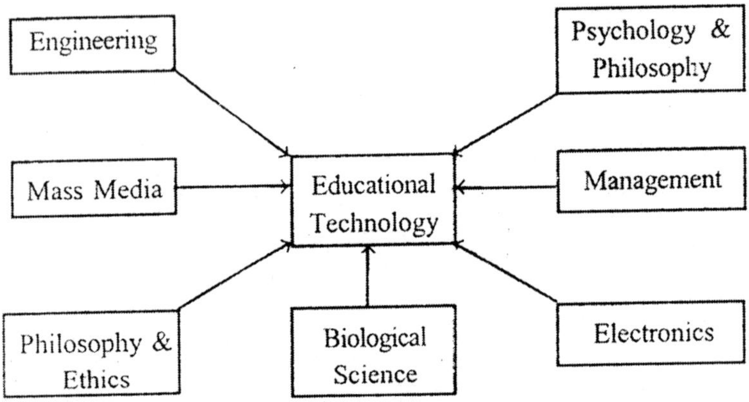

1.1 Educational Technology

1.2 Definitions of Educational Technology

(1) According to **G.O. Leith**, "Educational Technology is the application of scientific knowledge and learning and the conditions of learning to improve the effectiveness and efficiency of teaching and training."

(2) According to **Robert A. Cox**, "Educational Technology is the application of scientific process to man's leraning conditions."

(3) According to **John P. Dececco**, "Educational Technology is the form of detailed application of psychology of learning to practical teaching problems."

(4) According to **E.E. Hadden**, "Educational Technology is that branch of educational theory and practice concerned primarily with the design and use of messages which control the learning process."

(5) According to **S.S. Kulkarni,** "Educational Technology may be defined as the application of the laws as well as recent discoveries of science and technology to the process of education."

(6) According to **S.K. Mitra,** "Educational Technology can be conceived as a sicence of techniques and methods by which educational goals could be realized."

(7) According to **Richmond**, "Educational Technology is con-cerned to provide appropriately designed leraning situations which, holding in view of objectives of the Teaching of Training, being to bear the best means of instruction."

(8) According to **D.E.S. Working Party** (U.K.), "Educational Technology is the development, application and evaluation of systems, techniques and aids in the field of human learning."

(9) According to **Robert M. Gange** defined Educational Tech-nology as "The Development of a set of systematic techniques and accompanying practical knowledge for designing, testing and operating schools as educational systems."

1.3 Characteristics of Educational Technology

Characteristics of Educational Technology are as follows:

1. It is based on scientific and technological advancements.
2. It is more a practical discipline and less a theoritical one.
3. It is a fast growing modern discipline.
4. It brings pupils, teachers and technical means together in an effective way.
5. It makes use of the research findings of psychology, sociology, engineering, sciences and social psychology etc., and applies the same to the field of education.

6. It is the science of techniques and methods. It locates the problems in the field of education, remedies them and ultimately aims at improving the education system.

7. It is bound to improve the teacher, the learner and the teaching learning process.

1.4 Nature of Educational Technology

Educational Technology in its grater and wider sense, includes the entire process of setting of objectives, it deals with the systematic application of the resources of scientific knowledge to the process that each individual has to pass through in order to acquire and use knowledge according to National Council of ET (1974). ET is the Complement of curriculum reform concerned with the content, its basicly process of improving learning method. According G.O. Leith, "Educational Technology is the applicational scientific knowledge about learning and the conditions of learing to improve the effectiveness and efficiency of teaching and training". The Basic nature of ET is as follows:

1. The basis of educational technology is science and technical advancement.

2. Educational Technology studies the effect of science and technology upon education. In other words, science and technology are used under educational technology. Hence, it is the practical aspect of science.

3. Educational Technology is a continuous dynamic, progressive and effect-producing method.

4. New conceptions are prossible only due to educational technology such as programmed learning, micro-teaching, simulated teaching, interaction analysis, video-tape, tape-recorder, projector and computer, etc.

5. Educational Technology cannot solve each and every problem of education. It can be used successfully in teaching and instructional system only.

6. Audio-visual aids cannot be termed as educational technology. It is because its concern is only with the process-aspect of educational technology and not with the input and output aspects. But if these A.V. aids are used to achieve educational objectives, then it can be put in the category of Educational technology.

7. Programmed Instruction is also different from Educational Technology. Its main cause is that the student learns himself during the programmed instructions. It does not allow interaction between pupil and teacher. Hence, it can be used only for limited objectives and limited subject-matter. Therefore, programmed instruction is merely a part of educational technology.

8. Educational Technology accepts schools as a system. In this system, the school-building, furniture and teachers act as input while various methods, techniques, strategies and the teaching and examination with the help of audio-visual aids function in the form of a process. Lastly, the output is in of form of ability of the pupils.

9. Engineering Technology is not the educational technology because the engineering technology has manufactured radio, tape-recorder, video-tape and T.V., etc., which are used in teaching as audio-visual aids, but still engineering technology is different from educational technology. In education, it is accepted as hardware approach only.

10. Some people assume that educational technology will replace the teacher which will make the teacher unemployed one day. It is their mistake. Educational technology can never replace the teacher. It is because of three aspects of educational technology. These are—*(a)* Input, *(b)* Process and *(c)* Output. Input is the teacher's job and therefore, educational technology cannot snatch the place of a teacher. In spite of this, educational technology develops cognitive domain only and not the affective domain. Affective domain can only be developed when an interaction between teachers and pupils takes place. Hence, educational technology cannot replace the teacher.

1.5 General Objectives of Educational Technology

The objectives of Educational Technology at macro level or broad level are as under:

1. To identify educational needs of the community.
2. To achieve the aims of education.
3. To develop a suitable curriculum.
4. To determine appropriate strategies.
5. To suggest remedies to overcome the above traced out obstacles.
6. To manage the whole system of education.
7. To identify the resources—human and non-human.
8. To locate the major obstacles in the way of proper development of learners.

1.6 Specific Objectives

The objectives of educational technology at micro-level *i.e.*, in view of specific class-room teaching are as under:

1. To identify the educational needs of the pupils.
2. To determine the class-room objectives in behavioural terms.
3. To analyse the contents of instructions and organise them.
4. To evaluate class-room teaching in terms of students' performance.
5. To plan the teaching strategies.
6. To identify the resources—human and non-human.
7. To provide feedback to the teacher and the students for betterment of teaching-learning process.

Regarding objectives of Educational Technology, **Hilliard Joson** has given the following objectives:

1. Transmission of Information.
2. Serving as role model.
3. Contribution to the provision of feedback.
4. Assisting the practice of specific skills.

1.7 Main Objectives of Educational Technology

1. To help in the environment of facilities required in the teaching learning process.
2. To make the class-room teaching more effective.
3. To improve and update the methods of leraning.
4. To modify the behaviour of the teacher and the learner.

TECHNOLOGIZING EDUCATION IS TO OPTIMIZE LEARNING ENDEAVOURS

In Educational Technology, both hardware and software mechanisms are involved. Garrison (1989), opines "technology will be viewed here as having both a process (software) and a product (hardware) component, where process is the creative application of knowledge of purposeful activities. A subset of hardware is media, where media are the devices used to distribute information."

In Educational Technology, hardware covers TV, Computer, Overhead projector, Tape Recorder, Teaching machines etc. Software includes audio/video cassettes, Filmstrips, micro films, slides etc.

Educational Technology is comprehensive. It is associated with all aspects of educative process-methods, teaching strategies, learning materials, handling of various equipment etc.

1.8 Components of Educational Technology

The following 4 M's are the major components of Educational Technology:

(i) Methods, (ii) Materials, (iii) Media, (iv) Manpower.

(i) Methods. It is concerned with the devices such as Programmed Learning Team Teaching, Micro Teaching, Personalized System of Instruction in Teaching Learning situations.

(ii) Materials. Instructional materials such as Programmed Text-book. The material of this type may be handwritten or printed.

(iii) Media. The media used here are audio, or visual or audio-visual. A few examples are—radio, tape recorder, charts, films, educational television etc.

(iv) Man Power. Man power controls educational technology in every way. Educational Technology without man is zero.

1.9 Scope of Educational Technology

By scope of educational technology we mean the jurisdiction, the limits or the bounderies within which it works. It needs demarcation of the boundaries within which the process of education can go on. Being a fast growing modern discipline it is almost practical all through and is expanding with a tremendous speed, aiming at all-round development in the area of education.

National Policy on Education (1986), recommends that, "Educational Technology will be employed in the spread of useful, information, the training and retraining of teachers, to improve quality, sharpen awareness of art and culture, inculcate abiding values etc., both in the formal and non-formal sectors. Maximum use will be made of the available infrastructure."

The scope of Educational Technology can be assessed from the following points:

Educational Technology

↓

Objectives

↓

Teaching Learning Material

↓

Teaching Learning Process

↓

Teaching Learning Strategies

↓

Improvement

Educational Technology

↓

Development Curriculum

↓

Audio Visual Aids

↓

Hardware and Software

↓

Feed back

↓

Sub-System of Education

1. **Determination of Objectives.** Educational Technology provides different methods and techniques for writing instructional objectives in behavioural terms such as Bloom Taxonomy Magar's Approach and RCEM Approach.

   The needs and requirements of the people and hence education need be revised from moment to moment. Educational technology helps in fixing-up the right objectives in the light of the changed circumstances and changed environment.

2. **Development of Teaching Learning Material.** Teaching learning materials are also as important as anything else in the teaching learning process. In this

age of science and technology, the materials of teaching can not be unscientific. Everything of the society including values of life need be reflected in the materials. Only right type of material will be able to modify the behaviour of the learner suitably making him a fit person for the society.

3. **Improvement in Teaching Learning Process.** It helps in improving the teaching learning process and makes it more purposive. It tries to discuss the concept of teaching, analysis of teaching process, variables of teaching, phases and levels of teaching, principles of teaching, maxims of teaching and relationship between teaching and learning.

4. **Development of Teaching Learning Strategies.** A strategy plays an important role in the hands of a teacher in every learning situation. The strategy has to be the right one which should be according to the materials and is able to bring about effective teaching-learning. The differnt strategies are being evolved by educational technology. The knowledge of those strategies is a must for every teacher. Then only the teacher will be able to do justice to their jobs.

   It tries to describe the ways and means of discovering selecting and developing suitable startegies and tactics of teaching in terms of optimum learning and available teaching-learning resources; the availablity of the different types of teching methods, devices and models of teaching—their appropriate selection and use—for the optimum results.

5. **Improvement in Teaching Training.** The change of environment with new curriculum and new materials need be handled by the teachers. The teachers equipped with old strategies and methodologies of teaching will remain misfits. Right type of training to the teachers is the need of the hour. Educational Technology can render its

valuable help in the training of teachers also. The use of video tapes and close circuit T.V. will help the teachers to remodel and reshape their teaching behaviours suitably.

It includes micro teaching, simulated teaching, term-teaching, teacher effectiveness, modification of teacher-behaviour, class-room interaction and interaction analysis, etc.

6. **Development of Curriculum.** Educational Technology is concerned with the designing of a suitable curriculum for the achievment of the desired objectives. It is helpful in describing the ways and means of the selection of suitable learning experiences, organisation of the contents in a suitable framework in order to bring better results. It provides the scientific foundation to education as well as develops theories of teaching and learning.

7. **Proper Use of Audio Visual Aids.** Audio Visual aids have always played an important role in the teaching-learning process. They need be used according to the times. The software aids, the hardware aids, the computer and other such appliances, equipment etc., have to be used in the present type of teaching-learning environment. Computer assisted instructions will help the learner as well as the teacher to achieve the goals of education more conveniently/effectively.

8. **Utilization of the Sub-System of Education.** Educational Technology considers education as a system operating in a systematic and scientific way for the achievement of educational objectives. For the coverage of its systematic approach, it tries to include the topics dealing with the theory and principles of a system approach, explaining education as a system, its different sub-systems in terms of input and output. It is helpful in solving scientifically educational administrative problems with the help of system analysis.

9. **Provides Feedback.** It provides an appropriate feedback to the learners as well as teachers for bringing necessary improvement at the preparatory and implementation stages of their specific acts. For this purpose, educational technology discusses the ways and means of suitable evaluation techniques, their planning, development selection and appropriate use in relation to the objectives of teaching-learning system.

10. **Proper Use of Hardware and Software.** These days hardware and software are playing an effective role in the attainment of educational objectives. Educational Technology helps in the proper use of these aids. It tries to describe these resources in terms of their specific functions, their solution, proper handling and maintenance.

    In this way Educational Technology is concerned with all those who are connected in any way, directly or indirectly, to the processes and products of education. It teaches the teachers the art of teaching, the learners the science of learning the educational planners the structure of planning and administrators or managers the skill of managing or administering the task of teaching and learning. It works for the individualization of instructions as well for improving the group dynamics of the class-room.

Therefore, in any way, the scope of the educational technology should not be confined to the limited boundaries, but it should be left free for the necessary expansion and development for carrying out its mission, tasks and objectives.

1.10 Functions of Educational Technology

There are a variety of ways in which computers and communications technology can provide educational services. In some cases, different types of applications will require different technologies; in other cases, the same type of technology can be used to provide different types of services.

(i) Passive Instruction. The oldest instructional use of information technology is simply to present information. The textbook is the traditional passive instructional system. Projection media—slides. filmstrips, overhead transparencies, and pictures—are more modern forms. Educational radio and television have experienced quiet but steady growth since the late 1950's and early 1960's. Video cassettes and video disks will provide even more flexible tools for presenting video-based instructional material. The best known recent examples of passive instructional programming are the "**Sesame Street**" and "**Electric Company**" programmes produced by the Children's Television Workshop with partial Federal support. These programmes were intended to supplement, not replace, normal schooling. Sesame Street is intended to teach pre-school children somebasic concepts and learning attitudes. Electric Company is principally aimed at supplementing reading instruction at the grammar school level.

At the other extreme, a full alternative to traditional education is the "Open University" in Britain, which has conducted a full college degree programme for over 11 years, based principally on passive instruction using the broadcast networks. In the United States, the Corporation for Public Broadcasting is developing an educational programme along similar lines in cooperation with universities across the country. New technology for video production is also having an impact on educational uses. Computer animation systems have become considerably less expensive than older, hand animation techniques. Video processing uses computers to perform elaborate modification of video images. Both of these technologies are widely used in commercial television and motion pictures, but they are also particularly attractive for instructional application in which concepts and processes that are subtle and difficult to visualize need to be illustrated. Complex physical processes, such as fluid flow or load stresses on structures such as bridges, can be simultated on a computer and displayed as dynamic graphic images. In addition, video cassette recorders (VCRs) and video disks promise to relieve students from the dictates of schedule. The VCR, in particular, allows-copyright-law permitting-instructors, and students to copy instructional programmes off the air and play them back at some later time. Video cassettes and video disks will provide alternate mode of broadcasting for the distribution of instructional material.

Passive instruction systems have the following characteristics:

(A) All educational decisions are in the hands of the providers; what information is to be presented, for how long, in what sequence, and even-in the case of such current instructional broadcasting—the schedule when it is shown.

(B) The boundaries between entertainment, public information, and educational services can become blurred. A shakespeare play, a concert, or an informational series such as the successful Cosmos series carried by the Public Broadcasting System, may all the considered important instructional resources as well as entertainment.

(ii) Interactive Instruction. This technology is used to teach a specific subject or skill directly to a sudent, guiding the learner through a sequence of steps involving the presentation of information, drills and exercises designed by an instructor. Interactive instructional systems require the student to communicate with the device, allowing the system to vary the pace of instruction, select among alternate sequences of presentation, test for understanding, and alter the content according to the specific needs of the individual.

Computer-assisted instruction is the best known interactive technology. A student sitting at a computer terminal works through a series of "frames" that teach and test understanding. If the student is progressing slowly, the computer branches to an alternate style of presentation or a remedial section. If the student has mastered that section the computer jumps ahead to more advanced material. The Plato system was one of the better known experiments. It was developed by researchers at the University of Illinois and Control Data Crop. With principal funding from the Federal Government, the system originally combined a new type of interactive graphics terminal with a large multiterminal computer system and an elaborate language specifically designed to create instructional programmes. While Plato was originally a very expensive experimental system, most of its underlying concepts survive in commercial instructional systems now marketed by Control Data.

Four factors have more recently revived interest in interactive instruction:

(1) the rapidly declining costs of computers and the advent of the desktop computer,

(2) the escalating labour-intensive costs of traditionat schooling,

(3) the development of alternative delivery mechanisms that link the computer with other technologies, such as video disk and interactive cable, and

(4) an improved understanding of how to create instructional packages.

The video disk is good example of how new technologies can be combined to form instructional systems. The video disk contains an extensive data base of text, still images, and film. The computer controls the sequence of presentation and, using an educational programme contained on its floppy disk and information stored in the remote data base, interacts with the student. The video disk, for example, might contain several thousand images of microscope slides. The data base would have full descriptive information on the subjects illustrated by the slides, indexed in various ways. Educational software on the computer would take a student through sequences of slides and text presentation, providing information and administering tests. While the computer programme would be designed to achieve a specific instructional purpose, the slide catalog and data base would be intended to be more widely applicable for research and education.

Several experiments are under way to develop instructional packages using combinations of video disks and personal computers. The Minnesota Educational Computing Consortium is developing a series of video disks in basic economics. The first disk of a planned 6-disk series has been produced and tried in the classroom with favourable results." Other companies are developing products aimed at the industrial training market; and a few firms, such as IBM, are already using interactive video disks for employee training.

Interactive instructional technology has the following characteristics:

(1) It allows the system to customize teaching to the particular level of understanding learning style, and ability of each individual student.

(2) The system can be designed so that students can pace themselves.

(3) Because individualization and self-pacing may not fit well with traditional schooling, large-scale implementation of inter-active instructional technology in the schools may engender substantial institutional resistance.

(4) Instructional software is often divided into discrete packages, each designed to teach a specific skill or item of information. An instructional curriculum (say, a fifth grade mathematics course) is a collection of these packages, which, for a full course, may number into the hundreds.

(5) Because they are so carefully tailored, interactive curricular packages are inflexible. They are not generally

useful for any purpose, clientele, or environment other than the specific one for which they were designed.

(6) Extensive design effort is needed to create each module. The material to be taught must be broken down into framesized pieces. Tests of understanding must be devised, and the paths that students are most likely to take in going through the material must be anticipated.

(7) Some experts suggest that smaller instructional modules can be designed to fit into the regular course of instruction, permitting a gradual introduction of educational technology. Others maintain that the principal educational benefits of technology are lost with such an incremental approach.

(8) The skills required both to produce software and to assist students with its use are substantially different from traditional teaching skills.

(iii) Learning Environments. The interactive instruction technology described above can be used to create a special environment—a language, simulation, or data base—that can be manipulated by the student. For example, special computer languages, such as LOGO, can help learners gain particular problem-solving skills. Languages such as VISICALC, a system designed for business users of small computers, can be a powerful tool in teaching accounting principles and financial planning techniques.

Another form of learning environment is the simulation. A simulation of a laboratory experiment for a physics course, for instance, might present on a television screen a variety of weights and springs. The student would be allowed to "connect" them in various configurations, to apply forces of prescribed amounts at different points in the arrangement and to measure and record the results. Working with this system for only a few days, a student would learn some basic principles of mechanics. As another example, large-scale simulations can be made of physical processes or of equipment that might be too expansive or dangerous to use in person. Simulated nuclear powerplants provide vehicles, for training new operators; simulated aircraft are used for pilot training. For medical education, computer-controlled robots can be used to simulate injured or ill human beings. A small computer presents the student with an instructional sequence where proper techniques are illustrated using a computer-controlled video disk. The student then practices on a dummy equipped with sensors monitored by the computer, which in turn, presents the results to the student.

Using information technology to provide a learning environment has several implications:

(a) An instructional programme can be applicable over longer course periods and for a greater variety of educational uses than can an interactive module that concentrates on a single teaching unit.

(b) Since the interaction is so flexible and is directed in large part by the students, instructors and student need documentation and supplemental curriculum materials appropriate for using the system to meet their particular educational objectives. Except for large simulations (such as flight trainers) that may require special hardware, the principal cost of "learning environment" applications will be in developing these supplemental curricular materials. Developmental costs for the programmes will, in general, be written off against a much larger customer base.

(c) As it fundamentally changes both content and the way material is presented, use of an automated learning environment may require extensive changes in course content or even a broader redesign of an entire curriculum.

(iv) Information Resource. General information literacy is needed for all individuals to work and to participate fully in an information society. In addition, for most professions, specialized computer and communication-based systems are rapidly becoming indispensable tools of the trade. Students must learn how to use these services as part of their early training.

For these reasons, in addition to being an instructional tool, the computer in education is viewed as an intellectual and problem-solving resource, akin to the library or laboratory. Information services will need to be both broad enough to support general education and specialized enough for particular subject matter. Examples of specialized systems include computer-aided design systems for industrial engineering students, on-line legal or medical information retrieval systems for use by law students or doctors, and automated accounting and financial analysis systems for business students. In addition to these specialized resources, students in all fields will need constant access to information services and computer facilities for their work. One engineering school is experimenting with providing a desktop computer to some of its entering freshmen, with a view toward giving computers to all students in the future. A graduate school of business has already adopted a similar policy for its entering students. The leader of the movement to provide all undergraduate students with computer access has been Dartmouth College, which, for well over a decade, has operated with a policy of universal computer literacy and free student access to computer terminals. The role of the computer as an educational resource on campus is blending with the view of libraries as automated information centres. Many college and university libraries have been among the leaders in this movement-first in automating their management, then in providing users access to computerized bibliographic services. Their ultimate goal is to provide full text, on line retrieval. As these trends continue, the computer center and the library will actually merge into a single automated information utility.

(v) Distribution of Education. The distribution of services to those who need them has always been a difficult problem, for the educational system for as long as education has been provided by schools, the distribution problem has been responsible for institutional constraints of both time and location on the student. That schooling takes place on a physical campus, attended principally by young people, may be more reflective of the limitations of the traditional schooling system than it is or the current needs of society for education.

Information technology is a tool that can address these to distributional problems-distance and time. In the past, television and radio have been used for this purpose, often to good effect. However their applicability has been limited both by the need to use expensive and scarce broadcast facilities to serve a relatively small clientele and by the inhability to provide interactive services.

Modern technology removes these barriers. Communication facilities such as cable, direct broadcast sattellite, lowpower television, and video cassette and video disk will greatly increase the number of information channels coming into the home and office. Two way cable, remote conferencing facilities, and optical video disk microcomputer systems provide the capability for interactive education.

Among the particular applications of information technology for distribution are the following:

(1) **General Educational Services to Dispersed Populations.** Some geographical regions need to provide schooling to a sparse population spread over a large area. Communication technology such as direct broadcast satellite or low power television allows educational programming to be broadcast at low cost to small rural communities and even to individual residences. Vedio cassettes, video disks, and personal computer programmes can be distributed physically by mail.

(2) **Specialized Educational Services to Small Populations.** Some groups in society that have very specialized needs for educational services are not concentrated geographi-

cally. Only by providing courses regionally or nationally can a critical mass of students be assembled to justify the expense of the course. Information systems provide that wider market. For example:

(a) Advanced professional training, especially continuing education in such fields as medicine, law, and engineering, in which knowledge advances at a rapid rate.

(b) Unusual educational needs, such as accelerated science programmes for the gifted or courses conducted in a foreign language.

(c) Instruction in subjects for which experienced teachers are scarce or courses conducted by outstanding scholars and leaders in a field.

(3) **Education for the Homebound.** For a number of reasons—*e.g.*, illness physical handicap, or age—many individuals in society cannot travel physically to attend a class. Information technology can provide educational services directly to the home, hospital, or workplace.

(4) **Job-related Education and Training in the Work-place.** There are a number of barriers to workers who wish to take job-related instruction. Attending regular classes is difficult due to competing demands on their time, travel to a campus may be burdensome, and there is reluctance on the part of some order individuals to sit in a classroom and compete with younger students. Information technology, by bringing the course to the workplace, can remove some of these constraints.

(vi) Testing and Diagnosis. Computers have been used for some time to grade and analyze the results of college admission exams, intelligence tests, and a variety of psychometric examinations designed to explore the values, attitudes, and thinking patterns of individuals. Educa-tional testing can be thought of as having four basic roles:

(a) **Strategic.** Testing helps assess a student's general levels of understanding and learning strategies. It is used to determine what classes and courses of study a student should pursue, and what instructional approaches would be most effective for him.

(b) **Certification.** Testing plays an important role in certifying the knowledge and skill of individuals, qualifying them to pursue professions such as medicine or law, or attesting that they have progressed along certain educational or training paths.

(c) **Tactical.** Testing also takes place during instructional sequences to determine how the student is progressing through the course and to detect and diagnose difficulties the student might be having.

(d) **Gatekeeping.** Testing plays an increasingly important role in supporting decisions to institutions and to programmes of study. It is a basis for allocating scarce resures (*e.g.* admission to a prestigious college or university) and for the granting of licenses to practice professions.

Modern information technology will likely have several effects on testing:

(a) Automated teaching systems depend on continual testing and evaluation to direct the presentation of material.

(b) Continual testing of students progress and levels of understanding is an important pedagogical tool, even in a non-automated teaching environment. However it is very demanding of a teacher's time. Automated systems will allow much closer monitoring of student and class progress in a normal classroom environment.

(c) Automated instruction may lead to a decoupling of instruction from institutions—in the sense that a student moves freely between home, job, and school for course work. This trend will create greater need for strategic testing to determine appropriate instructional programmes for students.

(d) The accelerating growth of knowledge is pressuring professions such as medicine, law, and engineering to require retraining and periodic renewal of certifications.

(e) Institutional decoupling will also require more testing for purposes of certification. Traditionally, an engineering degree was obtained by following a course of study at one department. Certification was the degree earned by successfully completing the programme.

(f) If traditional forms of education become increasingly extensive and, hence scarce, gatekeeping requirements. will inevitably continue to grow in importance. The current competition for entry into medical school illustrates this trend.

(g) On the other hand, automated learning systems may make certain types of education and training far more accessible and affordable. If that occurs, gatekeeping may take place not on entry to the education programme, but in licensing to practice.

1.11 Forms of Educational Technology

The scientific, inventions and technological developments have influenced every walk of human life. There is rapid mechanization in the field of industries, defence, trade, administration, etc. The educational process does not remain untouched by these advances. It has necessitated introduction of technology in the field of education.

Hence Educational Technology came with its various forms which are as under:

Forms of Educational Technology

↓

Teaching Technology

↓

Instructional Technology

↓

Behavioural Technology

↓

Instructional design Technology

Teaching is purposeful activity. The ultimate goal of teaching is to bring allround development of a child. The knowledge and practice which help in realizing the goal is the content matter of teaching technology.

Teaching is an art as well as science because teaching can be studied objectively and scientifically. Teaching has the scientific foundation. This has evolved the concept of '**Teaching Technology**.'

Teaching technology is the application of philosophical, sociological and scientific knowledge to teaching for achieving some specific learning objectivies.

I.K. Davies, N.L. Gange, Robert Gange, Burner and Robert Glaser have contributed significantly in this area of education. Silverman has termed it as constructive educational technology.

1.12 Assumptions of Teaching Technology

'Technology of Teaching' is based on the following assumptions:

1. Teaching is a scientific process and it has two major components: Content and communication.
2. The teaching activities can be modified and improved.
3. A close relationship may be established between teaching and learning.

4. Teaching skills can be developed with the help of feedback devices.

5. The learning objectives may be achieved by performing teaching activities.

K. Davies and Robert Glaser (1962), have developed the content of Technology of Teaching and classified it into four elements:

1. Planning of Teaching,

2. Organization of Teaching,

3. Controlling of Teaching,

4. Leading of Teaching.

Main Features of Teaching Technology

1. All the three types of objectives: cognitive, affective and psychomotor can be achieved by this technology.

2. The philosophical, sociological and scientific knowledge can be applied to teaching process.

3. The teaching process can be made effective with the help of Teaching Technology.

4. The teaching can be organized from memory level to reflective level.

5. Teaching technology implies the input, process and output aspects side by side.

6. The teaching theories can be formulated by the use of teaching technology.

7. The pupil-teachers and in-service teachers can improve their teaching and make it more purposive.

8. The content structure can be related to communication structure for achieving the learning objectives.

1.13 Instructional Technology

The instruction has significant role in human learning. The systematic actions which induce learning is known as instruction. The instruction stands for development of knowledge and beliefs. Instructional technology means a net work of techniques or devices employed to accomplish certain defined set of learning objectives. It implies the application of psychological and scientific principles and knowledge to instruction for achieving the specific objectives of learning.

The origin of instructional technology is from psychological laboratory experiments. The most important example of instructional technology is 'programmed instruction'. The programmed instruction and instructional technology can be used interchangeably.

(i) Assumptions of Instructional Technology

The instructional technology involves the following assumptions:

1. Reinforcement can be provided continuously by the use of instruction.
2. The content matter can be divided into its elements and each element can be presented independently.
3. The external learning conditions can be created by arranging the elements in a logical sequence.
4. The student can learn according to his needs and rate of learning.
5. The student can learn successfully with out the physical presence of a teacher.
6. The strategies and tactics of instruction can be used for achieving certain well defined set of instructional objectives.

(ii) Characteristics of Instructional Technology

1. The cognitive objective can be achieved successfully by the use of Instructional Technology.
2. Reinforcement is provided with the help of right responses.
3. Individual differences are taken care of in his technology.
4. It makes use of the psychological learning theories and principles.
5. It provides deep insight into the content structure.
6. The students can learn at their own pace.

1.14 Behavioural Technology

Psychology is the science of behaviour. It studies the nature and structure of behaviour of the organisms. The learning is the modification of behaviour through activities and experiences. The educational activities are designed to bring desirable changes in the behaviour of the students. The psychology deals with every type of human behaviour. Thus, the behavioural technology has wider scope. It covers the area of industry, defence, commerce, communication, administration, health, motivation, training education, teaching and instruction.

The teaching and instruction activities are organised to achieve sepcific learning objectives by bringing desirable behavioural change among the students. Thus, teaching and instructional technology are two forms of behavioural technology. But in the field of education it refers mainly to the teacher behaviour. The behavioural technology is the application of scientific knowledge in modifying the teacher behaviour. Thus it is also termed as **'Training Technology'**.

(i) Assumptions of Behavioural Technology

The behavioural technology is based on the following assumptions:

1. Teacher behaviour is observable.
2. Teacher behaviour is measruable and quantifiable.
3. Teacher behaviour is relative.
4. Teacher behaviour is modifiable.
5. Teacher behaviour is social and psychological.

(ii) Characteristics of Behavioural Technology

1. The specific teaching skills can be developed.
2. It helps in developing the theory of teaching.
3. The achievement of teaching can be evaluated objectively and in a systematic manner.
4. The individual differences of pupils and teacher can be tackled.
5. Feedback devices can be used for the improvement of communication skills.
6. The knowledge and practice of behavioural technology may be an important instrument for training colleges to produce effective teachers.
7. In it mechanism of feedback devices for modification of teacher behaviour are also employed for developing teaching skills.
8. In class-room, behaviour technology concentrates on elements of behaviour.
9. In behavioural technology the theory and practice of class-room teacher behaviour are included.

1.15 Approaches of Educational Technology

Approaches of Educational Technology are as follows:

I. Hardware Approach. Hardware Approach has physical science and applied engineering as its basis. They have mechanised the whole teaching-learning process. There is even reduction in the cost of education. Educational Technology that way, has almost revolutionised the total teaching-learning. The new mechanism of teaching-learning with improved technology as its basis is suggesting innumerable new ways of doing things to the class-room teachers. A good many gadgets of teaching-learning find their place in the class-room situations and many more of that type are expected to enter into the class-rooms in the near future. The job and the duties of the teacher are likely to have multi-faceted changes.

As a result of Hardware technology, electro-mechanical equipments have been developed which are used for instructional pruposes. In the overcrowded class-room, the teacher uses microphones for making his voice fully audible to the learners. Radio, T.V., tape recorder, epidiascope, projector, closed circuit television (C.C.T.V.), teaching machines, computers are used for teaching the students. Silverman (1968), called this type of educational technology 'Relative Technology'. According to Marilym Nickson (1971), educational technology deals with the application of many fields of science to the educational needs of the individual as well as of society.

Davis (1971), thinks that the hardware approach is based on the application of physical science to the education and training system which mechanizes the process of teaching gradually so that teachers would be able to deal with more students, resulting in less cost and economy in finances.

Hardware approach, undoubtedly, is bound to work wonders in the area of education. It has a few draw-backs which are given below:

(a) Hardware material, equipment were devised by science for use in science but now they have been borrowed from there and are being used in education.

(b) While operating in the field of education, it works in isolation and not as an integral part of that system where it existed earlier.

II. Software Approach. In software approach, the basis of all thinking and working is behavioural science and psychology of learning. The scholar can exploit psychology of learning to any extent to attain the different objectives. With every new thinking he can evolve something new for teaching purposes. The teacher with added knowledge of software approach can use the films, flash-cards, tapes etc., for various purposes. There is not end to his thinking. Decidely he can plan better teaching which results into better learning.

Software approach uses the principles of psychology for the purpose of behaviour modification. In this connection, **Davis** (1971), observes, "This view of educational technology is closely associated with the modern principles of programmed learning and is characterised by task analysis, wirting precise objectives, selection of appropriate learning strategies, reinforcement of correct responses and constant educ^tion."

Silverman (1968), termed this educational technology as 'constructive educational technology.'

Both software and hardware approaches are so interlinked that they cannot be sparated from each other. One without the other is incomplete. It is software approach which makes the hardware approach function well. Mitchell (1973), writes, "By directing attention to the achievement of educational aims of standards through knowledge and control relation between inputs in man-machine systems and organisations, educational technology can be expected to make more contributions to behavioural science than science has made to educational technology."

III. System Approach. This new technology has influenced the educational administration and organisation to a great extent. This is the modren approach. It acts as a link between hardware and software approach. It is also known as 'Management Technology'. It has brought to educational management a scientific approach for solving educational administrative problems.

It is essentially a new management approach, influencing management decisions in business, industry and education. Education is regard as a system and system approach is a systematic way of designing an effective and economical educational system.

System is defined in the dictionary as "an assemblage of objects united by some form of regular interaction or inter-dependence; as organic or organised whole as the solar system or a new telegraph system". System may be divided into three broad categories. For instance, there are natural systems as solar system; there are systems which have been designed by man as telegraph system and lastly, there are systems which are combinations of natural and man-made systems like hydro-electric plants or modern dairies.

(A) Aspects of System Approach

System approach has three major aspects:

(1) Input

(2) Output

(3) Process

Input. It involves the entering behaviour of the learner.

(1) It involves previous achievements, abilities of student and level of motivation.

(2) It concerns with the comprehension level of the learner.

(3) It includes the skill of teaching and awareness of teaching and training methods.

(4) It considers availability and skill for teaching aids.

(B) Teaching Learning Process. It involves the means and devices of learning experiences.

(1) To generate situation for presenting the subject-matter systematically.

(2) To select and use appropriate teaching strategies and tactics for desired learning structures.

(3) To employ appropriate teaching aids for desired behavioural change.

(4) To ideantify and use suitable communication techniques for the comprehension of the subject-matter.

(5) To use suitable schedules of reinforcement for effective learning.

(6) To establish rapport with students for effective teaching.

(7) To evolve appropriate school environment by developing good relations among students.

Output. It includes mainly the terminal behaviour of the learner.

(1) To identify the characteristics of content.

(2) To clarify the objectives achieved through are content.

(3) To analyse the stimuli.

(4) To determine the characteristics of students' desired activities.

(C) Advantages of System Approach

(1) It provides conceptual framework to build plans for implementing change for education.

(2) It helps to identify the suitability of the resource material to achieve the specifc goal.

(3) It helps to assess the resource needs, their sources and facilities in relation to quantities, time and other factors.

(4) Technological advance could be used to provide integration of machines, media and people for attaining the defined goals.

(5) It permits an orderly introduction of components demonstrated to be required for systems success in terms of student learning.

1.16 Devices of Teaching

A device is not the same thing as a method of teaching. A method is an orderly and systematised arrangement of the material of instruction, keeping in view the way in which it would produce the best effect on the pupil's mind. A device, on the other hand, is just a tool of the trade. It is a contrivance which enables the teacher to succeed in his efforts, when he is actually on the job. A teacher may arrange the subject-matter in various ways and, thus, use different methods. He may use the concentric method of teaching History or the experimental method of teaching Science. But for gaining success in the use of these methods, the teacher must make use of certain external forms or modes or materials. For example, he may use a film projector, a chart, a map or a model in the teaching of social studies. He may narrate an incident or ask a question or dramatise an event in the teaching of language and literature. Such external modes or forms, like dramatisation, illustration and exposition etc. do not imply any orderly or systematic arrangement of subject matter They are merely devices, which the teacher uses to his best advantage, form time to time for fostering the development of knowledge and attitudes among his pupils.

(i) Types or Devices

Teaching devices are basicly of two types:

(1) Artificial Devices, which give learning through indirect experience. These devices consist of oral communication through narration, exposition, explanation and description etc.

(2) Natural Devices which give learning through direct experience. *e.g.* School excursions and field trips, visits to museums, hikes etc.

(3) Fixing Devices. In addition to the above two types of teaching devices, there are also fixing devices, such as drill, review or revision and recapitulation. These Devices help in fixing the impresssions and are, therefore, very important. Nc learning, worth the name, takes place until the knowledge imparted, is thoroughly understood and fixed. Hence the importance of repetition and practice.

(4) Audio-visual Aid, like film-strip, gramophone, tape-recorder etc.

(ii) Important Devices of Teaching

Below we discuss briefly some very important devices of teaching, which must be profitably made use of by all teachers, in their daily lessons.

(A) Narration. Narration is story-telling or giving accounts of events to others. It is one of the most important means of communicating knowledge from one person to another. In subject like social studies, history, descriptive geography and literature, narration can be used as one of the most effective devices of teaching. Children love stories. It, therefore, pays the teacher a lot, if he or she is a good storyteller. Narration, in fact, is one of the most useful skills which must be possesed by all those persons who intend to become successful teachers.

In the words of Panton, "Narration is an art in itself which aims at presenting to the pupils, through the medium of speech, a clear vivd, interesting and ordered sequence of events, in such a way that their minds reconstruct those happenings and they live in imagination through the experiences recounted, either as spectators or possibly as participators"

A good teacher can develcp his powers of narration by observing the work of other good narrators, by reading children's books of successful writers and by practising story-telling. He should keep in mind the following points, if he wants to achieve real success in the use of this effective device:

(1) He should himself feel the story or the event and take genuine interest in it. His narration will then be inspirational and interesting for his students and he will definitely achieve the purpose in view.

(2) He should come prepared for the narration. Off hand narration is neither interesting nor effective. If prepared before hand, it will be narrated is an orderly manner and hence effective.

(3) Narration must be suited to the audience. Interests of particular age-groups should always be kept in view, while selecting a story or event for narration.

(4) A clear-cut aim should always be kept-in view. I will give due effect to the entire activity. Mere enjoyment must not be the sole aim of narration. The narration must-develop the pupils' imagination and taste.

(5) Children are more interested in action than mere description. It is therefore, that there must always be some action in one's narration. Narration can be made more interesting if the teacher, sometimes, takes the role of the main character in the event or the story and then delivers his speech in the direct from of narration.

(6) A skilful use of language and speech should be made in narration. The language used, should be appropriate to the situations and events depicted, as well as to the mental level of the children.

(7) The story or the event should not be read out from a book or a magazine or a newspaper. It should always be narrated in one's own words in a natural tone and in a pleasant manner.

(8) The teacher should also make an effective use of humour in his narration. Catchy words and phrases in humourous and pleasing tone add a lot of charm and interest to narration.

(B) Description. Description is "the act of representing a thing by words." In other words, description means portrayal of a person, thing or event in words. Thus there is not much difference between narration and description. While narration deals with some story or event, decription aims at narrating something about a lifeless thing or an object on a person or a problem. Thus description requires much move imaginative power than narration. It involves a good use of language and speech. It is a device which is needed in lesson of all school subjects, especially in the lessons of social studies and general science. The following points should be rememeberd in the use of this device:

(1) Description should be simple and meaningful. It should always be clear and vivid to serve its purpose.

(2) Since description requires strong imaginative power. It is essential that the teacher must possess a clear image of the object. It is better if he has actually seen the real source or object, connected with the lesson in hand.

(3) Mere word-pictures are not enough. Models, pictures, charts and other illustrations should also be used on proper occasions, to make the description effective and interesting.

(4) Description should not contain many details, otherwise it will baffle the imagination of pupils. It should be as brief as possible and its important points should be repeated and stressed.

(C) Explanation. Another very important device of teaching is explanation. It means removing difficulties and obscurities about the theme or subject-matter of a story or an event and thus to make it more intelligible to students. In the words of Pantan, "Explanation forms a kind of bridge between telling and revealing knowledge to the learners and it involves number of other techniques as well as narration and description. Throughout the process, the teacher must keep in close touch with the minds of his pupils, suggesting lines of thought, questioning them, assuming their questions, setting them on practical work, examining the results obtained and discussing significant problems etc."

In the use of this device, the following points must be remembered:

(1) A definite aim should always be kept in view both by the teacher and the students, otherwise they may be lost in useless details and elaborations.

(2) Essential, and important points should be stressed, repeated and written on the black-board.

(3) There should be a systematic and logical division and arrangement of different sections of the theme in hand.

(4) The language used in explanation should be simple and according to the age and capacity of the pupils.

(5) Various types of illustrative aids should be used to make the explanation more effective.

(6) At the end of the lesson, a summary of the whole theme or lesson should be given. This will drive home all the important points, to the pupils.

(7) Questions may be asked at different steps to ensure whether the subject-matter is quite clear to them or not. Students should also be encouraged to ask questions to clear their doubts, if any.

(D) Exposition. Exposition means opening, disclosing or bringing to light. In simpler words exposition means making clear the new information to the child in a way that may enable him to grasp intelligently the meaning or sense of the subject-matter, presented to him. Thus exposition is more than explanation. It helps in making the theme or point clear where mere explanation or description fails. In exposition, meaning of the subject-matter in hand, is given in a more comprehensive form. Pupils are also encouraged to co-operate in exposing further details. Thus their mental activity is directed to useful and educative channels. Effective teaching depends upon clear and graphic exposition. However the following points should be kept in view for the effective use of of this device:

(1) As in case of the other devices, the aim should be kept in view both by the teacher and the pupils. It will save time, labour and useless elaborations.

(2) A systematic and logical arrangment of the procedure should be followed with essential pauses in between the lesson. This will enable the pupils to grasp new knowledge hit by hit without much difficulty.

(3) Co-operation of pupils is essential in exposition. On occasions when the whole class is backwards, a lot of repetition is a must. Sometimes, in place of repetition. the teacher shall have to find out new ways of presenting the same information.

(4) Simple and intelligible language should be used in exposition. Voice and manner of speach should neither be too slow nor too fast. In other words, language, voice and speech should be used in accordance with the age and capacity of pupils.

(E) Questioning. Questioning is one of the most important devices of trading. It is by means of this device that teachers keep in close touch with their classes. According to Raymont, **"The acquisition of a good style of questioning, may be laid down definitelty as one of the essential ambitions of a young teacher:"** Questioning is an art and it requires all the skill of an expert to handle it properly. To a very large extent, the efficiency of a teacher depends on his master of the art of questioning. A good teacher must be a good questioner.

Ability to ask suitable questions, has long been regarded as one of the chief qualifications of a successful teacher. The question and answer method is old type recitation, was almost a universal method of teaching. The Upanishad as mention that questioning and answering is the binding force between the teacher and the taught. Times have changed and along with them, methods of teaching have also been altered to suit new conditions. But questioning as one of the devices of teaching, still holds the ground. Even today, no teacher worth the name, can do without qnestioning.

(I) Type of Questions

Generally questions are asked for finding out what the child knows and what he does not know. This type of questions are called introductory or preliminary questions.

Then questions asked to keep the child attentive in the class and also to know whether he is following the step in the lesson. This type of questions are called developing on teaching questions.

Lastly questions are asked to revise the lesson and to fit it clearly in the minds of pupils. Such questions are known as testing or recapitulatory questions.

1. Introductory or Preliminary Questions. These questions are asked in the beginning of the lesson to find out the depth of the child's previous knowledge and also to arouse his curiosity in what he is going to learn. Introductory questions should be very few in number. They should be asked briskly so that the pupils' attention be focussed on the topic in hand.

2. Testing or Recapitulatory Questions. These questions are asked at the end of each section in a lesson as well as at the end of the whole lesson. It is by means of Testing questions that sectional revision and final recapitulation are undertaken by the teacher. These questions ensure the teacher that knowledge has been properly learnt and grasped. Such questions not only require a re-statement of the facts, learnt in a lesson but also the explanation of the work done by the teacher, in a logical and orderly manner. It should, however, be noted that recapitulatory questions are differently worded from questions at the stage of sectional revision.

3. Developing of Teaching Question. These questions are asked by the teacher in the course of a lesson. It is by means of these developing questions that the teacher develops a particular line of thought and leads his pupils to grasp the new ideas step by step. Again it is through these questions that pupils' memory, imagination and judgment are called into play. These questions, therefore, should be asked in a way that pupils are led to discover facts and formulate new generalizations for themselves.

4. Characteristics of a Good Question. As we have stated in the beginning, questioning is an art and it should be learned and practised with great care by all teachers. Asking questions purposefully and effectively, requires understanding insight and experience. It is therefore, essential for all teachers to know the characteristics of a good question in order to take proper care in the formulation and asking of questions. A good question should have the following main characteristics:

1. ***Clarity.*** The question should be so worded that the child may easily understand what is wanted even though he may not know the answer to the question. The vocabulary used in the question, should be within the age and ability of the pupils. If the question puzzles the class or some students in the class, it may be recast in simpler words and tried again.

2. ***Simplicity.*** As stated above, the content and language of the question should be as simple as possible. As far as possible the language of the child should be used in formulating questions. Unusual terms and uncommon usages must be avoided in all cases. In other words, a good question should never go beyond the learners' vocabulary.

3. ***Briefness.*** In asking a good question, only a few simple words should be used, All unnecessary words and long phrases should be excluded. The question should be stated in a few words as possible and must not contain any ambiguity or doubt.

4. ***Challenging.*** A good question should promote mental effort and stimulate thinking. It should arouse all pupils the class and set them to observe, think and remember. It is therefore, essential that good questioning should not be confined to memory or recall questions only. There must be a reasonable proportion of questions, designed for stimulating thought.

5. ***Specificness.*** A good question should be definite and not vague or general. Vague questions admit of more than one answer and sometimes encourage the pupils to bluff. Moreover it should not be a question which can be answered in "yes" or "no". The teacher should make his question specific and precise to get specific answer.

6. ***Relevancy.*** A good question should be relevant to the theme in hand. If in lesson, the teacher has to ask a number of questions, these should be connected with each other in such a way that they may help in unifying learning. Link between different sub-units should, thus, be maintained and strengthened through the sequence in questioning, "Good questioning which proceeds in a logical sequence should aim to unify concepts that might otherwise be isolated."

In the words of Theodore Struck, "Good questions are educative and they have a very prominant place in all kinds of learning. If used in the right way, at the proper time, questions lead to new realms of understanding. They serve as means of organising knowledge, of correlating the result of educative experiences; of trying together units of learning and of integrating personality."

(II) Proper Technique of Asking Questions

Being a very important and frequently use device of teaching, all teachers must learn the proper technique of asking questions. This technique is given below:

(1) **Address your Question to the Whole Class.** If addressed to a particular pupil or pupils, the rest of the

class will sit idle and become inattentive. If addressed to the whole class, all pupils in the class will participate in the development of the lesson which is very vital for successful teaching.

(2) **Distribute Your Questions Evenly.** As far as possible, distribute your questions evenly among all the pupils. Some teachers concentrate only on the brighter section of the class. Such a habit brings about increasing indifference in weaker pupils. Slow learners and non-learners must also be goaded. It is therefore, that appropriate questions should also be put to such pupils. Also do not follow a fixed order of putting questions to the class because those who have had their chance will become inattentive.

(3) **Do not Repeat or Change Your Question.** The habit of repeating a question unneccessarily as well as that of changing or re-phrasing it should be avoided Repetiton and sudden change disturb the mind of a pupil and encourage inattention.

(4) **Give Sufficient Time to Think and Formulate Answer.** After a question is addressed, give sufficient time to the class to think and formulate the answer. Many lessons are spoiled because of the unnecesary inpatience of the teacher. If a question is worth asking, it is worth-waiting till pupils offer a correct answer.

(5) **Observe Some Logical Sequence in Questioning.** Once a lesson is started, there should be no gaps in the working of the pupil's mind. Such gaps are often caused by stray questining, which must be avoided. As Theodore Struck has said, "Good questioning which proceeds in a logical sequence, should aim at unity concepts that might otherwise be isolated. It correlates the result of study ahd experience and relates one subject with others."

(6) **Be Pleasant and Cheerful.** Put question in pleasant and sympathetic manner. This will make learning delightful, cooperative and profitable. Also avoid putting a volley of questions in a rapid-fire manner because the children are sure to lose interest and pay due attention.

(III) Answering of Questions

The problem of dealing with answer is closely connected with that of dealing with questions. Generally teacher's success is judged by the type of answers given by his pupils. Good answers are the result of good questioning. It is, therefore, that the teacher should make full use of the answer which the pupils give to his questioning. He should build them into the structure of his lesson and make them an integral part of his procedure. Pupils should also be ȅncouraged to ask questions for information and for further explanation of points, not clearly understood by them. In fact the success of class-teaching depends upon the manner in which answers of pupils are received and dealt with. Sympathy, patience and encouragement rather than harshness, impatience and snubbing are better means of evoking good response.

Generally the puplis' answers can be classified into the following types:

(1) Those which are all correct.

(2) Those which are all wrong.

(3) Those which are partly wrrect and partly wrong.

(4) Those which are correct but incomplete.

All correct answers must be welcomed and appreciated. Such cases do not require any skill all the teacher's part to deal with. A totally wrong answer should be rejected without ridicule. The teacher should ask another student to give correct answer. If he has succeeded in getting it, he should ask the child who gave all wrong answer, to repeat the correct answer. Similarly in case of a partly correct and partly wrong answer, the teacher should accept the correct part of it and reject the wrong part. He should then put a supplementary question to get the wrong part righted. He can, similary, get the incomplete part completed by asking a contributory question. It is on such occasions that resourcefulness and intelligence of the teacher are put to test. A conscientious teacher always accepts such a situation as a challenge. He tries to find out the real cause of the mistake and then deals with the very basis at the wrong response. He may also correct himself and modify his teaching procedure if he finds, that the wrong answer is due to his wrong questioning or use of difficult words at the presentation stage.

(IV) Illustration

Illustration means throwing light upon a certain thing. In teaching, the term "illustration means the employment of those aids which help in making things clearer and more understandable to children. The utility of illustrations depends upon the skill with which easy and familiar things are used for explaining new and difficult ideas in various subjects. At the elementary or kindergarten stage their value is great. It is at this stage that lesson can only be taught rightly and profitally with the help of thing that can be seen and handled. It is, however, essential to use illustrations of various types at all stages and in all subjects. They are the real soul of teaching. Good illustrations make intellectually dead presentations come to life. As illustrations have a direct appeal to senses, they arouse interest in the lesson and make it pleasing and easily understandable. The knowledge, thus gained, is retained much longer than otherwise. In addition to all this, illustrations are the best means of cultivating the power of observations and judgment, So wisely selected, timely exhibited and tactfully used, they can be great asset to teaching.

(A) Kinds of Illustrations

According to Raymont, there are five main kinds of illustrations:

(1) Actual Objects. These are concrete materials which include specimens of actual objects like grains, fruit, rocks and minerals etc, visits to factories, mills, rivers or hill side and handling of insects, flowers, leaves and feathers etc. Such actual objects give first hand knowledge and experience to children, especially in primary and junior classes.

(2) Pictorial or Photographic Representation of Objects. Some times it is not easy to prepare good models. In such cases, pictures and photographs of the objects required, can serve the purpose. Beautiful and attractive, pictures of all sizes are available from publishing houses and educational book-sellers. Every school must have a good variety of them, for profitable use in the teaching of social studies, languages, nature study and general science etc, especially for lower and junior classes.

(3) Models and Solid Representation of Objects. Very often it becomes almost impossible to bring to class room all the concrete materials needed for all types of lessons. It is also not possible to take children out on all occasions to see an actual place or thing, referred to in the lesson. On such occasions, models and solid representations of objects are the most convenient means of illustrations. A nicely prepared model of Bhakra Dam or that of the Panama Canal can prove an effective aid in a Geograply or Social Studies lesson. Similarly models of human heart, or human eye and ear, can give clear ideas about them in a general science or Physiology lesson.

(4) Blakboard Sketches, Diagrams, Maps and Graphs. It is not desirable to depend entirely on concrete objects, models and pictures. The teacher should also possess some illustrative talent. He should be able to illustrate his lesson by drawing a sketch or a diagram on the blackboard. The parts of a flower or a leaf, and the bones of a human body can best be explained by means of drawing sketches on the blackboard in front of the class. Such sketches and diagrams are often more useful than pictures because they allow little chance of producing vague impressions.

Maps, graphs, charts and experiments in Geography and General Science are other very useful material illustrations. In higher classes, pupils should be encouraged to prepare maps, graphs and chart, themselves, under the guidance of their teachers. Experiments in science subjects are concrete illustrations which must be encouraged in middle and high classes.

(5) Verbal Illustrations. These are illustrations "which influence the mind through the medium of related ideas expressed in words." They include comparisons, similis, word-pictures and analogies etc, and their main function is to make clear the meaning of a general statement or an abstract idea.

(B) How to Use Illustrations?

Illustrations are used differently at different stages. Their use depends upon the state of pupils, growth as well as the requirements of the subject while at the primary school stage, actual object and their solid representations would be mostly used, in secondary and higher, they must give place to pictures, sketches, diagrams, charts, and verbal comparisons. It should, however be remembered that illustrations are only a means and not an end in themselves. Their proper use does help but their misuse or overuse may spoil the lesson in band. They should therefore, be used with care and caution. The following points may be noted in the proper use of illustrations:

(1) Illustrations should be simple, direct and obvious. They should be easily understood, without any comment or explanation.

(2) Illustrations should be relevant to the topic in hand and suited to the children for which they are meant to be used.

(3) Illustrations should be chosen carefully and exhibited tactfully at the time when they actully needed should be exhibited in a manner that every child in the class can see them clearly and easily.

(4) Too many illustrations must not be used in a single lesson as they will surely spoil their value. Too much of everything is bad, is a well-known saying.

(5) Highly finished illustrations should be avoided as far as possible. These illustrations are the best which can be drawn and developed readily before the class itself.

(6) Some teachers, expecially the pupil teachers, layout a number of illustrations on the table before the entire class, in the beginning of the lesson. This practice must be avoided because pupils become more interested in the illustrations than in the lesson itself.

(V) Home Work

Home work is also a practical device of teaching. But unfortunately it has been subjected to a severe criticism in recent years both by the educationists and the parents. Educationists are of the opinion that home work is useless because pupils do not understand its importance and utility. They consider it as an extra burden or a kind of job, done for the teacher. For many of the publics, it means spending a few dual, and dreary hours on some dry job They cannot enjoy the amenities of home-life because they are always under the constant worry of doing the so-called home-work. Moreover, conditions in many of the homes especially in the rural area are not conducive to independent acamdemic work at home.

Thus parents also sometimes object to home work because deprives them of getting a helping hand form their children in farms, shops and in the home itself. Some parents also feel that it puts extra strain on their delicate children and thus endangers their health. Children are also deprived of many social duties and activities at home and in the neighbourhood which leave great educative value.

On the other hand, there are educationists and parents also advocate that home work is essential. They feel that only five a or six hour's work at school is not enough. It must be supplemented by work done at home at night or in the morning. Moreover home work provides opportunities to children to work independently of the teachers and learn to stand on their own legs. It also helps in fostering Co-operation between home and school because real education cannot be confined to the four-walls of the school alone. Home also plays a very important role in educating children. Then, home-work establishes a habit of reading and writing regularly, which goes a long way in the pursuit of knowledge.

From the above discussion, we may conclude that too much of technique of teaching But for making use of assignments everything is bad. Too much of home-work may endanger the pupils' health and freedom and it may also create disgust in the pupils' mind for the subject, for the teacher and even for the school. Expecting too much of children, is making them careless and indifferent. But it does not mean that home-work should be abolished altogether. It is necessary as well as desirable under the present circumstances. In fact, syllabus in different subjects for almost all classes, is so heavy that it is impossible to cover it without the help of home-work. Right type of home-work does assist the pupil in the direction of independent study and it, thus, makes him self-reliant. it widens his mental horizon, creates new interest for him and develops in him a taste for creative work. If rightly understood, skilfully planned, intelligently given and regularly checked by the teacher concerned, home-work is invaluable and indispensable.

(VI) Assignments

Some people confuse assignment with home work. They feel that home work and assignment are identical terms. But this is not a correct view. The term 'Assignment', as used in education, is quite different from home work. While home work enables children to revise the lessons, taught in the class; assignment is mainly meant for substituting teaching work in the class. A good portion of the text-book can be covered through this useful device. Assignment provides direction and expert guidance in pupils' curricular activities.

During very recent years, a large number of new-type assignments, contracts, study guide, work-books and work-sheets etc. are being very profitably used in modern progressive schools. These new forms of assignments are very helpful to the teacher for improving his technique of teaching But for making use of assignments sccessfully, teachers must have mastery over their subject possess a broard understanding of children and their interests for preparing good assignments.

(a) Characteristics of a Good Assignment

The following are the main characteristics of a good assignment:

1. A Good Assignment must be Definite and Clear. The student must be clear as to what they have to do and up to what time they have to complete and submit thier assignment. Approximate length of the assignment must also be fixed before hand. A definite list of sources, including books, magazines, papers, source-books, reference-books, maintaining definite chapters and pages to be consulted, must be given by the teacher. But all this material should readily by available in the school library.

2. Assignment should Provide for Individual Differences. A single assignment for all pupils, may be too difficult for some and too easy for others. Then there may also be difficulty of providing similar sources to all the pupils. So it is advisable to divide the class into sub-groups according to abilities, aptitudes and resoursefulness and then give different assignments to these different groups of pupils. Detailed instructions as stated at number one above, must be given in case of each assignment.

3. A Good Assignment must be Challenging and Motivating. When an assignment has been selected cooperatively by the students and the teacher, it should provide a challenge to pupils to work enthusiastically. Since it is purposeful and meaningful, it is sure to motivate pupils to put in their best efforts.

4. It must Develop Insight and Understanding. A good assignment must provide for both individual and group work. It should start from cooperative thinking and discussion and then lead to individual thinking and understanding. It is an outgrowth of better organisation of the learning situation and better lesson planning in a socialized atmosphere. It is thus, based as a democratic theory of teaching and learning.

5. It must be Related to Purpose. A good assignment is prepared and given with some definite purpose in view and as such, it must contribute to the desired learning outcomes. It is not something to keep pupils busy and occupied after school hours. Instead, it must be pertinent to the goals of instruction and pupils must be made to recognise the relationship of the assignment to those learning objectives.

(b) Evaluation of the Assignment

The progress of independent work, done by the pupils, must be measured because without evaluation the assignment will have no value. If pupils definitely show some progress in their study-periods and exhibit more interest in the subject, we can attribute a part of it to the effectiveness of the assignment. Although the definite effectiveness of the assignment is very difficult to measure, yet it may be done, to some extent, by means of good check-lists, prepared before hand by the teacher. Some teachers may feel that it is an extra burden on them, but it has to be done for successful teaching and for realizing the immediate objective of instruction, in view.

Conclusion. This chapter is meant to give proper understanding of educational technology. Educational Technology is not an issoliated field. This area has a great importance always. Educational Technology implies to use of all educational resource men, material, method, means and media is an integrated and systematic manner for optimizing learning. The NPE (1986) have laid emphasis on the approaches of Educational Technology. Now Educational Technology has a great importance in all the fields of education including nursary to university education. It spreaded to find to non formal and distance education. The essence and objective of education which is all round development of the personality can easily achieve through Educational Technology effectively.

REFERENCES

Allen, W.H.—Media Stimulus and Types of Learning, Audio-Visual Instruction, 1967.

Apter, M.J.—The New Technology of Education, Macmillan, London, 1968.

Bloom, Benjamin ***et al.***,—Taxonomy of Educational Objectives. The Classification of Educational Goals New York Mackay, 1956.

Diev Zcide, H.—Educational Technology and Development of Education UNESCO, ILY, 1970.

Government of India—National Policy on Education (MHRD) Education, New Delhi, 1986/1992.

Government of India—Programme of Active (MHRD)/ Education, New Delhi, 1986/1992.

Mohanty, J.—Educational Technology, Deep & Deep publications, New Delhi, 1992.

Sampath, K, ***et at***—Introduction to Educational Technology, Sterling, New Delhi, 1981.

Spalding, Seth—Advanced Educational Technology Prospects in Education UNESCO, Vol. 31.

❒

2

Teaching Strategy

2. Introduction

The teaching is much more difficult task. It requires different type of methods, techniques and teaching aids. The selection of these methods and techniques depends upon the nature of content, learning objectives, learner abilities and student's entering behaviour. The learning objectives and content analysis provide the basis for effective presentation of teaching. In order to bring desirable change in the behaviour of the learner, teacher has to employ the devices: Teaching strategies and teaching tactics.

'Teaching strategy is the means to achieve learning objectives'. **E. Stones and S. Morris** have defined the term 'teaching strategy' comprehensively in the following manner:

> "Teaching strategy is a generalized plan for a lesson which includes structure, desired learner behaviour in terms of goals of instruction and an outline of planned tactics necessary to implement the strategy. The lesson strategy is a part of a larger development scheme of the curriculum."

This definition of teaching strategy involves two aspects: *(1)* a generalized plane for the presentation of a lesson; and *(2)* it includes desired learner behaviour in terms of goals of instruction.

Teaching strategy seeks to establish the relationship between teaching and learning in view of achieving the objectives.

Teaching strategies include broad methods of instruction, *e.g.*, a lecture strategy, a tutorial strategy, a case-study strategy and programmed instruction strategy. They can be regarded as a broad way of operation.

2.1 Definition of Teaching Method

Teaching method is a style of the presentation of content in classroom. **M. Varma** has defined the term method in the following manner:

> "Method is an abstract as logical entities that we can distinguish between manner and methods, in reality, they form an organic whole and matter determines method analogously as objective determines means; content and spirit determine style and form of literature".

M. Varma has presented broad meaning of the term 'method'. According to him matter is important for determining method. The common teaching 'matter may be of three types, hence all the methods can be classified under three heads—

1. Telling Methods—Lecture, Questioning, Discussion, etc.
2. Showing Methods—Demonstration, Excursion, Laboratory work etc.
3. Doing Methods—Project, Role playing, Practical, etc.

Broudy (1963) has stated that "Method refers to the formal structure of the sequence of acts commonly denoted by instruction. The term 'method' covers both strategies and tactics of teaching and involves the choice of what is to be taught and in which order is it to be presented".

Method is more general, it includes techniques also. The teaching techniques are ways of implementing a method. Different techniques may be employed within one method of teaching.

2.2 Difference between Teaching Strategy and Method

Teaching strategies and method are used for the same meaning but they are quite different from one another. Some points of difference have been discussed here:

1. Teaching method is based on classical theory of human organization task-entered, whereas teaching strategy is based on modern theory of organization task and relationship centred.

2. The content and mode of presentation are the main elements of teaching method. The matter determines the method (telling, showing and doing). The behavioural objectives and learning conditions are two basic elements of teaching strategy. The objective determines the strategy of (Cognitive, Affective and Psychomotor) teaching.

3. The assumption regarding teaching strategy is that teaching is a science and method assumes that teaching is an art.

4. The term strategy has been borrowed from military science (technology) and method is the term of pedagogy.

5. Teaching strategy employs micro-approach to teaching, whereas method uses micro-approach to teaching.

6. The effectiveness of teaching strategy is evaluated in terms of achieving objectives by administering criterion test. The teaching methods are evaluated in terms of mastery over the subject master by using achievement test.

7. The strategies are implemented by tactics of teaching and methods are implemented by techniques of teaching. The tactics are more concerned with learning structure, whereas techniques are concerned with mode of presentation and nature of content.

8. The main focus of a teaching strategy is to achieve the objective by creating appropriate learning conditions. The teaching method aims at the effective presentation of subject-matter to have the mastery over it.

Some teaching methods are also termed as teaching strategies, *e.g.*, lecture is used both method as well as strategy. The lecture strategy refers to realizing some specific objectives but lecture method refers to mode of presentation of some specific content. In selecting appropriate teaching strategy task analysis, learning conditions and learning objectives are crucial factors, but subject-matter determines the method though the same subject content can be used for achieving different types of objectives.

2.3 Features of Teaching Strategies

Teaching strategies are of various types because there is great variation in teaching. Some of the various features have been given in the following basis:

1. Teaching Objectives: Cognitive, affective and psychomotor.
2. Nature of Components of Content Terms, Concepts: facts, rules, principles, theories, creativity, interest, attitudes, values, skill verbal concepts, linguistic and habit formation.
3. Types of Activities: Knowing or telling, showing of feelings and doing.
4. Nature of Teaching: Teacher centred, Learner centred and activity-centred or group-activities or action oriented.
5. Types of maxim teaching used in teaching strategies. Inductive and deductive teaching strategies employ the maxims-General to specific or Rule to example.
6. Involving senses of the learners in gaining experiences. The field trips, laboratory and field work involves multi-sensory instruction which provides true knowledge.

7. Some of the teaching strategies are used in teaching specific subject, thus the nature of subject determines the type of teaching strategies. For example—Regional method in geography teaching, Chronological in history teaching, Analysis and synthesis strategy in Geometry teaching. Language laboratory in language teaching and demonstration in science teaching.

8. The teaching strategy are also determined by the level of students. The story telling and play way are used for small children. Group discussion and seminar strategies are used at higher level.

9. The strategies of teaching are used inview of levels of teaching. In memory level Herbartion approach and understanding Morrison approach are used.

10. The micro teaching device is the real teaching but it is used for training purpose in developing teaching skills.

2.4 Classification of Teaching Strategies on the Basis of Some Special Features

There are various types of teaching strategies which are used in classroom. There teaching strategies have been classified on the basis of the following special features.

(1) Teaching learning objectives or Instructional objectives.

(2) Components or elements of content of teaching.

(3) Nature of Teaching Strategies.

(4) Teaching competency.

Some details of the above classification of teaching strategies have been in the following paragraphs:

(1) Teaching Learning Objectives or Instruction Objectives. Inview of teaching objectives the teaching strategies are broadly classified into three categories—knowing, feeling and doing strategies.

TEACHING STRATEGIES ON BASIS OF OBJECTIVES

Teaching Objectives	*Type of Strategies*
1. Cognitive objectives.	(a) Knowing Instructional, Strategies.
2. Affective objective.	(b) Feeling Instruction Strategies.
3. Psychomotor objectives.	(c) Doing Instructional Strategies.

(2) Nature of Teaching Strategies. Teaching strategies are generally classified on the basis of its nature and roles of teaching variables.

Types of Teaching Strategies on the basis of roles of teaching variables.

1. Teacher-Controlled Teaching (TCT),

2. Learner-Controlled Teaching (LCT) and

3. Group-Controlled Teaching (GCT), and Action oriented

As teaching method determines the role of teacher and learners in teaching-learning situations. An instructional method is selected in view of subject-content to be taught. In the following table, instructional methods and nature of teaching learning situations have been provided:

NATURE OF TEACHING STRATEGIES

Teaching Stidiegies	*Nature of Teaching-Learning*
1. Lecture Method. 2. Demonstration Method. 3. Team Teaching Method. 4. Chalk and Talk Method.	(a) Teacher, Controlled Teaching (TCT) (Monologue Teaching) (Autocratic Teaching)
1. Questions Answer Method. 2. Interactive Procedure.	(b) Interactive Procedure of Teaching (T-LCT)

3. Group Discussion Method.	(Dialogue Teaching)
4. Tutorial Method.	(Democratic Teaching)
1. Programmed Instruction.	(c) Learner-Controlled Teaching (LCT)
2. Library Method.	(Self-Study)
3. Computer Assisted Instruction.	(Lassies-Faire Teaching)
4. Laboratory Method.	
5. Assignments.	
1. Project Method.	(d) Group-Controlled Teaching (GCT)
2. Simulated Instruction.	(Action Oriented Teaching)
3. Field Trips.	(Democratic Teaching)
4. Field work.	

There are various ways to classify instructional methods. Teacher controlled Instructions are also known autocratic style or authoritarian methods. Learners-controlled Instructions are termed as permissive style or democratic methods.

(3) Aspects of Development and Components of Content. An Instructional method is used for developing certain aspects of learners. The method involves some components of content, which is the part of school curriculum. The content components are the means for developing the cognitive, affective and psychomotor aspects of the learner. In the following table aspects of development and components of content have been classified.

ASPECTS OF DEVELOPMENT AND COMPONENTS OF CONTENT

Aspect of Development	*Components of Content*
1. Cognitive Aspects-knowing	1.1 Terms and words.
(Cognitive Objectives)	1.2 Concepts.
	1.3 Facts and Events.
	1.4 Rules and Principle.

	1.5	Theories.
	1.6	Problem solving.
	1.7	Creativity.
2. Affective Aspect-Feeling (Affective Objectives)	2.1	Interest and feelings.
	2.2	Attitudes and beliefs.
	2.3	Values and character.
3. Psychomotor Aspects-Doing (Psychomotor Objectives)	3.1	Skill Training.
	3.2	Verbal - concepts.
	3.3	Linguistic training.
	3.4	Habit formation.

(4) Teaching Learning Competency. The knowledge and skill of these instructional methods is essential for classroom teacher because he is the manager of classroom activities whether these are teacher-controlled or learner-controlled or group controlled instruction. The effective teaching can be classified into four type competencies.

1. Competency of Subject matter,
2. Competency of Teaching skills,
3. Competency of Problem solving, and
4. Competency of Teaching behaviour.

These competency develop the quality of teaching which are related to content and instructional methods. The following are the good qualities of teaching-learning:

(1) Managing classroom activities—Organized dominar.

(2) Dynamism in teaching style.

(3) Warmth and acceptance in teaching,

(4) Flexibility in teaching, and

(5) Creative teaching style.

The competencies and quality of teaching enables the teachers to understand four stages of learning.

(a) Learning to know,

(b) Learning to learn,

(c) Learning to do,

(d) Learning to be, and

(e) Learning to live cooperatively.

The awareness of these aspects of teaching is essential for selecting appropriate instruction method. It is not the easy because teaching learning is very complex activity, which involves several components in various subjects method. The details of teaching strategies included in the classification have been discussed below:

2.5 Teacher-Controlled Strategies

A teacher plays significant and main role in classroom teaching learning situations. All the activities of teaching are controlled by the teacher. The dominates the classroom climate. It is assumed that teacher has the mastery of subject and possessor of matured personality while students have less mature personality. It further assumes that the learner have the capacity to carry out the order and obey the teacher. Then, they are the passive listeners in the classroom. They can not argue or ask question in the classroom. This type of instruction has authoritarian type climate. The curriculum is content centred, The concept of teaching is explained in the following manner by H. C. Morrison.

"Teaching is an intimate contact between a move mature personality and a less mature which is designed to further the education of the later (student)."

This type of teaching and instruction confines to memory level, there is no place for developing feelings. Attitude and values. This type of instruction methods have their advantages and limitations, which have been discussed along each instructional method. Even a teacher and teach wrong thing to the students. The following are the instruction methods, which are known as Teacher controlled instruction. These are task-centred methods.

(1) Lecture Method Strategy

It is an oldest teaching method given by idealism philosophy. It is still most important teaching method in our schools. It is one of the autocratic teaching strategies.

Focus. It may be used to achieve the cognitive and affective objectives. Lecture can be used to realize the highest order of cognitive objectives.

Structure. Lecture lays emphasis on the presentation of the content. Teacher is more active and students are passive participants but he uses question-answer technique to keep them attentive in the class. Teacher controls and plans for all students act.

Principles of Teaching. It employs the following principles:

(a) The content is presented as whole.

(b) The main stress is on presentation.

(c) The students learn better through listening.

(d) The subject-content in correlated with other subject.

(e) The new knowledge is linked with student's previous knowledge.

Applications. The presentation can be made effective but it should be used with great precaution. Teacher should make use of the teaching aids in the description and explaining concepts. Developing questions should be asked to make the presentation purposeful and interesting.

Advantages. The following are the major advantages of lecture strategy.

1. The habit of concentration may be developed among the students.
2. It is an economical teaching strategy. A large subject content may be taught relatively in small duration.
3. It provides the opportunity to the teacher to use different types of teaching aids.
4. Very high order of cognitive objectives may be achieved.
5. Teacher can employ his full verbal communication.
6. The new content can be easily introduced.
7. The personality of teacher influences the learner's personality.

Limitations. It has the following limitations:

1. It has more emphasis on teacher presentation and has no place for the participation of the students.
2. Teaching activities are dominated by the teacher and there is no place for student's abilities, interests and their learning.
3. This strategy can be used in higher classes but it can not easily used in elementary classes.
4. It is not based upon the principle of psychology. The individual differences are not considered in implementing teaching strategy.
5. Usually teacher deviates from the subject-content and teaching points. Therefore, student can not perform well in examination.
6. It can not be used for achieving the psychomotor objectives and the highest order of affective objectives.

7. An effective teacher can use this strategy effectively, because teacher should have mastery over the content.

Suggestions. The following precautions should be observed to use this strategy effectively:

1. The language of the lecture should be simple, easy and comprehensive.
2. The developing question should be asked to make the students attentive in the class.
3. The teacher should explore their previous knowledge and make the efforts to link with new one.
4. The strategy should be used from secondary level to upward classes.
5. The students remain inactive and passive participants, hence the teacher use humour to release their tension and monotony of the class.
6. The strategy should be supported by question-answer technique and appropriate teaching aids, maps, charts, diagrams, pictures, etc.

(a) Lecture-cum-Demonstration Method/Strategy

In this method, the spoken word is supplemented with demonstration using varied aids resulting in auditory and visual learning; concrete demonstrations through aids is reinforced instruction through two channels, eye and the ear. Development demonstration involves getting answers from pupils as the demonstration proceeds gradually in stages.

Advantages of Lecture-cum-Demonstrations

(1) Much matter could be covered in a short time.

(2) Much time and energy of pupils and teacher is saved.

(3) Only one set of apparatus necessary is required; so the lecture demonstration is economical.

(4) Demonstration will be most effective to stimulate the thoughts of pupils.

(5) Delicate and dangerous experiments which require delicate manipulation can be performed by the teacher only with pupils as active observers.

(6) By the expressions on the faces of pupils as lesson progresses the method of delivery of the lecture could be varied and changed to suit the needs.

(7) Demonstration will be useful before pupils launch on independent work.

Precautions of Lecture-cum-Demonstration

(1) All the aids must be arranged in the order in which they are to be used, leading to orderly thinking. Fumbling for things will destroy for communion between teachers and pupils.

(2) There must be an element of wonder or surprise associated with the demonstration.

(3) The experiments must be simple and effective and must not take a long time.

(4) Qualitative experiments should be preferred to quantitative experiments involving time.

(5) Control experiments would play a great part to clarify details.

(6) The aids must not be arranged mechanically in a straight line.

(7) Demonstrations which are simple should be chosen in preference to complicated ones to demonstrate the same aspect.

(8) When effects are of small magnitude they must be shown on a magnified scale with suitable aids.

(9) Pupils also may be made to assist in the demonstration.

(10) Clear and suitable background should be provided for the demonstration set up so that the same could be completely seen be all pupils.

(11) All the pupils should be able to see the demonstration.

(12) Any demonstration made must be with a purpose and the define objective clearly stated.

(b) Lecture-cum-Discussion Strategy

It has been evident form above discussion about lecture method that it is teacher-centred method. Teacher is more active and learners are the passive listeners. The students do not remain attentive in the class. It is a least effective method of teaching because only one sense remains active in teaching learning process. It is uni-sense or monologue approach of teaching. Therefore it is essential that lecture method must be supported by other technique of teaching *e.g.* Question-answer technique or discussion technique. It the lecture method is supported by discussion technique, it is known as lecture-cum-discussion method. In a democratic form of government teaching is considered as an interactive process. It means that participation of both teacher and students is must. Thus lecture-cum-discussion is an improvement method which is very conducive for learning.

Structure of the Method. The teacher introduce the topic by lecture and raises some related issues for students participation. Some time he puts question. So that students should participate in teaching. It involves more senses of students which facilitate true knowledge of the content. The learning situation created by this method are effective. They should remain active in classroom. After discussion the teacher has to explain the concept or summarizes the discussion by his lecture under this method teaching activities are performed by the both agents the discussion is initiated by questions answer teaching of teaching.

Principles of Lecture-cum-Discussion. This method involves the following principles of teaching:

1. The content of teaching is presented into it components.
2. Teaching is organized in an interactive way participation of both students and teacher.
3. It involves more than one sense in learning process.
4. The students learns better through participation.
5. The learnt content can be retained for a longer line.
6. The students get reinforcement in discussion.
7. It is based on appreciative mass theory of learning.
8. The methods creates very conducive learning situations for the students.

Application of this Method. The following are major application of lecture-cum discussion method.

1. The presentation can be made effective.
2. The teacher has to organize the discussion during presentation.
3. The teacher has to employ question-answer technique for discussion.
4. The discussion should be interesting and purposeful.
5. The teacher has to plan his lesson appropriate so that discussion can be held.

Advantages of the Method. It has the following advantages:

1. It develops the habit and interest in discussion among students.
2. It is helpful for realizing high order of cognitive objectives.
3. The new content can be easily introduced.
4. It involves more senses of students in learning process.
5. It makes teaching as an interactive process.
6. The teacher .can used his best competency of teaching.
7. It provides the better understanding of the content.

Limitations of the Method. It has the following disadvantage:

1. Every teacher can with used this method appropriately.
2. In the discussion only few students dominate.
3. It is also difficult and organize appropriately.
4. It requires proper training and practice.
5. The nature of content permits the application of the method narrative content of a subjected.
6. It requires some adequate requires lecture-discussion and followed lecture-discussion with the help of questions answer technique.
7. The required weightage to lecture and discussion on a topic is the logical activity depends on the students.

Suggestions for Using the Method. The precaution should be observed for using this method.

1. The proper training and practice should be done before using this method.
2. The teacher should plan his lesson according to this method.

3. The question-answer technique should be used properly for intuiting the discussion.

4. The method should be higher-secondary level of social science teaching.

5. The method should be supported by teaching aids and devices of teaching.

6. Teacher should employ proper technique, devices and maxim of teaching.

7. Teacher should try to made teaching as an interactive process.

(2) Demonstration Method or Strategy

The lesson demonstration strategy is a traditional classroom method, which is used in technical schools and training colleges. It is widely used by teacher-educators during teaching practice, as a permissive than a discussion.

Focus. It is used for achieving the psychomotor and cognitive objectives.

Structure. It consists of three successive steps:

(a) Introduction, *(b)* Development, and *(c)* Integration.

In the first step of introduction, the aims are stated. The second phase involves a good deal of question-answers and other class activities. The last step, in which the Jesson material is rehearsed, revised and evaluated.

Principles. It is mainly used as a teaching strategy for average and below average students or untrained and inexperienced teacher. The cognitive and psychomotor objectives can be realized. It is more useful for pupil teachers to develop his own lesson in classroom teaching.

Limitations. It suffers from the following limitations:

(1) It does not provide an opportunity to develop originality of pupil teachers. They try to imitate the model lesson in their teaching.

(2) Teacher-educators can not demonstrate the lesson correctly and effectively.

Suggestions. The following precautions should be taken in demonstrating the lesson:

(1) An effective or skilled teacher should demonstrate the lesson.

(2) The lesson-demonstration should be followed by discussion.

(3) The pupil-teacher should be given an opportunity to seek the clarification of their problems.

(4) The lesson-demonstration should be used as a supplementary techniques in simulated social skill training.

(3) Tutorials Method or Strategy

Tutorials strategy is considered both autocratic and permissive type of teaching. It is generally considered to be one of the most valuable educational experiences. Lecture strategy is followed by tutorials because individual difficulties can be solved in lecture. Tutorials are highly individualized type of teaching.

Focus. Tutorials aim at to provide remedial help of the learner or to help individual difficulties of the learner. The cognitive and affective objectives may be achieved by the tutorials.

Structure. Tutorial classes are formed by considering the homogeneous type of difficulties of the learner. The small homogeneous group is assigned by one teacher. He has to give remedial help to the learner. Tutorial is a follow up programme.

Principles. It is based upon the following teaching principles:

(1) It considers the individual difference.

(2) It establishes the rapport with learners.

(3) It organizes as remedial help to the weak learner.

(4) It provides educational guidance.

Type of Tutorials. Tutorial covers a wide range of teaching activities.

These may be classified under three heads:

(a) Supervision Tutorials. In this type of tutorial students and teacher meeting are arranged regularly. A student reads an essay and defends it with arguments. This strategy can provide an opportunity to dependant, his understanding of subject can provide an opportunity to deepen his understanding of subject for able student. It stresses on the mastery over the basic skills of scholarship.

(b) Practical Tutorials. These tutorials are commonly used for both group and individual basis to achieve psychomotor skills wil laboratory, workshop and rehearsal. These tutorials are basically employed to achieve the psychmotor objectives.

(c) Group Tutorials. These tutorials are useful for an average students. These can satisfy the needs of less exceptional students. The teacher should have the background of social psychology and group dynamics so that he can deal with group tutorials effectively in solving their problems.

Group tutorials are more useful in adult teaching. A tutorial strategy is more useful for achieving higher-order cognitive, affective and psychomotor objectives.

Advantages of Tutorials Strategy. The following are major advantages of tutorials:

(1) It is a valuable teaching strategy from individual differences point of view.

(2) It provides an opportunity to organize remedial teaching.

(3) It provides full freedom to the learner to seek the clarification of their problems and can raise their level of performance.

(4) It can fulfil the need of entering behaviour of the learner.

Limitations of Tutorials. It has the following disadvantages:

(1) One teacher cannot solve the difficulties related to different subjects and different students.

(2) Usually some students dominate the tutorials group and all students can not get actual opportunity to participate.

(3) The teacher becomes bias and docs not take interest in the problem of each and every student.

(4) Tutorial-group develops the feeling of Jealousy.

Suggestions for Tutoral Strategy. Tutorials may be improved by observing the following suggestions:

(1) Tutorial groups should be formed of some background, abilities and entering behaviours.

(2) Teacher should have very objective dealing with the students.

(3) The tutorial groups should be formed on the basis of students difficulties in different subjects.

(4) Teacher should provide the remedial help in the subject of his won interest.

2.6 Learner-Centred Strategies

The participation of teacher and students is equally important in this type method. This type of instruction methods are used in democratic form of government. The transaction curriculum is objective-centred and teaching is an interactive proctess. B.A. Smith has rightly defined as follow.

> "Teaching is a system of actions and activities which induce learning through interpersonal relationship."

This type teaching helps in developing students as will as teacher.

Interaction means development of both teacher and students.

Similarly Edmuned Anidoll (1967) has defined teaching in view of the democratic model of behaviour.

This type teaching in relationship centred rather than task-centred. Due weightage is given to the feeling and beliefs of the students in classroom teaching. The students are encouraged to ask questions and initiate the classroom talk. A students can argue with teacher, even they can critise the teacher. Teacher role is like a guide and friend.

The teaching activities and action in this type instruction-method are planning, organizing leading or motivating, counselling and evaluation (feedback to both), the conductive classroom climate. The following are the methods which are used as dialogue in classroom.

(1) Question-answer teaching method or strategies.

(2) Heuristics teaching method or strategies.

(3) Group-discussion teaching method or strategies.

The defects of these methods or strategies have been given in the following paragraphs.

(1) Question-Answer Teaching Method or Strategy

The Socratic method is known as question-answer method. It is developed by the famous philosopher. Socrates. He assumes that all knowledge within the learner and teacher has to unfold it. He further assumes that teacher should present the subject-matter in such a way that learner recognizes the truth and he can identify himself with it.

Focus. The strategy aims at achieving the cognitive objective and bringing knowledge at the conscious level.

Structure. Socrates has suggested three steps:

(1) To prepare questions and arrange them in a sequence.

(2) To present the questions in appropriate way so that curiosity may be created among the learners.

(3) To ask new questions by liking with the learner's responses. Teacher is able to recognize the intention of learner and provides motivation accordingly.

He has to identify the three phases of learning process: observation, experience and testing.

Principles. The question-answer strategy based upon the following principles:

(1) Theory of unfoldment. All knowledge is within the learner, teacher can not teach any new knowledge to students.

(2) The knowledge can be emitted by liking the questions with his answers.

Example. Lesson on Indian population?

Teacher — Where does most of Indian population live in?

Pupil — Villages.

Teacher — What is their main occupation?

Pupil — Farming or Agriculture.

Teacher — What are the main agriculture crops in our country?

Pupil — Rice, Wheat and Sugarcane.

Thus, the teacher develops his lesson with the help of appropriate questions.

Advantages. The following are major advantages of question-answer strategy.

(1) The classroom verbal interaction can only be encouraged.

(2) The learner remains active and participates in teaching acts.

(3) It reduces the chances of incisciplinc in classroom teaching.

(4) The new knowledge is imparted by liking with earlier acquired knowledge.

(5) While asking the questions, teacher should keep in mind the abilities, needs and interests of the learners.

(6) It is more useful at primary and secondary level.

(7) It involves psychological principles of learning.

Limitations. It has the following disadvantages:

(1) It is very difficult to prepare good questions and arrange them in psychological sequence.

(2) It is a mechanical strategy and creates memory in the classroom climate.

(3) All knowledge can not be imparted by questions-answer strategy.

(4) It can be used in the teaching of higher classes.

Suggestions. The following precautions should be taken:

(1) It should be supplemented by lecture and narration devices.

(2) The questions should be evenly distributed among the whole class.

(3) The strategy should be used only by those teachers who can prepare question immediately even at the time of teaching.

(4) The teacher should try to reduce the tension of the class by humour.

(2) Heuristics Teaching Strategy (Heurism)

The term 'Heuristics' has been borrowed from the word 'Heurises', it means, "discover or investigate". The purpose of communication is to develop the tendency of investigation. Arm Strong is the exponent of this strategy. It is based upon the assumption of Herbert Spencer that the learner should be told as little as possible and he should be encouraged to learn himself as much as possible.

Pollio and Dankar (1945) have mentioned this method in their article entitled 'Problem Solving.' The strategy involves 'trial and error' and invention techniques. This strategy is very economical and speedy. It requires more logical and imaginative thinking in formulating the number of tentative solutions for the problem.

Objectives. The following are the main objectives of 'Heuristics Strategy of Teaching:

(1) To develop problem-solving tendency.

(2) To develop logical cum imaginative thinking ability.

(3) To develop scientific attitude towards the problem.

(4) To encourage free thinking for performing the task.

Structure. A problem is placed before the learners and they attempt to seek the solutions of the problem. The learners get full freedom of working and thinking. The number of devices are used for solving the problem. The problem is analysed in possible elements. The learner discuss themselves about the problem. The learners discuss themselves about the problem. The teacher encourages the students to work in laboratory and to study in the library. The teacher attempts to acquaint the learner with relevance of the problems.

Advantages. The following are the main advantages of Heuristic strategy of teaching:

(1) It develops the scientific attitude of the learner and tendency of observation.

(2) It evolves the feeling of self confidence and self reliance.

(3) The teacher provides the individual guidance to the learner.

(4) It creates the situation for divergent thinking.

(5) The teacher remains active.

(6) It is based upon psychological principles of learning.

(7) It develops logical and imaginative thinking among the learner.

Limitations. It suffers from the following limitations:

(1) It can not be used for lower classes.

(2) It is very time consuming strategy.

(3) It can be employed for a large number of students.

(4) It can not be used for the dull or poor students even for higher of classes.

(3) Group Discussion Method

There is no comprehensive definition of 'group discussion' but it is considered as a democratic teaching strategy. The pupils are more active in it. Teacher's job is to supervise, and to provide guidance to pupils activities. It is child-centred teaching strategy. It may be of two types: *(1)* By the teacher and *(2)* By the students.

(1) ***By the Teacher.*** This type of discussion is more autocratic in style.

(2) ***By the Student.*** In this situation, discussion is more permissive or democratic in style.

Objectives. The affective objectives and higher order cognitive objectives may be achieved.

Structure. The group discussion is organized in two forms: Formally and informally. In formal group discussion, proper schedule is prepared and certain rules are absence of a teacher, pupils have to select a student to act as a leader of the group. The leader of the group prepares a plan for discussion. The leader of the group prepares a plan for discussion. In the group discussion, due weightage is given to the answers and questions of the Pupils.

Principles. This strategy is based upon the following principles of teaching:

(1) Principle of active participation.

(2) Principle of freedom for work.

(3) Principle of group work and equal opportunities to as questions and to answer them.

Advantages. The following are the main advantages of this strategy.

(1) It has the greater scope of criticism for incorrect approaches ideas and concepts.

(2) It develops the feeling of group work and group participation.

(3) It develops the problem solving attitude and the tolerance to hear one's own criticism.

(4) It helps in developing the creative ability and thinking among pupils.

(5) The higher order of cognitive and affective objectives of teaching are achieved.

(6) It helps in develcping the feeling of cooperation.

Limitations: It has the following limitations:

(1) It has chances for deviation from the main topic.

(2) In the discussion, only few students dominate and to discuss more and large number of students do not participate in the discussion.

(3) It involves more criticism rather than relevant discussion.

(4) Generally group are formed in this strategy and they are critical to one another.

Suggestions. It may be improved and can be effectively employed by observing the following precautions:

(1) Every student should be provided an opportunity to participate in the discussion.

(2) Students should be encouraged and motivated to participate in the discussions.

(3) Irrelevant criticism should not be encouraged.

2.7 Group-Centred Strategies

There are some methods of teaching which are learning activities oriented. These methods are also known as learner-controlled method (LCM) in which learners are active and teacher has the secondary role just guide and help the learners. The following methods of teaching are included in this classification:

(1) Assignment Strategy. Assignments and home work are the supporting devices of teaching. It provides the opportunity for doing some things. It is self-study techniques of teaching. In teacher-controlled instruction, teacher remains more active, the learners are passive listener's. At the end of teaching, some assignments are given to the students to do and complete their own. Thus, the students have to assimilate the content through self-study. Home work and assignment technique is the stage of assimilation.

Morrison has used the step of assimitation in his understanding model of teaching. If the students activities are supervised by the teacher, then it is called supervised study in which student remains more active in his learning.

(2) Project Method or Strategy. It is a new teaching strategy and it has been evolved as a result of social tendency of education. The advocates are of this opinion that the education should be related to life situations. It is experience-centred teaching strategy. The exponent of project method is W.H. Kilpatrick. The main focus of this strategy is to socialize a child.

(3) Role Playing or Dramatization Strategy. A number of techniques are being used currently in India as well as in other countries for the modification of teacher-behaviour. The simulated social skill training (SSST) is one of them. Cruick Shanik has developed a teacher training system. This system of training is being denoted by several terms such as : Role playing, Artificial teaching, Pilot training, Laboratory method, Clinical method and Inductive scientific method.

The Drama is a form of English literature like prose and poetry. It is also an effective method of teaching as well as device of training. It is effectively used for teaching historical stories and events. The events of history cannot be repeated but can only be dramatized by role-playing. The historical content can be made more effective and interesting for the students.

(4) **Brain Storming Strategy.** It is completely permissive style of teaching strategy. It is based upon an assumption that a student can learn better in a group rather than in individual study. It is a problem oriented strategy teaching.

The higher order cognitive and affective objectives in which learners are assigned a problem and they are asked to discuss any idea which come to their mind. The group is encouraged to provide even unusual suggestions. They have to analyse and evaluate the workability of their own suggestions of the problem.

(5) **Discovery Strategy.** J.S. Brunner has development this teaching strategy. The discovery and heuristics are used for the same meaning but they are quite different from one another. The discovery strategy is used for teaching social subjects whereas heuristic strategy is meant for teaching science subjects. The heurism is used to provide the knowledge of science concepts whereas discovery is used for the historical facts. There is a scope for direct observation in the heuristic, but discovery provides the factual information about the past events, remains or records.

(6) **Deductive and Inductive Method or Strategy.** This strategy has two forms:

(a) Deductive Method and

(b) Inductive Method

The detailes of Deductive and Inductive method have been in following paragraphs:

(a) Deductive Strategy. By deduction, the pupil arrives at particular facts by applying previously established laws, conclusions, propositions, or generalizations.

In other words, his reasoning proceeds from the general to the particular.

Shipley defined deductive strategy as "a method in teaching that proceeds from rules or generalizations to examples and subsequently to conclusions or to the application of the generalization".

If a teacher refers to rules, actions, principles, or other generalizations that the pupil knows, she causes him to apply those general conclusions to the particular problem of the moment.

Eggen *et.al.*, divided deduclive model in two models Ausubel model and General deduclive model. The Ausubel model is a deductive informalion processing model designed to teach inler related bodies of content. In deductive model the broader or more inclusive ideas are presented first and are followed by less inclusive ideas. In addition in the Ausubel's model an organizing statement, called an advance organizer presented at the beginning of the lesson acts as a connection between the material to be learned and the learner's cognitive structure. This advance organizer acts as a cognitive roadmap, guiding the student over the new content be learned.

(b) Inductive Strategy. In inductive teaching process the thinking proceeds from specific to general. Inductive reasoning is a method of seeking relationships among phenomena toward the development of a principle or generalization to explain the observed relationships and is always hopeful for establishing a theory.

Megrath defined inductive strategy as "a method that proceeds from known data to a generalization, such as a theory or hypothesis that will explain the evidence at hand".

Herbert called inductive strategy as synthetic learning. According to him learner himself synthesizes from his study of the cases the broad principle.

Conclusion. So again we say teaching needs lots of efforts and planning. We can only find good result and achieve objectives through proper teaching strategies and teaching tactics for that

Educational Technology has to be taken up as a comprehensive and continuous programme. The Educational Technology can immensely contribute in the development of the personality of the learner.

REFERENCES

Apter Michael, J.—Educational Technology, Macmillan, London, 1968

Allen, Dwight and K. Ryan—Micro-Teaching (Addison Wasley)

Apter M. J.—The New Technology of Education (Macmillan)

Bajpal, AC, & J.F. Leeham—Aspects of Educational Technology.

Dicuzeide, Henri—Educational Technology and development of Education IEY (1970).

❒

3

Micro-Teaching

3. Introduction

Micro-Teaching is one of the most recent innovations in teacher education programmes which aims to modify teacher's behaviour according to the specified objectives. Educationists in our country have recently recognised the importance of Micro-Teaching in preparing efficient class-room teachers. A beginning has been made at some centres in the country, in the direction of conducting researches on Micro-Teaching to replace traditional methods of class-room teaching in teachers' training institutions. It is assumed that if a person is trained to acquire the sub-skills of teaching one by one, and then if all these sub-skills are integrated together he becomes an efficient teacher. The systematic training that a would-be-teacher or a practising teacher, receives for each sub-skill of teaching is called Micro-Teaching.

3.1 Background of Micro-Teaching

Micro-Teaching was developed by Professor Dwight Allen and Robert Bush in the teacher preparation programme at Stanford University between 1960-1967. It can be used for pre-service and in-service teacher training programmes. It is a laboratory technique of teacher training in which the complexities of normal class-room teaching are simplified. It is based on Skinner's operant conditioning. It is not a teaching technique. It is a training technique. It is described as a 'Scaled down teaching encounter in class size and class time. The student-teacher teaches a class of 5 to 10 pupils for 5 to 10 minutes. It is also scaled down with respect to teaching complexity.

Teaching is considered to be made up of skills and each teaching skill is a set of related teaching behaviour which tends to facilitate pupils' learning. Such skills can be defined, practised, controlled, observed and evaluated. A particular lesson may involve any number of skills.

A teacher should be trained in all these skills for developing the ability to teaching. These skills are developed by Micro-Teaching.

1. According to **Allen and Eve** (1968), "Micro-Teaching is a system of controlled practice that makes it possible to concentrate on specific teaching behaviour and to practise teaching under controlled conditions."

2. According to **N.K. Jangira and Ajit Singh**, "Micro-Teaching is a training setting for the student teacher where complexities of the normal class-room teaching are reduced by:

(i) Practising one component of skill at a time.

(ii) Limiting the content to a single concept.

(iii) Reducing the size to 5 to 10 pupils, and

(iv) Reducing the duration of the lesson to 5 to 10 minutes.

According to L.C. Singh (1977). "Micro-Teaching is a 'scaled down teaching encounter' in which a teacher teaches a small unit to a group of 5 pupils for a small period of 5 to 20 minutes. Such a situation offers a helpful setting for an experienced or inexperienced teacher to acquire new teaching skills and to refine old ones".

3.2 Micro-Teaching in India

Micro-Teaching was introduced in India in 1967, with the humble attempt made by D.D. Tiwari of Government Central Padagogical Institute, Allahabad.

In 1970, G.B. Shaw experimented with Micro-Teaching at M.S. University, Baroda. Then the Technical Teachers Training Institute, Madras introduced Micro-Teaching to train the technical teachers. In 1947, Dr. N.L. Dosajh used Micro-Teaching as a teaching device in Teachers Training Institute, Chandigarh. He also wrote a book namely: Modification of Teacher Behaviour through Micro-Teaching' NCERT, SCERT, in the different states have been propagation this concept.

3.3 Definitions of Micro-Teaching

1. According to **D. W. Allen** (1966), "Micro-Teaching is a scaled down teaching encounter in class size and time."

2. According to **Buch** (1968), "Micro-Teaching is a teacher education technique which allows teachers to apply clearly defined teaching skills to carefully prepared lessons in a planned series of five to ten minutes encounters with a small group of real students, often with an opportunity to observe the result on video tape."

3. According to **David B. Young** defined Micro-Teaching as "a device which provides the novice and experienced teacher alike, new opportunities to improve teaching."

4. According to **Allen and Eve** (1968), "Micro-Teaching is defined as a system of controlled practice that makes it possible to concentrate on specific teaching behaviour and to practise teaching under controlled conditions."

5. According to **Clift and Others** (1976), "Micro-Teaching is a teacher training procedure which reduces the teaching situation ot simpler and more controlled encounter achieved by limiting the practice teaching to a specific skill and reducing teaching time and class size."

6. According to **MC Alleese and Unwin** (1970), "The term Micro-Teaching is most often applied to the use of Closed Circuit Television (CCTV) to give immediate feedback of a trainee teacher's performance in a simplified environment."

7. According to **Passi, B.K.** (1976) says, "It is a training technique which requires pupil-teachers to teach a single concept using specified teaching skills to a small number of pupils in a short duration of time."

3.4 Nature of Micro-Teaching

On the basis of these definitions, the nature of Micro-Teaching can be concluled as follows:

(a) Micro-Teaching is an innovation in the field of teacher education.

(b) It is a techer training technique.

(c) It is micro in the sense that it scales down the complexities of real teaching.

(d) Duration of each micro lesson is 5 to 10 minutes.

(e) It is a highly individualised training device.

(f) In Micro-Teaching only one skill at a time practised.

(g) The size of the class is reduced and the number of the students is just 5 to 10.

(h) The use of video tape and CC TV make the observations very objective.

(i) In Micro-Teaching 'feedback' is provided immediately after the complextion of the lesson.

3.5 Characteristics of Micro-Teaching

A few characteristics of Micro-Teaching are as under:

1. It is a teacher training technique and not a method of class-room instruction.
2. It is micro in the sense that if scales down the complexities of real teaching.

(a) Out of contents, a single concept is taken up at a time.

(b) Only one skill at a time is practised.

(c) Size of the class is reduced and thus the number of students is just 5 to 7.

(d) Duration of each micro lesson is 5 to 7 minutes.

3. Feedback is provided immediately after the completion of the lesson.

4. The use of Video Tape and Closed Circuit Television makes the observation very objective.

5. There is a high degree of control in practising a skill when this technique is used.

6. It is highly individualized training device.

7. Micro-Teaching is an analytic approach to training.

Micro-Teaching involves actually teaching a real lesson to real pupils with none of the role-playing of earlier modelled teaching situations.

(i) Micro-Teaching lessons are constructed for the benefit of the teacher and student's learning is incidental.

(ii) Micro-Teaching provides a significant way to bring specific educational problems into manageable focus.

3.6 Components of Micro-Teaching

The components of Micro-Teaching are:

(i) a teacher,

(ii) the pupils (usually 4 or 5),

(iii) a brief lesson,

(iv) the objectives of the specific Micro-Teaching occasion,

(v) feedback by the supervisor, or by using audio tape recordings, video tape recordings and closed circuit television.

3.7 Assumptions of Micro-Teaching

The assumptions on which Micro-Teaching is based are as under:

1. Teaching behaviour of a teacher can be observed in class-room situations.
2. Drawbacks in the teaching competency can be traced out and then they can be improved upon.
3. Complexities of normal class-room situation can be reduced. The size of the class, the duration of teaching, teaching contents etc., can be reduced for giving training to the beginner teachers.
4. Practice of teaching can be controlled by providing regular feedback.
5. Training of specific skills can be given very well by taking up one skill at a time.
6. Teacher training programme can be highly individualised.
7. In-service teachers can also be better trained through Micro-Teaching technique.
8. Feedback to the teacher trainee can be possible immediately. The earlier the feedback to the teacher trainee, the better is his learning the different skills of teaching.
9. Observation of teaching can be done objectively by using video-tape and Closed Circuit Television.

3.8 Procedure Adopted in Micro-Teaching

The following steps are used for conducting a micro lesson successfully:

1. There is general discussion about Micro-Teaching. Theory of Micro-Teaching with all details is discussed. The teacher under training reads related literature and through discussions, clarifications are sought.
2. Different skills involved in teaching are explained to the pupil-teachers.
3. An expert the subject gives a demonstration lesson on that particular skill.
4. Out of the various skills, one skill for mastery purpose is selected. Full details of that skill are given to the pupil-teachers.
5. The demonstration lesson is followed by discussions in which the learner teachers discuss things and seek all type of clarifications.
6. The pupil-teacher teaches the lesson to a small group of students (*i.e.*, 5 to 10 students). The lesson is observed by the supervisor (the teacher) or by the peers or video tape.
7. The pupil-teacher writes the micro lesson plan on the skill already selected. He does this in consultation with the supervisor.
8. Immediately after the lesson, feedback is proved. All type of suggestions are given for the improvement of the lesson.
9. In the light of discussion and suggestions, the pupil-teacher replans the lesson. It is done again under the guidance of the supervisor.

10. The lesson replanned, is retaught to the small group of students.

Thus, we find that through Micro-Teaching, the pupil-teacher is able to acquire 5 R's *i.e.*

1. Recording
2. Reviewing
3. Responding
4. Refining and
5. Redoing.

3.9 Phases of Micro Teaching Procedures

According to Clift and Others (1976), Micro-Teaching procedure have the following three phases:

1. Knowledge Acquisition Phase. At this stage, the student teacher tries to get knowledge of the skill to be practised. He reads revlevant literature concerning that skill. He is also made to observe a demonstration lesson in which that skill figures prominently. The person who demonstrates the skill is an expert of the subject and the skill. By observing that lesson, the teacher under training gets theoretical as well as practical knowledge of that skill.

2. Skill Acquisition Phase. The student teacher acquires the skill in hand through a lot of practice. He prepares the micro-lesson, teaches it to have practice and then through feedback the evaluates his performance. Then he replans the lesson with modifications and improvement and then reteaches that lesson. Again there is re-feedback in order to enable him to have mastery of the teaching skill. In this way, different skills are learnt by the student teacher one by one.

3. Transfer Phase. At this stage, teacher integrates the different skills. Instead of artificial situation he teaches in the real class-room where the number of students full class. His lesson is of 30 to 35 minutes duration and there he tries to integrate all the skills for which he made efforts in Phase Nos. I and II.

3.10 Principles Underlying Micro-Teaching

Micro-Teaching is based on a few sound principles which are briefly explained below:

1. Principle of One Skill at a Time. In Micro-Teaching, training of one skill is given till the person has acquired mastery over it. Then the second skill is taken up and so on. Thus, we find that Micro-Teaching is based on the principle of giving training of one skill at a time.

2. Principle of Limited Contents. In Micro-Teaching, limited contents are taken up and the teacher is required to use those contents only. It helps the beginner teacher teach that limited material easily and confidently.

3. Principle of Experimentation. A lot of Experimentation is involved in Micro-Teaching. The experiment consists of objective observation of actions performed under controlled conditions. The pupil-teacher and the supervisor conduct experiment on teaching skills under controlled conditions. Variables like time duration of the lesson, contents of the lesson to be taught, number of students sitting in the class etc., can be easily controlled.

4. Principle of Practice. Micro-Teaching is based on the sound principle of practice. Here lot of practice is given by taking up on skill at a time. Practice makes a man perfect. It helps the pupil-teacher in becoming better and better.

5. Principle of Immediate Feedback. The micro lesson lasts for four or five minutes only. Thereafter, feedback is provided to the pupil-teacher. It helps the pupil-teacher to know his drawbacks and improve them effectively without any delay.

6. Principle of Individualised Training. In Micro-Teaching, each trainee is given training very thoroughly. There is individual attention by the supervisor. The drawbacks in teaching are pointed out, suggestions given one by one and thus improvement is brought about.

7. Principle of Evaluation. In Micro-Teaching, there is continuous assessment of the performance of the pupil-teacher. Evaluation helps the learner know his drawback and then he is able to improve it. In Micro-Teaching, each micro lesson is supervised by the supervisor or the peers. Drawbacks in teaching are pointed out and suggestion for improvement are given. Self-evaluation is also possible. Thus, evaluation ensures good learning by the pupil-teacher.

8. Principle of Continuity. Learning of different skills of teaching is a continuous process in Micro-Teaching programme. The pupil-teacher is learning one skill at a time and learning continues till he has mastered the skill. For each skill, the principle of continuity is implied. It makes the teacher good and effective.

3.11 Micro-Teaching Procedures/Steps of Micro-Teaching

A Micro-Teaching programme is organised to expose the trainees to an organised curriculum of miniature teaching encounters, moving from the less complex to the more complex. At each step along the way, a teaching strategy is discussed until it can be incorporated into a short teaching lesson of approximately 5 minutes duration. The trainee then teaches this lesson with a small group of four to six pupils in front of a video camera (if it is available), a supervisor, and often some trainee peers. The pupils are sent out after filling a short rating form, and the video recording is replayed and criticised by the supervisor and trainee peers. Then the trainee is given time to think about this criticism and to make modifications in his teaching strategy.

Micro-Teaching process includes the following steps:

(i) Orientation. In this step teacher provides orientation *i.e.*, lectures on Micro-Teaching, its process, aspects, merits and limitations, to the popil-teachers.

(ii) Discussion of Teaching Skill. Under this step the pupil-teachers should be introduced with various teaching skills. Teacher discusses and explains the psychological rationale behind a particular skill under use.

(iii) Presentation of Micro-Teaching Model. The teacher educator gives a model Micro-Teaching (5 to 10 minutes) for the particular skill. His model-examplifies the use of the particular skill and its components. There are following different ways for providing the model lesson:

(a) The teacher himself can present the model-lesson.

(b) The model-lesson can be given with the help of a film or video-tape.

(c) It can be provided with the help of a audio-tape.

(d) Written or printed model-lesson can be distributed among the pupil-teachers.

(iv) Observation Schedule. The pupil-teachers should be provided the 'Observation Schedule' for the observation of the specific skill. Each skill has different observation schedule. The observation and criticism of the model lesson provide feedback to the demonstrator.

(v) Teaching Session. The teacher teaches a group of four or five pupils (or his own peers). The teacher educator or a peer can observe the micro lesson by the trainee and note down the observations in a specially developed proforma. The micro lesson may be video taped or atleast recorded using cassette recorder.

(vi) Preparation of Micro-lesson-Plan. Under this step pupil-teachers are required to prepare micro-lesson-plan related to the specifically selected teaching skill. The pupil-teacher should preferably select one unit concept for micro-lesson.

(vii) Feedback. Under this step, immediate feedback is provided to the trainee for his micro lesson. This feedback is provided by playing the video or audio-tape. The trainee observes his own lesson and analyses it with the teacher educator and his peers. If video and audio tape recorders are not available, the observation schedule maintained by the teacher educator and the peers can serve as a good basis of the feedback. This feedback session helps the trainee to know what acts of his teaching are to be consolidated and what acts be eliminated.

(viii) Replan. In the light of the feedback and the educator's comments the trainee re-plans the micro lesson. Duration of this session is 12 minutes.

(ix) Re-Feed Back. After re-teach, re-feedback is provided to the pupil-teacher. The duration of re-feedback is 6 minutes.

(x) Re-Teach. The trainee re-teaches the micro lesson to a different but comparable group of pupils. This time also the micro lesson is video or audio-taped and the observations are noted in the proforma. Feedback is again provided on the re-teach lesson.

(xi) Repetition of the Micro-Teaching Cycle. The Micro-Teaching cycle is repeated till the pupil-teacher acquires the mastery in the teaching skill. The Micro-Teaching cycle consists of planning, teaching, feedback, re-planning, re-teaching and re-feedback.

(xii) Creation of Micro-Teaching Setting. Under this step, consideration is made for creating proper conditions and providing appropriate facilities for the practice of a teaching skill. In the Indian model of Micro-Teaching developed by NCERT the standard setting for a micro class as below:

(a) Number of pupils: 5-10

(b) Type of pupils: Real pupils or preferably peers.

(c) Type of supervisor: Teacher educators and peers.

(d) Time duration of a micro lesson: 6 minutes.

(e) Time duration of a Micro-Teaching cycle: 36 minutes.

This duration is divided as under:

Teaching session: 6 minutes

Feedback session: 6 minutes

Replan session: 12 minutes

Re-teach session: 6 minutes

Re-feedback session: 6 minutes

Total: 36 minutes

3.12 Merits of Micro-Teaching

Micro-Teaching is an innovation which has sound basis of principles of learning and application of technology. The advantages of Micro-Teaching are as follows:

1. It is an effective feedback device for the modification of teacher's behaviour.
2. It is highly individualized type to teacher training.
3. It is useful for developing teaching efficiency in pre-service and in-service teacher training programme.
4. It helps in acquiring various types of skills which ultimately form the basis of successful teaching.
5. It helps in systematic and objective observation by providing specific observation schedule.
6. It reduces the complexities of normal class-room teaching such as size of class, time and problem of discipline.
7. Teaching is a complicated type of activity. Micro-Teaching simplifies it so as to make it suitable for the beginner teachers.

8. It is a training device for improving teaching practice and to prepare effective teachers.

9. It develops the feeling of confidence among the teachers.

10. It provides economy in mastering the teaching skills. The use of video-tape enables the trainee to analyse his own teaching performance.

11. It can be done either in real class-room conditions or simulated conditions.

12. It permits increased control and regulates teaching practice.

13. It focuses on training for the acomplishment of special tasks such as practice of instructional skills, mastery of certain curricular materials and practice of techniques of teaching.

14. It enables the trainee to make progress in developing teaching skills at his own rating depending upon ability.

15. Trainees get staisfaction when they hear and see themselves through audio-video-tapes.

3.13 Demerits of Micro-Teaching

The drawbacks of Micro-Teaching are as follows:

1. Through Micro-Teaching one trainee is trained at a time.

2. It is more time consuming as a trainee will take 35 minutes to practice one skill only.

3. It presents fragmented view of teaching.

4. The immediate feedback which is a must, may not be feasible in all conditions.

5. It may enable a trainee to seek mastery over the isolated teaching skills but hardly trains him to meet the needs of the real teaching encounter.

6. Due to short lesson of 6 minutes, a trainee cannot get training in evaluation, diagnostic and remedial skills.

7. It can not fit in Indian conditions and situations due to its short practice period which may create academic and administrative problems in the schools.

8. Micro-Teaching can be carried on successfully only in controlled environment but generally it is found class-room situations are flexible.

9. It depresses the creativity of teachers. During teaching a teacher evolves something new but he has to stop as the micro lesson ends.

10. It wastes a lot of time of students. Each micro lesson goes on for 5 to 10 minutes where the main emphasis is on teaching technique, learning by students is almost ignored.

3.14 Micro-Teaching and Traditional Teaching—A Comparison

Micro-Teaching is a new idea in the field of teacher education. People who have traditional outlook don't want to change their ideologies. They face problems in accepting the innovation of Micro-Teaching. This type of situation always arises whenever new things will come up. The old nations need be converted into the modern ones because the modern ones are undoubtedly unique. The comparison of the two teachniques-brings home clearly the view point that Micro-Teaching is an inproved teachinque in every way and is better as compared to the traditional teaching:

Micro-Teaching	*Traditional Teaching*
1. Teaching is relatively simple.	1. Teaching as experienced by the teacher is complicated and difficult.

2. It does not pose a big threat or fear to the teacher.	2. It poses a big threat and a challenge to the teacher.
3. It usually encourages the beginner teacher for better job performance in future.	3. It may lead to failure and cause frustration.
4. Here the objective are given in behavioural terms.	4. The objectives are not stated in behavioural terms.
5. The number of students in a class is less. It is rather a small group of 5 to 10 students.	5. It is an over-crowded class where the number of students is 60 to 90.
6. There is provision of immediate feedback. That helps the teacher to know his drawbacks and improve upon them.	6. Mediate feedback is not provided.
7. Teaching is carried on under fully controlled situations. The supervisor is there who is determined to improve teaching.	7. There is no control as such over teaching. There is no supervision.
8. The teacher practices one skill at a time. He continues the practice till he is able to have mastery of it.	8. The teacher practices the whole teaching behaviour which consists of many skills.
9. Duration of time for teaching is 5 to 10 minutes.	9. Time duration is 35 to 40 minutes.
10. Patterns of class-room interaction can be studied objectively.	10. Patterns of class-room interaction cannot be studied easily.

TEACHING SKILLS

Teaching is a complex phenomenon that comprises of various specific teaching skills. Through Micro-Teaching, complexities of class-room teaching are reduced. The different skills are identified and then mastery of each skill is acquired. Here two important questions crop up which need consideration. The first one is to know what is a skill. The second one is how many skills are involved in the teaching process.

What is a Teaching Skill? N.L. Gage (1968) says, "Teaching skills are specific instructional activities and procedures that a teacher may use in his class-room. These are related to the various stages of teaching or in the continuous flow of the teacher performance."

To know how many skills are involved in the teaching process is rather an interesting study. A few research workers have tried to identify several sets of component teaching skills. Some of them are common with a little different terminology.

Allen and Ryan (1969), of Stanford University put forth the view that fourteen skills are involved. Borg and his associates (1970), increased the number to eighteen.

In India, **B.K. Passi** (1976), on the basis of work done in CASE, Baroda has given a list of twenty one skills. Jangira and his associates (1979), gave a list of twenty.

None of the lists suggested by the researchers are exhaustive and final. We can add or subtract from the lists as per need of the situation. The list of skills given by Allen and Ryan (1969), is as under:

1. **Stimulus Variation.** Teaching depends upon the stimulus provided by the teacher during teaching. A good teacher goes on varying the stimulus in order to bring in variety in his teaching. That way he is able to attract the attention of the students. Thus, the teachers

are trained in movements, gestures, focussing, interactional styles etc.

2. **Closure.** It is related with the finishing up of a stage in teaching. It helps the students to relate the new knowledge with the previous one.

3. **Set Induction.** Set induction helps the students to induce maximum. The teacher uses their present knowledge and skills and tries to involve them in the lesson.

4. **Higher Order Questions.** In every good lesson, the teacher puts some questions which are of higher order. This type of questions enable the students to form generalizations or to reach some definite principles.

5. **Silence and Non-Verbal Cues.** During teaching, the teacher provides cues to the students in order to encourage them. Sometimes he puts a thought provoking question. The students speak on it. The discussion goes on and on when the teacher does not give his personal comments. He rather remains silent. It makes many other students to come forward and speak.

6. **Reinforcement of Student Participation.** The pupil-teacher in every way tries to encourage students's participation in the lesson. As fas as possible, he accepts their responses with a smile. Only positive reinforcers are used by him. He makes every effort to avoid the use of negative reinforcers which may result into any type of discouragement for the students.

7. **Probing Questions.** The teacher puts such questions with the help of which he is able to dig out something from the students. With the help of probing questions, the teacher is able to lead the students to correct responses.

8. **Divergent Questions.** Putting divergent questions is another skill which makes the students think creatively.

9. **Fluency in Making Questions.** While putting questions to the class, the teacher should have fluency. He tries to have as many questions as possible in the scheduled period of teaching.

10. **Recognising Attending Behaviour.** Every good teacher has the ability to judge while teaching how far the students are taking interest in the lesson. The teacher is able to do so through visual cues.

11. **Planned Repetition.** Sometimes during teaching the teacher repeats things in a planned manner. He does so in order to focus the attention of the students over some important points.

12. **Completeness.** Communication of teaching is a two way traffic. Through teaching, the teacher is able to communicate himself fully. He is able to give knowledge, develop attitude and interest of the students.

13. **Illustrations and use of Examples.** A good teacher has the skill of clear teaching. For this purpose he is able to give good examples. Through illustrations, he is able to capture the attention of all.

14. **Lecturing.** The teacher is able to present the material effectively by using the right type of techniques.

B. K. Passi (1976), described 13 skills in his book 'Becoming Better Teacher—Micro-Teaching Approach.' The different skills are as under:

(i) Writing instructional objectives.

(ii) Introducing a lesson.

(iii) Fluency in questioning.

(iv) Probing questions.

(v) Explaining.

(vi) Illustrating with examples.

(vii) Stimulus variation.

(viii) Silence and non-verbal cues.

(ix) Reinforcement.

(x) Increasing pupil participation.

(xi) Using blackboard.

(xii) Achieving closure.

(xiii) Recognising attending behaviour.

The Baroda General Teaching Competence Scale (BGTC) has divided teaching skills into three categories:

(a) Pre-instructional Skills.

(b) Presentation Skills.

(c) Closing, Evaluation and Managerial Skills.

3.15 List of Probable Teaching Skills For Different Stages of a Lesson

Below is given a list of probable teaching skills which are required at different stages of a lesson:

I. Planning Stage

This stage involves the following skills.

1. Writing Instructional Objectives.
2. Selecting the content.
3. Selection of Audio Visual Aids material.
4. Organising content.

II. Introductory Stage

1. Creating set induction.
2. Introducing the lesson.

III. Presentation Stage

The Presentation Stage has four sub-stages. Each sub-stage needs different type of teaching skills which are given below:

(a) Questioning Skills

(i) Structuring Class-room questions.

(ii) Fluency in asking questions.

(iii) Probing questions.

(iv) Question-delivery and distribution.

(v) Divergent questions.

(vi) Responses Management.

(vii) Higher order questions.

(b) Presentation Skills

(i) Packing of the lesson.

(ii) Lecturing.

(iii) Explaining.

(iv) Illustrating with examples.

(v) Demonstrating.

(vi) Discussing.

(c) Aid Using Skills

(i) Using teaching Aids.

(ii) Using blackboard.

(iii) Silence and Non-verbal cues.

(iv) Reinforcement.

(v) Stimulus variation.

(d) Management Skills

(i) Promoting pupil participation.

(ii) Recognising attending behaviour.

(iii) Management of the class.

Teaching is a very complex activity having atleast three levels of teacher behaviours *viz.*, component teaching skills, component teaching behaviours having the component skill and atomistic teaching behaviours. This is primary level of teaching skills. These component teaching skills can be classified into individual sets of component teaching behaviours at the secondary level. The component teaching skills can be defined as a set of inter-related component teaching behaviours for the realisation of specific instructional objectives. To help the student teachers at the beginning stage to prepare the lesson, a component teaching skill and its component teaching behaviours are selected as units and not the complex teaching as a whole. Thus, we may say that the Micro-Teaching is an analytic approach to teacher training.

There is a feeling that teaching cannot be broken into pieces in the form of various teaching skills and component behaviours. Teaching is not just a combination of these isolated bits and therefore mastery over the different teaching skills does not make one an effective teacher.

There should be some bridge between training in isolated skills and the real teaching situations. The concept of integration of teaching skills may perform the role of such bridge.

Inegration of skills means a process of selection, organistation and utilization of different teaching skills to form an effective pattern for realizing the specified instructinal objectives in a given teaching-learning situation.

Objectives. The major objectives of the integration of teaching skills are as follows:

1. Helping in the transition from Micro-Teaching situation to real teaching situation.
2. Providing practice in making decision regarding the synthesis of teaching skills in view of the teaching situation and instructional objectives.

Integration in parts and integration as a whole are the strategies for the integration of skills.

Integration in Parts. First of all decision is made with respect to the number of individually mastered skills required to be integrated. The time duration of the teaching excercise for integration depends upon the number of teaching skills to be integrated. It is increased four time if there are four skills to the integrated and five times in case of five skills and so on. All the steps like teach, feedback, re-plan, re-teach, re-feedback are planned and carried out in the controlled setting (as in the case of Micro-Teaching) and this process continues till the student teacher acquires a reasonable level of mastery in the integration of the skills in hand. After acquiring mastery in the integration of these skills he is required to apply it in a real class-room setting and have sufficient practice in such real teaching.

Integration as Whole. In this approach, opportunity is provided to integrate all the individual teaching skills by taking them as a whole and not in parts. It is a sort of mini-teaching, bridging the gap between Micro-Teaching and teaching in real situation.

Student teacher should have full knowledge of the content, instructional objectives, teaching learning situations and scope of utilization of the learned individual teaching skill.

Conclusion. Teaching is a very complex activity and teaching considered to be made up of skills and each teaching skill is related with teaching behaviour, if we want desirable changes in learners personality we need trained skills and these all skills are the main thrust of Micro-teaching, Micro-teaching, is considered as a revolution in teaching field. Its an approach to replace traditional methods of class-room teaching in teachers, training institutions etc. The knowledge of Micro-teaching would help and facilitate would be teacher or practising teacher to perform well and received excellent results or learning output.

REFERENCES

Allen, D.W. & Eve, A.—A Micro-teaching Theory into Practice (1968).

Bloom, B.S.—Human Characteristics and School Learning Harper, New York, 1976.

Bloom B.S. ***et al***—Texonomy of Educational Objectives: The Classification of Educational Goals/Congnitive Domain and effective Domain, New York, Mackey 1965.

Das R.C.—Educational Technology, Sterling Publisher, New Delhi, 1993.

Dececloo, J.—The Psychology of Learning & Instruction, Prentice Hall, New Jersey, 1968.

L.C. Singh—Micro-teaching.

Mohanty, J.—Educational Technology, Deep and Deep Publication, New Delhi, 1991.

Gange, R.M.—The Conditions of Learning, New York, Holt, Rinchart & Winston, 1965.

❐

4

Lecture Presentation in Class

4. Introduction

Lecturing occurs whenever a teacher is talking and students are listening. It flourishes in an age of cheap paperback books and affordable videotape technology. Its survival is not solely due to the old-fashioned preferences of conservative college faculties. Many students, especially those who seek information and high marks, prefer lectures as well. Innovative course formats eventually fade from listings of departmental offerings when students are given a choice between them and traditionally taught courses. The lecture also survives because at its best it can be magnificent. Enough instructors at almost every school are accomplished lecturers for the form to remain the norm in spite of poor examples. The economic advantages of teaching classes by means of the lecture, especially those offering very large sections, are numerous, though they are insufficient to account for the lecture's popularity.

4.1 Forms of the Lecture

A graduate instructor once supervised eschewed lecturing in favor of discussion. He said he didn't believe in lecturing. Asked to describe the lecturing he did not believe in, he realized that lecturing symbolized for him a rejecting, dominating attitude toward students, not a variety of teacher presentation.

What are the major types of lecture? At one end of a continuum is the formal oral essay, the tightly constructed, highly polished kind of lecture that presents information primarily to support a summative point or conclusion. In this kind of lecture the professor has reviewed and selected from a large body of knowledge the theories, research studies, and arguments that support his or her conclusion. The most formal of such lectures are written out and read to the students.

At their best, oral essays are by no means boring. Listening to one can be an emotionally and intellectually significant experience. However, lectures such as these rarely occur in college classes for a very practical reason. A formal lecture for a fifty-minute class needs to be about 7,500 words long. At three classes per week for a fifteen-week semester, a teacher giving only oral essays would have to compose 337,500 tightly constructed words, producing over 1,000 pages of typed manuscript a feat well beyond the powers of most faculty members.

There are other problems with this kind of lecture as well. Formal essays can achieve the highest level of Dimension I teaching, but a course consisting solely of them fails to meet educational objectives that require dialogue with students. Because formal lectures ignore the interpersonal dimension, they are not likely to fully motivate or satisfy most students. A long series of such lectures would wear out students' ability to concentrate on them as well as the teacher's ability to construct them.

The most common kind of college lectures are called expository lectures because they primarily define and set forth information. Most students think of this sort of lecture when they hear that a professor "lectures a lot." In these lectures the instructor does most of the talking, with only occasional questions from the bolder students. Such lectures are less elaborately planned than oral essays, but nothing prevents them from being outstanding and satisfying to students if they are skillfully prepared and delivered.

A related form is the provocative lecture. As in formal and expository lectures, the instructor does most of the talking, but here there is more intention of provoking thought. In these lectures the teacher challenges students' existing knowledge and values and helps them to form a more complex and integrated perspective. Provocative lectures are better suited to the humanities than to the sciences, but lectures that challenge and question student assumptions are appropriate in any discipline, especially near the end of a term when a common set of knowledge has been shared. Instructors rely more on discussion than on lectures to help students question their personal values and attitudes, but a first-quality provocative lecture can achieve the 'same objective.

In a lecture-discussion the college teacher encourages students to comment or express concern rather than simply raise questions. The typical lecture-discussion class begins with the instructor speaking for five to fifteen minutes and then stimulating a few minutes of discussion around a key point in his or her remarks. During such discussion the instructor offers brief clarification or integration between student comments, but students do most of the talking. Lecture-discussions vary in the amount of time spent in lecture and in discussion, but most instructors using this format pause for discussion at least twice in a period.

Another common variation of the formal lecture is lecture-recitation, in which the teacher stops to ask specific questions or request students to read prepared material aloud. Lecture-recitations are the reverse of question-lecture classes because in this case the teacher provides the questions and the students share what they know or have prepared. Class time in American colleges was once spent almost exclusively on recitation and some teachers and subjects (especially languages) still use it heavily.

A final variation is the lecture-laboratory, in which students follow short lectures by making their own observations, experiments, or other independent work. Science courses most often use this method, but studio art and writing classes can be lecture-laboratories as well.

4.2 What the Lecture Can and Cannot Do Well

A common criticism of lectures is that if a speaker does not write out a lecture beforehand, what is said is likely to be inferior to something already written in a book; and if a lecture is already written, why bother to read the words aloud rather than simply assigning students to read the text?

This is indeed a conundrum if one accepts the premise that the sole purpose of a lecture is to present information. Available research consistently concludes that lectures are one of the least effective methods of conveying information. Though lectures sometimes produce better immediate recall than reading, tests of recall several hours or days later indicate that a single lecture does not produce more learning of information than a single reading of the same material. Since most students can read faster than a lecturer can talk, it is easily argued that lectures are an inefficient use of students' and teachers' time.

Fortunately, this narrow view of the objectives of the lecture is neither universal nor necessary. Lectures do much more than readings. Research suggests that a first-rate lecture is better than written material at emphasizing conceptual organization, clarifying ticklish issues, reiterating critical points, and inspiring students to appreciate the importance of key information. The high clarity of an excellent lecture aids understanding, as do the emotionally tinged associations created when students learn in a state of intellectual excitement.

The lecture is probably most effective at motivating students to learn more about a topic. Good lectures are very difficult to ignore. They are, above all else, engaging. Any student's mind wanders more often while reading assigned chapters or articles than when listening to an instructor who makes his or her knowledge about a subject seem exciting and important. The intellectual excitement resulting from good lectures can make students more likely to read assignments attentively.

Lectures, then, are not superfluous. When formal essays, expository lectures, or provocative lectures are combined with any of the modes requiring student participation, such as discussion or laboratory, a number of educational goals can be accomplished. Students can question their values and attitudes and increase their problem-solving and thinking skills. A professor can model the kind of thinking he or she wishes students to emulate and then give them an opportunity to try it themselves.

To organize lectures well, teachers must consider how students learn. The next section contains a brief summary of what psychological research has demonstrated about learning. These general principles apply to all human learning, but they are especially relevant to the way content should be selected and organized for presentation in a college lecture.

4.3 Choosing What to Present in a Lecture

This section deals with ways of organizing outstanding lectures. The preparation is the same whether the instructor only lectures or combines lecturing with other activities. My recommendations in the remainder of this chapter concern both what a college teacher chooses to present in a lecture and how he or she presents it.

Deciding How Much to Present. As instructors quickly learn, only a small number of major points can be presented effectively in a single class meeting. Research on what can be remembered following classes indicates that most college students can absorb only three to four points in a fifty-minute period and four to five in a seventy-five-minute class, regardless of the subject being taught. Students can remember details about each point, but the number of general ideas that can be absorbed is limited. Attempting to cover too much causes the coverage of each point to be superficial and the pace to be rushed for the instructor and frantic for the students. Time to answer questions or to pause for individual ideas to sink in will be eliminated.

Selecting Points for Presentation. Since relatively few major points can be presented in each lecture (and in a semester), choosing what to present becomes critical. A first choice is whether to survey course content comprehensively or select only key or critical topics for presentation. Though most teachers in theory endorse concentrating on points of fundamental importance, in practice they seem to believe that if they do not cover everything, their teaching is somehow suspect, shoddy, or superficial. Introductory or survey courses particularly evoke this feeling. When, as is common, beginning college teachers fall hopelessly behind schedule near the end of the term, they wrestle in obvious discomfort over which important topics to omit. Without guidelines on ways to select material, the easiest course for an instructor to take is to attempt to present it all, however sketchily.

Experienced instructors know that lectures cannot carry the major responsibility for conveying information. Readings should do that. Points for lectures should be chosen using the following criteria:

1. Central points or general themes that tie together as many other topics as possible should be presented. Details will be associated to central points more easily. The lecturing practice of placing topics in brief historical perspective is common because of this advantage of organizing points.

2. Points should also be selected for their high interest to students. If the most provocative topic in the assigned reading for a given class is ignored in favor of more theoretically critical topics, students are likely to be disappointed. Satisfying students' initial curiosity about certain topics is a good way to lead them to appreciate the importance, beauty, or relevance of other ideas that seem less appealing at first and to motivate them to read assigned materials outside of class.

3. Of most importance in choosing what to present is the depth and complexity of a given topic. A lecture should not be so simplistic or obvious that students are unlikely to learn anything new from it (especially if they have done the assigned reading); neither should it be so sophisticated and terse that many will be overwhelmed with the intricacy of the remarks. Finding the appropriate depth of presentation for a group whose members differ significantly in ability is one of the greatest challenges in giving fine lectures. Experience can help a teacher calibrate his or her presentation, but careful observation of student reactions is the most effective way to fine-tune the level of complexity on the spot.

4. A teacher should occasionally choose a topic because it is especially difficult for students. Though class time would be drudgery if it were spent only on difficult or abstract points, selecting commonly misunderstood topics is frequently appropriate.

4.4 Organizing the Lecture

A lecture should begin by stimulating students' curiosity. Any playwright, screenwriter, or novelist knows the importance of starting with a "grabber," a tension-producing statement or juxtaposition that attracts the audience and holds their involvement as the plot and characters are developed further. The opening of a lecture should also create in students an expectation that something important will follow.

Many lecturers begin with a key question or paradox that the day's lecture will attempt to answer or explain ("What can we learn about changes in British images of the heroic through comparison of nineteenth and twentieth century novels?"). Another option is to call attention to an intriguing example of or exception to a general phenomenon. Sometimes lecturers approach a familiar concept from a fresh direction. Lectures aimed at students who have had considerable prior coursework in a subject are especially appropriate for beginnings that re-examine familiar ideas.

After the attention-getter is chosen, there are several options for organizing the remaining points in a lecture. A common method is to proceed in a linear and logical fashion, gradually building to a final concluding point. Some lecturers, however, prefer non-linear organization, in which students may not understand at the beginning where the lecturer is heading. Jacob Bronowski, in his television series "The Ascent of Man", typified non-linear organization. Another common tack is to present two separate topics in some detail and conclude by contrasting and comparing them.

Whatever the organization of a given lecture (and one should vary the approach from one class meeting to another), it is advisable to approach the structure of the formal lecture as much as possible. Ploughing through loosely related topics without emphasizing the relationships among them promotes neither understanding nor satisfaction. When organizing a lecture, the instructor should remember that it is a dramatic presentation needing boundaries: an engaging beginning and a concluding ending.

4.5 Presenting of Contents

This section focuses on general lecture style and the use of audiovisual technology to enhance interest and organization. Carefully selected and organized points constitute a lecture of only moderate quality unless they are delivered well. Increasing the interest value of a lecture is the best way, to prevent students from dozing off in class or staying away altogether.

(i) Lecturing with Immediacy and Spontaneity. Classical Greek orators spent an incredibly large amount of time preparing their speeches for contests. Every word, every gesture, and every inflection was planned and practiced before-hand so it would have the desired effect on the audience. Yet the effect the orators sought was the appearance of speaking extemporaneously to express genuine emotions.

Regardless of how carefully a teacher has prepared a lecture, the actual delivery should have a sense of immediacy, as if the speaker is having for the first time many of the thoughts he or she is sharing with the students. This quality of conversational intimacy involves the students more readily in the flow of ideas than does a didactic style. The instructor should avoid at all costs the stern, moralizing tone commonly associated with a lecture from a disapproving superior.

Beginning college instructors sometimes indicate that they plan to prepare for their courses by writing out all their lectures beforehand. Such energy would be highly misplaced. The elegance of written lectures is admirable, but such lectures take too much time to prepare and cannot seem spontaneous when delivered. Rather, teachers should think first about the major points they wish to present. If they want to plan specific classes ahead of time, they should write brief outlines for at most the first three class meetings.

Until an instructor has actually used notes, he or she will not know how much detail is needed or how much material can be covered in a given class. Because most beginners fear they will not be sufficiently prepared and will run out of content before the class hour is up, they almost always prepare too much and write notes in too much detail. After a few months' experience, they gradually shorten their lecture notes and come to realize that their initial fantasy about writing out all lectures ahead of time was quite impractical.

Lecture notes should contain in outline the major topics selected for presentation and the key points under each. Experienced instructors know that complete sentences in notes are both unnecessary and difficult to read quickly. Words or brief phrases suffice. Any formulas or definitions to be read to the class may be written out, though quoting from memory or reading them from a book is often more impressive to students. The purpose of lecture notes is to remind the instructor of what he or she thought about while preparing the class, not to provide something to read. There are no definitive criteria for the length of lecture notes for a single class, but less than one page is probably too short and more than three is surely too long. To achieve a sense of immediacy and spontaneity, a college teacher must create a lecture to some extent while presenting it, and writing notes out in too much detail risks sapping creativity and making the speaker too dependent on them. Many outstanding teachers report that they commonly have new ideas or insights into their material while actually giving a lecture.

(ii) Introducing Variety. An instructor must not only capture but also hold students' attention throughout each class meeting. "Never do any single thing for very long" is a good rule for keeping attention. Students will tire of anything, even humor or anecdotes, if it is done for too long without a change of pace. A lecturer should plan for some change in format every ten minutes or so. The organization of content need not be broken, only the manner in which ideas are presented.

An instructor might vary a presentation by giving a specific example of the topic under consideration, asking a series of rhetorical questions, or saying something humorous. Humor is an especially good way to introduce variety and let everyone (the instructor included) relax a bit. A teacher should note, however, that the best humor in college classes is not canned jokes; satirical or witty comments about the subject, individuals studied, or oneself are more appreciated.

(iii) Seeking Feedback During Class. Fortunately, college teachers need not worry about sensing when they should shift gears to maintain the class's interest—the students will tell them. All that instructors need do is note the messages that students send their way. Students' faces give the best indication of the way a presentation is being received. Students signal when they are no longer caught up in a lecture and are having to work to pay attention.

Yawns, chair shuffling, sighs, or whispered asides to fellow students clearly tell an instructor that it is time to do something different. More subtle cues give the same message. There is a certain glassed-over quality in students' eyes that shows they are no longer fully engaged. The wise instructor looks for it constantly to fine-tune the pacing of a lecture and to indicate when it is time to ask a question, give an example, or in some other way break stride for a short while.

Another technique to solicit feedback from students is to ask questions such as "Am I going too fast?" or "Should I slow down a bit to let all this sink in?" Highet suggests keeping a running joke with the students in the back row of a large room: Every week or so the teacher can break up slow spots in a lecture by suddenly asking, "Can you people in the back row still hear me okay?"

4.6 Suggestions for Bad Lecturing

1. Begin a course with no introduction to the subject or to your own bias. Simply start with the first topic you wish to present.

2. Make no references to the broader context related to the specific topic being considered.

3. Do not acknowledge the students' interests or previous knowledge and experience.

4. Give excessive attention to the trivial details of the subject or to those parts that most interest you; omit topics of more central importance or interest.

5. Become preoccupied with the historical context of a topic, neglecting the central subject of the course.

6. Dwell extensively on your private scholarly quarrels with other authorities over esoteric points without showing how your concerns relate to the larger subject.

7. Present learned quotations without connecting them to the content.

8. Qualify terms so excessively that students will not be able to explain them to a friend immediately after class. Be so specific and sophisticated in the definitions you present that students will have to memorize what you say word for word and will be unable to define terms meaningfully in their own language.

9. Justify conclusions on the basis of tradition or authority without explaining why the authorities believe as they do.

10. Rarely look at your audience. With a fixed posture, keep your eyes on your notes, the floor, the ceiling, or the side walls.

11. Use arcane terms and make no attempt to define them; do not acknowledge that students may not know what you mean.

12. Speak in a monotonous voice, showing little emphasis, force, or enthusiasm.

13. Show little sense that time is passing and insist on presenting points in the orderly manner you have planned, even if individual classes end in mid topic or you fall far behind the course syllabus.

14. Hesitate frequently in the middle of sentences, but rarely pause at the end of major lecture sections.

15. Indicate that you know the students are confused or impatient, but then do nothing differently.

4.7 Suggestions for Good Lecturing

1. Seek concise ways to present and illustrate content. Express concepts in the simplest terms possible and define technical terms when using them.

2. Fit the material you present to the time you have available.

3. Begin each course and class by pricking the students' interest, expressing positive expectations, and sharing the objectives you have for them.

4. Use a wide range of voices, gestures, and physical movements, but be yourself: Develop a varied and interesting style consistent with your values and personality.

5. Follow a prepared outline but include improvised material or illustrations. Appear spontaneous even when you are following the outline closely.

6. Break up the monotony of lectures by varying methods of presentation.

7. Give students regular places to catch their breath and ask questions. It is "better to talk too little and stop short than to go on for too long".

8. Be guided by your students during your lectures. Continually observe their reactions, acknowledge them, and modify your approach when indicated.

9. End each lecture with a conclusion that connects what has happened today with what will be covered during the next meeting.

10. Remember in your relationships with students that all of you are persons first, students and teacher second. Remember that you, as a teacher, "are both host and guest".

Conclusion. Lecture preparing is basicly an art. A well articulated lecture is always dilogue oriented which gives due credit to learness desire. Good lectures are very difficult to ignore. Through good lecture teacher may arouse interest in the subjects. The intellectual excitement resulting from good lectures can make students more likely to read assignments attentively. The main aim of any good lecture must be-impart-indepth knowledge of the subject concerned and should develop critical and analytical ability which is the core objective of total educational system at last we can quate Sec. Edu. Com. (1952-53) which clearly pointed out "every teacher and educationist of experience knows that even the best curriculum and the most perfect syllabus remain dead unless quickened in to life by the right methods of teaching and the right kind of teachers".

REFRENCES

Bloom B.S. (Ed.)—Taxonomy of Education Objectives Classficiation of Educational Goal, Handbook of Cognitive Domain, New York Longmans, 1965.

Govt. of India—National Policy on Education 1986 M.H.R.D. (Edu.), New Delhi.

Govt. of India—Report of the Secondary Education Commission, New Delhi, 1952-53.

Kochhar, S.K.—Methods & Techniques of Teaching Sterling Publishers Pvt Ltd. New Delhi, 1978.

Lowman—Mastering the Techniques of Teaching Prentice-Hall of India, 1987, New Delhi.

Mohanty J.—Dynamics of Higher Education, Deep & Deep Publication, New Delhi, 1992.

Sharma R.C.—Modern Science Teaching, Dhanpat Rai & Sons, New Delhi.

Sharma G.D & Ahmed, S.R. (Retd.)—Methodologies of Teachings in Colleges, Sterling Publishers, New Delhi, 1989.

Vedanayogam—Teaching Technology for College Teachers, Sterling Publications Pvt. Ltd., New Delhi 1989.

❑

5

Guiding Principles in Teaching

5. Introduction

The method of teaching refers to the regular ways or orderly procedures employed by the teacher in guiding the pupils in order to accomplish the aims of the learning situations. By methods in general is meant the process of reaching a definite end by a series of related acts which tend to secure that end. As applied to class-room teaching, method is a series of related and progressive acts performed by the teacher and the pupils to accomplish the general and specific aims of the lesson. Method has to do with the way a teacher communicates the subject to the student. Method involves regular steps to guide the mental processes of the learner in mastering the subject-matter being presented to him. It implies arrangement. Psychological studies reveal to us that the mental processes involve senseperception, memory, imagination, judgment and reasoning. The processes are involved in every learning situation, but they are not employed with the same degree of intensity in learning different types of subject-matter. Risk classifies methods of teaching into two general types, namely; the authoritative and the developmental. According to Risk, "the authoritative method is a procedure by which the teacher teaches by means of some kind of exposition, either oral or written, and developmental method is a procedure by which the pupil goes through the necessary learning experiences under the leadership and guidance of the teacher." Much has been written on the types of methods but no one has proven one method superior to another in every situation. In other words, there is no one best method of teaching for all situations. It should be obvious that different forms of learning require appropriate teaching methods. Likewise, there is no way to teach a particular process effectively, but there are certain fundamental principles of learning and sound philosophies of education which cannot be violated without affecting teaching methods and procedures adversely. As long as sound principles of learning are applied in the classrooms, and as long as the real aims of education are understood and are the ends toward which pupils and teachers are working, teaching methods and techniques can differ widely, even in learning the same thing.

5.1 Method of Teaching and Technique of Teaching

Writings on educational theory and practice have presented different classroom procedures as methods of teaching or techniques of teaching. These two terms have different meanings and values, but both are integrated in any teaching and learning situation. The method of teaching covers the psychological processes involved in learning, and the technique of teaching covers the use of devices and the application of principles in teaching in order to effect the proper development of the individual pupil. The term technique is also applied in the selection of devices and method to be used as well as to the way in which they are used. Method relates to the learning performance rather than to the teaching performance, and method of teaching involves steps to guide the mental process. In brief, we may say that method of teaching refers to the arrangement of the ways or procedures through which learning is achieved while technique of teaching refers to the skill employed by the teacher in carrying on the procedure or act of teaching. Method is the course or procedure; technique is the manner of performing the various steps of the procedure. In general, method involves teacher and pupils activity, while technique limits itself to the actual performance of the teacher. Method is the key to teaching and learning, and how to use this key is what we may call technique. Teachers gain techniques and skill in teaching through experience and training. Teaching has but one prime objective—to effect the proper development of the individual pupil. To accomplish this fundamental aim, the teacher must utilize specialized teaching procedure and apply properly the accepted principles of teaching and technique. Classroom instruction cannot be sucessfully accomplished with method alone, it requires some particular teaching technique as well. Different methods call for different techniques although both are basic factors in learning.

5.2 The Old and the New Methods of Teaching

The old or traditional methods are characterized by mastery of logically organized subject-matter through drills, repetition, and memorization, fixed ourriculum or activities formulated by adults, strict classroom discipline, formalized instructional patterns, and fixed standards to be achieved by all pupils. Classroom activities are governed by the processes of compulsion, rigid control, formality, fear, and tension. They are based on the concepts that education is a preparation for adult life, mental discipline, transfer of training, acquiring knowledge for its sake, seeking truth and perfection, and habit formation. The tradtioaal methods are subject-centered and teacher-dominated activities because their main concern is to get the pupils to master the subject-matter presented. The new progressive methods are based on the philosophy of John Dewey that education is life growth, reconstruction of human experiences, and a social process. The main goal of the new methods is personality development through proper stimulation, direction, and guidance. Guidance and counseling of the pupils go hand in hand with the regular methods and technique of teaching. The new methods place more emphasis on thinking and less upon memorizing, more on understanding and less on merely accumulating facts, and more through genuine interest and less learning through coercion. Classroom activities are governed by the democratic principles and ideals, group-planning and selected activities, freedom from rigid regulations and control of authority, and friendly attitude between teacher and pupils.

Most educators agree that certain fundamental principles underlie all learning, and that responsible teaching must correspond to them. However, there are the progressive educators who object to traditional methods with fixed and formalized educational procedures and standards. They advocate informality, freedom, encouragement of creative expression, recognition of the rights of the child as a free personality, life-like situation, and the fundamental importance of the interests and needs of the learner. In contrast to the foregoing philosophy, the traditionalists condemn the progressivist's easy-going tendencies, and urge the maintenance or mastery of subject-matter and mental discipline which prepares one to meet unpleasant but inevitable duties of life in a democracy. However, there are reasons why dictation, or coercion cannot be completely eliminated in the educative process.

With regards to our modern school curriculum, however the writer believes that there are subjects which can be taught effectively by using the traditional methods advocated by the old school, and there are subjects which can be taught with good effect by following the practices of the progressive school as practised in the Phillippine Normal College and in the Elementary, Department of Silliman University. In the teaching of Arithmetic, a systematic and logical procedure or series of steps is better for solving problems than an undirected one, as shown in the experiment conducted by Newcomb. The experiment conducted by Washborne and Osborne on the same subject gave the same result. Wrightstone concluded that in the teaching of social studies the new practices of the progressive school are not inferior to the traditional methods used for developing academic achievement and skill; that these practices induce the pupils to take a more literal, tolerant, and scientific attitude; and that they provide more opportunities for developing initiative, responsibility, curiosity, and the power of criticism. The modern schools call for the integration of the two points of view in moulding the child into an intelligent and social being. The wise and efficient teacher will not throw aside traditional methods because they are old, nor will he embrace progressive methods merely because they are new. Any method should be used where it would be most effective. We must bear in mind that methods, both traditional and progressive, are means to an end. They are tools at the disposal of both the teacher and the pupils. The traditional methods when properly motivated, directed and evaluated by democratic teachers are perhaps more democratic than the progressive methods under autocratic teachers. There are elements in both methods which must be utilized if we are to attempt to teach the coming generation effectively.

Whatever method is to be used, the teacher must know the conditions prevailing at a given time. The most appropriate conditions for progressive or new methods are the following:

(1) availability of funds,

(2) small classes,

(3) bright pupils,

(4) variety of equipment,

(5) freedom to adjust curriculum to local conditions or needs,

(6) command of the language,

(7) good teachers who have mastered progressive methods and techniques, and

(8) understanding of principles and ideals of democracy.

It cannot be denied that language handicap, lack of needed equipment, textbooks and teaching aids, poor educational background, and poorly trained trachers are roadblocks to the effective uses of the progressive method. A good teaching procedure will inevitably fails if its application is misunderstood or misapplied.

5.3 Factors Which Determine the Method to be Used

The following factors must be taken into consideration in selecting the method to be used for successful teaching:

1. The Aims of Education. The general aims and objectives of education must be considered in selecting the method to be used because they embody the democratic ideals to which the schools are committed. They are the basis of educational theories and practices. The general and specific aims give direction to the needs and purposes of the teachers and the pupils and to the educational programmes and activities of the school. The effectiveness of instruction is determined largely by the presence or absence of educational aims. If the purpose of the school is conceived as growth in terms of knowledge, habits, skills, abilities, and attitudes, the method of teaching which will most effectively accomplish that purpose must be employed. Method is a fundamental thing in the educative process. Educational aims and objectives give directions to the educational programmes and activities in and out of the classrooms.

2. The Nature of the Child. In modern educational priactice the child is made the center of all educational programmes and activities. The nature of the child therefore should determine the nature of teaching. The method of teaching to be used must be brought into harmony with the experiences, ability, health, interest, and needs of the pupil, and with his progress and growth. The individual pupils comprising a class vary widely in mental ability. The teacher must also bear in mind that the child's interests and needs are many and varied and they change with his changing nature. For teaching and learning to be effective, it is imperative that the teachers possess a thorough understanding of the psychological factors and principles basic to pupil growth and development. Correct method of teaching is based upon the psychological laws and principles affecting child growth and achievement—his wants, needs, and potentialities.

3. School Environment. The recent educational trends in this country calls for a new type of classrooms equipped with modern facilities. Each classroom should have sufficient desks for the meeting of the entire class. Besides adequate classrooms, availability of instructional materials, such as references, textbooks, apparatus, audio-visual aids, and supplies, must be taken into account. Absence of the necessary instructional materials affects teaching and learning. The most effective teaching and learning can take place only when the environmental condition is most advantageous. It is quite difficult to do a good job of teaching in a poor building and without adequate equipment.

4. The Nature of the Subject-Matter. The nature of the subject-matter or lesson must be well considered in selecting the method of teaching. The term subject matter refers to what is needed to secure the desired specific knowledge or to develop the understanding, abilities, habits, skills, and attitudes. It must include tentative selection of the principal items of content that appear to be essential and desirable for the pupil experiences in attaining the goals and objectives of the course. Different types of subject-matter or lessons call for different methods and techniques of teaching. If the aim of the teacher is to develop ability to reason, the method of teaching which will accomplish that aim should be employed, and subject-matter to be selected should meet the same purpose.

5. Training of the Teacher. Mastery of the psychological principles of learning, methods and techniques of teaching are fundamental to effective teaching and learning. The method to be used must be well known to the teacher. He must have a clear understanding of the principles and techniques involved. The teacher must not select or use a method which he is not well acquainted. He must acquire knowledge of, and skill in, the proper methods of presenting his subject-matter to the pupils who differ widely in interest and in capacity to learn.

5.4 Characteristics of Effective Method

Any method, to be effective, must have the following characteristics:

1. The Method must Utilize the Theory of Self-activity. Learning is the result of the pupil's activity. It is essentially experiencing reacting, doing, and undergoing. This principle states that one learns only through reaction or through self-activity which is the foundation of all learning. Teaching must be done through first-hand learning.

2. The Method must Aid the Learner in Defining his Own Purposes by Setting the Situation for the Emergence of a Desirable Purpose. The learner must start with the purpose through originating it or accepting it. Teaching is best when the learner accomplishes his purpose and receives satisfaction.

3. The Method must Utilize the Laws of Learning. The mental activity of learning proceeds in an orderly and efficient way according to the fundamental laws governing its operation. The primary laws of readiness, exercise, and effect, must be well considered in all types of teaching and learning. It is important for us to know that all kinds of learning activities are influenced in some measure by readiness, use, and effect. Good teaching provides an opportunity for motivation, exercise, review, examination, and emulation.

4. The method must provide for individual differences and make use of procedures that will suit individual characteristics such as needs, interest, and mental and physical maturity.

5. The Method must be Based on the Accepted Well integrated educational theory and practice which is designed to unify the work of teaching and learning. It can be said that theory without practise is futile, and practice without theory becomes dangerous.

6. The method must stimulate the thinking and reasoning powers of the pupils. The procedure must provide opportunity for thinking activity and thorough organizing activity. The principle of self-activity is of great importance in teaching pupils to reason.

7. The method must be suited to the progress of the pupils in skills, abilities, habits, knowledge, ideas and attitudes. All these are the basis of psychological aims of the subject-matter.

8. The method must challenge the encourage the learner to farther activities which involve the process of differentiation and

integration. The process of unifying experiences contributes much to the formation of integrated behavior. This can be accomplished best through the use of integration method of teaching.

9. The methods to be used must be supplemented or implemented by other methods. Question-and-answer method, demonstration method, picture-method, the use of filmstrips, field trips, discussion method, and project method can be used to supplement lecture method or problem method. It is an accepted fact that a good method is a synthesis of many methods or procedures. This is based on the principle that the best learning takes place when the greater number of senses are stimulated.

10. The method must provide the learners with numerous and diverse learning experiences or activities. The numerous and varied activities must be provide to guarantee the acquisition of learning outcomes and to insure understanding. The activities or experiences must be unified around a central core.

5.5 Factors Affect the Teaching Process

In order to be able to teach effectively, it is necessary that the teacher must be conscious of the factors which condition the teaching process. Some of the factors which affect the teaching process are the following:

1. Physical Factors. Teaching process is conditioned by physical factors. Such poor physical condition of the pupil as defective hearing, poor eyesight, malnutrition, constant headaches, and sleepiness are hindrances to effective teaching because it cannot be denied that to a large extent, the pupil's ability to learn is determined by his physical condition. Similarly, the teacher's efficiency is conditioned by his health.

2. Mental Factors. Mental factors refer to the child's intelligence and mental habits. The teacher will be able to adjust his teaching more effectively if he has scientific evidence concerning the mental ability of each pupil. Such evidence can he obtained by the use of intelligence or mental tests. It is difficult to carry on the teaching process in a classroom where the majority of the pupils are mentally poor.

3. Social Factors. These factors refer to the pupil's social background or past experiences. The social background of each pupil has a tremendous effect on the teaching process. The teachers should therefore gather as much information as he can about the cultural background economic differences of each pupil if he desires to approach his teaching intelligently.

4. Language Factors. This refer to the language or medium of communication used by the pupils. Language is the instrument which the pupil employs in thinking and reasoning. His deficiency of the language will greatly affect the learning process. Many recent experiments point to the fact that a child's difficulty in reasoning is often one of language. Likewise, the difficulty of the pupil in expressing himself in English is a roadblock to understanding; hence, makes teaching process difficult.

5. Emotional Factors. Emotional factors refer to the interests, desires, or attitudes of the pupil. Attitude is one of the major factors if the pupil has a genuine desire for learning, or a need for the mastery of subject-matter.

5.6 Integration Method of Teaching

According to Ayer, "integration is unifying process that affects almost every phase of growth, thinking, and personal and social development." As a method integration denotes unity, wholeness, harmony or adequate adjustment. In teaching, integration is the process of unifying the child's mental, physical, social, emotional, and spiritual energies through learning experiences. This method of teaching emphasizes learning as conceived in terms of total growth of the child rather than in mastery of the subject-matter. Emphasis is placed on the development of integrated personality of the child—his abilities, habits, knowledge, skills, attitudes, and needs. Pupils are provided with a wide variety of learning activities and outcomes, with plenty of opportunities for participating in group planning, group discussion or execution, and group evaluation of learning activities. In the integration method of teaching, learning activities are organized in terms of larger units rather than on an assigned isolated task. Experiences are so organized that they may become meaningful and functional in the integration of pupil's behaviour and personality. In integration, the various experimental behaviour in different subjects of the curriculum are fused to effect a general pattern of behavior which must subscribe to the accomplishment of the general aims of education outlined in the Philippine Constitution. In utilizing this method, the teacher must bear in mind the aims of education, the pupil's abilities, knowledge, habits, skills, attitudes, and modes of social behaviour. Likewise, the teacher must know her pupil's likes, dislikes, tastes, and their individual differences. The child's nature and experience must be made the starting points in planning and organizing school programmes. Conscious of the objective of the school and the nature of the pupils, the teacher must assume full responsibility in introducing the unit through abilities, interests and needs and the resources of the community. The integration method of teaching consists simply of the major steps that are followed psychologically in developing a unit. The three major steps to be followed, irrespective of the type of unit used, are the following:

1. Introduction of the Unit. The aim of this steps is to motivate the learners so that they may be interested in getting the worked started. A good teacher naturally selects a unit of work that will stimulate the pupil's abilities and experiences to worth-while learning activities, and should be guided by the laws of child growth and development. The teacher plans the means of motivating and stimulating the minds of the pupils so that they may be interested in pursuing the study of the unit. The unit may be introduced by using the following devices:

(1) stating the objectives of the work of the unit and helping the pupils to see their worth and importance,

(2) presenting a bird's-eye-view of the entire unit and the important aspects to be developed,

(3) placing before the class illustrative materials such as pictures, objects, drawing, maps, globes, charts, films, and slides,

(4) correlating the new work with past experiences,

(5) giving the assignment through the use of outlines, guide sheets, problems, questions, and projects to be used as guides for the study of the unit, and

(6) administering pre-tests or written examinations. This step includes cooperative planning of the work by the teacher and the pupils.

2. Point of Experiencing. This step is devoted to the development or accomplishment of a larger goal and is essentially an assimilative period. There is no generally accepted uniform procedure to follow in this step of unit development because of the varying needs of the pupils and the various types of units. The procedure to be used therefore depends largely upon the unit or the learning situations. The methods which may be used during this period of development or point of experiencing are the following:

(1) excursions,

(2) fieldtrips,

(3) reading references,

(4) constructions,

(5) discussions or reports,

(6) interviews,

(7) experimentation,

(8) demonstrations,

(9) projects, and

(10) problem solving.

3. Culmination and Evaluation of the Unit. The aim of this step is to integrate and evaluate the work of the unit. This can be achieved best through the use of the following activities:

(1) final test or examination,

(2) demonstration,

(3) programme,

(4) exhibit,

(5) play,

(6) final report,

(7) debate,

(8) puppet show,

(9) re-teaching, and

(10) outlining or summarizing the unit.

During this period of culmination the teacher and the pupil must sit together and appraise the pupil's progress with the aid of checklists, rating scales, results of tests, cumulative records, anecdotal records, and objectives of the course or unit studied. The teacher, in guiding the pupil, should endeavour to develop in them the consciousness of continual self-evaluation of their experience. This step will give the pupils opportunity to do reflective thinking, summarizing or organizing ideas, training in expression, and evaluation of results; thus, developing the habits of self-criticism and self-evaluation. This step further serves to completely integrate the unit.

The following important points must be taken into consideration in using the integration method:

1. The learner must be considered as an organized whole and with a unique personality. He reacts in totality with a definite aim and purpose. The outstanding fact which must be taken into theoritical account is that the learner is at all times a totally organized system and he must be given more importance than the subject-matter. The fundamental aim of the integration method is to organize dynamic systems into unified whole.

2. Learning activities or programme must be planned in advance and organized in terms of long or large and unified units ather than isolated or daily assigned tasks. The plan must be revived as the work in the unit advances thus, a systematic check must be kept regularly on the progress of the class.

3. Learning activities must provide opportunities for group planning, group executing, and group evaluating. Opportunties for pupils' cooperative group work must be provided. However, the teacher who is more mature and more informed, should be the leader in a shared activity although he should let the pupils decide all matters of policy.

4. Learning must be conceived in terms of total growth and development of the child rather than the mere mastery of the subject-matter. Total growth of the child refers to mental, physical, social, emotional, and spiritual development of the individual. They are to be developed in as a whole and not in isolation as they function in meaningful and problem-solving situations. Education is now conceived in terms of integrated personality and social control.

5. Learning activities or programmes must be selected and organized atound real life problems, pupils' abilities, needs, interests, and levels of maturity. They must be initiated by the real needs and purposes of the learners. Interests and needs must be taken into amount and should be used as guides in developing the child. A properly aroused interest, related to the natural powers of the pupils, furnishes the sustaining drive in learning.

6. Teaching in and out of the classroom must be governed by democratic principles. The learner must be given freedom to attain his maximum growth. There should be no harshness, compulsion, or coercion in directing and guiding the child into what he was not intended to be. Integration is best accomplished through guided action---with love and understanding.

7. Teaching must be conceived as a process of stimulating, directing, guiding, and encouraging the learner. The teacher must guide and direct the natural activities of the learner toward the desired needs and purposes. By virtue of the teacher's wider experience and professional training, he should play the role of leader and counsellor. He must consider himself a part of the group.

8. Individual differences should be met, not by sectioning pupils according to ability, but through the use of varied activities, assignments, materials, and chosen goals or objectives. Pupils must be provided with a wide variety of learning activities and outcomes.

9. Integrated personality as has been mentioned, can only be developed through love and understanding. It is an inner process achieved within each human spirit; it can only be attained in an atmosphere which permits that spirit to discover its goals. Integration of personality is the fundamental aim of modern methods.

10. More emphasis should be given in helping each child develop as a unique personality rather than on minimum standards or grades. Total personality development is the fundamental aim of the integrated method of teaching.

5.7 Project Method of Teaching

According to educational literature the term project was first used by Richards in 1900. Project, as applied to teaching, had its origin in the activities introduced into the classroom procedure when manual training, home economics, and agriculture were added to the school curriculum. It was applied to the planning and completing of some activity which was primarily manual in nature. Kilpatrick wrote in order to change the essential meaning of "project" as it was employed in educational circles. He was greatly influenced by the idea of motivation which was so prominent in Dewey's educational theories. He defined project as "any unit or purposeful experience, any instance of purposeful activity where the dominating purpose is an inner urge." Monroe recognizes the philosophical nature of Kilpatrick's definition of the term project.

The project method is one name given to the method of learning through experiencing, and it emphasizes purposeful activities carried on in a life-like situation. Practically all pedagogical writers agree on four steps in the project-method procedure and agree likewise on the nomenclature of those steps, which are:

1. **Purposing.** The purpose is created in this step if the pupils have been able to select and determine the nature of the project. In purposeful activity the child feels the aim himself or the children feel the objective of the group. It is with the inherent features of purposeful activity that the teacher begins in simulating the present interest of the pupils. The importance and educational values are also considered. The teacher's role is mainly to stimulate and to guide the pupils.

2. **Planning.** In this step the pupils plan the work to be done and the procedure to be followed. The materials and other necessary expenses must also be considered in planning. The pupil or the class should carry the chief responsibility of planning the project. The planning and preparation, although in the hands of the pupils, should proceed under the guidance of a thoroughly informed teacher whose part is active, not passive; cooperation, not aggressive. The teacher must participate in planning the project.

3. **Executing.** This refers to the actual carrying out of the project according to the plan made. This execution varies with the nature of the project and the character of the subject-matter. The project must be executed in the class under the supervision of the teacher. Every phase of the activity should be directed toward the realization of the objectives that brought the project

into being. In this step the teacher has an active part to play, both as a guide and as helper. He needs to observe closely the progress made while the execution phase is going on. He must stimulate and encourage. He must also see to it that the plan is being followed carefully.

4. Judging. This refers to the evaluation of the results which may take the various forms. They maybe in the form of an exhibition of materials, a report, a floor talk given before the class, a dramatic production or a debate, or the publication of the product. The pupils should be trained to judge the products. of their own efforts. Psychologically, it is a well-established fact that self-criticism will be received more graciously than good suggestions from others.

The four steps given above apply to all other kinds of projects as well, such as: the producer project, the consumer project, the problem project and the drill project. In using the project method of teaching the following points must be taken into consideration:

1. The project must bave an educational value which can be appreciated by the pupil. It should take the pupil's interests and needs into consideration. To be of interest, it must be adapted to the mental level and maturity of the pupils. The time consumed must be commensurate with the values received from the execution of the project.

2. The project method can be used effectively if one starts with a purpose or an object in view, instead of an assigned lesson. Activities which aim to attain a purpose are always satisfying. Creating a purpose or a desire to do the work, which is based on the principle that effective learning is purposeful, is an important phase of the project method.

3. The project method should be carried out in its natural setting or in given life-like situations. Rather than

artificial, the approach must be practical or functional. If education is thought of as a life process, pupils should live under circumstances in school that are hot artificial.

4. The project method should be used occasionally but not regularly. It must be used to supplement or to coordinate with other teaching processes. Individual projects may be assigned to bright pupils to supplement other methods used by the teacher.

5. The project metbod must be based on the principles of creativity and cooperation. Creativity denotes and encourages growth, and cooperation improves personal and social relationsbips essential in a democracy the project method is a creative and cooperative enterprise in which initiative, originality, experimentation, and cooperation are encouraged.

6. The project method must be used according to the needs of the course so that an orderly development of learning may take place. This method is not adaptable to all units in the course of study; however, it can be used successfully in such subjects as English, physics, biology, and history. It is also used best in the teaching of industrial arts and vocational subjects where manipulation and construction are involved.

7. The project method must be evaluated in terms of educational values received by the participants. The teacher must exercise judiciousness in evaluating its merits for a specific learning need.

8. The project method involving construction or experimentation must be used only when materials needed are available. The cost of the materials should also be considered in the selection of a project. Many worthwhile projects are impossible because of the scarcity and high cost of the materials needed.

5.8 Development Method

The developmental method refers to the procedure whereby the learner follows the steps of the learning process to attain understanding; interpretation, and generalization. This method is generally used if the aim of the teacher is to formulate rule, principle, definition and general conclusion regarding important relationship. In this procedure, a rule, a general principle, or a generalization is arrived at through the study of many examples or particular situations. The learner goes through the different steps of the learning process in order to reach a conclusion or generalizations. This method provides a direct learning procedure wherein the pupils react under the wise stimulation, direction and guidance of the teacher.

The developmental method may be classified as a general method of teaching. This method is considered as one general method of wide application in the educative process. This teaching procedure is adaptable. Developmental method is the teacher's application of some theory of educational experience and learning principles. What the teacher should do in this method depends upon what is required to secure the qualities of experiences he seeks. The teacher considers such qualities of experience in selecting ends and means while planning, teaching, and evaluating the activities of the learning-teaching relationship.

When used to develop thinking which involves the manipulation of idea, data, or facts, the developmental method is the best procedure. The ultimate aim of thinking is to reach a conclusion or generalization. It is a process of inquiring, of investigating, of seeking, and of looking into things. Thinking is acting with the aims and purposes in view. Teaching, to be of real value, must provide the opportunity and urge for thinking. This method is also valuable as a means uf diagnosing class and pupil's needs, abilities, and difficulties. It also provides for the psychological application of the principles and laws of learning. A teaching method is good when it stimulates thinking and reasoning on the part of the pupils.

The developmental method will be effective insofar as the teacher provides the following steps:

1. Motivation (Prepare the Learner). The aim in this step is to prepare the learner for the work or lesson to be learned. Preparing the pupil for learning is the first step in a good teachi ng procedure. How the learner is to be motivated or stimulated is conditioned by the aims of the lesson, the nature of the learner, the nature of the subject-matter, and the instructional materials available. In other words, how the learner is actually motivated depends upon the circumstances of the particular learning situation.

2. Development (Direct and Guide Learning). The purpose of this step is to realize the aims of the teacher and the pupils. Actual learning takes place in this step wherein the teachers helps the pupils to compare, contrast, generalize, and evaluate the facts experienced or ideas presented. Pupils are led to formulate a generalization or general summary. Generalization gives assurance of real learning. Guidance and analysis are the teacher's most instructive functions in this step. Generalization or conclusion is the function of the pupils.

3. Application (Evaluate Learning). This step refers to the application of the facts learned, or principle, or rule through the cooperation of the teacher and the pupils. Application of facts learned or experiences gained to the actual situation completes the teaching pattern and makes learning more meaningful. Real learning comes only when facts or skills learned are used in real situatious. Application affords a natural means for "reviewing old knowledge," and offers the best opportunity for drill work. The application of facts learned or principle formulated is the test of the whole process. This step is also important in determining as to whether re-teaching is necessary.

The following points must be taken into consideration by the teacher in the use of the developmental method:

1. This method should be used only if the teacher has a thorough mastery of the subject-matter and when the

pupils have the ability and experience necessary to understanding. This method is a reasoning procedure; hence, the teacher must be a master of the learning situation.

2. The teacher must bear in mind that effectiveness of this method depends upon the direction and guidance given by the teacher and the participation of the pupils in the learning process. This method must be employed under the careful guidance of the teacher.

3. The materials or activities to be experienced must be planned and organized psychologically. In other words, activities or subject-matter must be organized according to the interests and needs of the pupils. The teacher should select those activities essential and desirable for the particular learning situations.

4. First-hand experiences of the pupils must be utilized in the formulation or generalization. Conclusion or generalization must be the product of their own thinking.

5. The principle of belongingness must be utilized in developing the lesson. Only the experiences of the pupils belonging to the new lesson must be brought out in the discussion. They must belong to the content of learning that the pupils had already experienced. Knowledges and skills learned in the classroom could be of real use to the pupils if these are in some way related to past learning.

6. The use of this method varies from one learning situation to another. There is no one best procedure in developing a lesson or organizing the activities. Both inductive and deductive procedures may be used in developing the lesson or subject-matter. Skillful questioning is essential in bringing out relationships sought.

7. There should be judicial use of illustrative materials in developing the lesson. Illustrations facilitate under-standing

and are a source of interest. Illustrative materials or devices must be made regular parts of the developmental method.

8. The principle of exercise plays an important part in the last step of this method. Exercise or use is a powerful aid to learning. Application must be planned to make maximum use of recall or exercise. Subject-matter is mastered by use, drill, and review. Practice in applying insight is the best test of real mastery of understanding.

5.9 Unit Mastery Plan

This method which has been briefly described in several courses of study issued by the Bureau of Public Schools is the one suggested for teaching the different units in such subjects as geography, history, government, and economics. In the educational field the Unit-Mastery Plan is sometimes called the Morrisonian Plan of Instruction. Since this method is built around group instruction, provisions for individual differences must be made through such means as special coaching for the slower pupils and extra work for brighter or superior pupils. The popularity of unit-teaching in the elementary and secondary schools in this country in recent years cannot be denied. Practically all our next textbooks in history and other social science subjects are organized on the basis of unit-teaching. It is this type of teaching that a teacher who is trained in subject-matter can best appreciate and use to advantage. This method has this formula to observe: pretest, 'teach, test the result, adapt procedure, teach and test again to the point of actual learning. The following steps are suggested:

1. **Exploration.** the teacher explores the pupils' knowledge of the lesson to be learned by written tests, oral questions, or informal discussion. The purpose of the test is to find out what they already know and what they do not know about the new lesson or unit. It serves also to eliminate needless repetitions of what has been previously studied by acquainting the teacher with the pupil's background for the unit to be studied. It also

serves to tie up the experiences of the pupils with the problem or problems to be studied. The main purpose of this step is, therefore, to enable the teacher to discover what is known and what is not known to the pupils and to stimulate the interest of the learners in the new activity or lesson.

2. **Presentation.** Here the teacher present to the class by lecture or demonstration. the essential features of the unit to be covered. In this presentation the details of the unit are omitted. The general idea can be presented by means of lectures, with the help of illustrative materials such as maps, pictures, outlines, etc. A presentation test is given to determine what the pupils failed to understand. The objective in this steps is, therefore, to give the pupils a preview of the entire unit so that they may approach it intelligently and without waste of time, and at the same time stimulate and maintain the interest already aroused. This step has no other purpose than to motivate and arouse interest and to establish goals or objectives.

3. **Assimilation.** In this state the pupil's work is to assimilate or to gather information through, the use of guide, sheets which give the problems and the reference books to be read. The work is individualized or socialized and the pupils make progress according to their individual abilities. Before going to the next step, the teacher must give a test to aid the pupil in determining whether he has sufficient information of the proper kind to enable him to organize and present sound conclusions relative to his work. The fundamental aim of this step is to place the whole responsibility of the learning process on the pupils.

4. **Organization.** In this step the information assimilated or gathered is put together in the form of an outline or conclusion. The organization may be a cooperative

understanding of the class. This is the acid test of the pupil's understanding of the whole unit. In brief this step calls for the construction of the students' outlines of the unit without resource to notes assimilated.

5.10 The Problem Method

This method is usable in associational or integrated learning. The procedure in this method is similar to the unit-mastery plan of Morrison. The primary purpose of the problem-solving procedure in the classroom is to develop the thinking and reasoning power of the pupils. The importance of reflective thinking as an educational goal is the essence of this method. Dewey points out that reflective thinking is characterized by a process of careful, conscious consideration of facts, beliefs, or other items of mental experience for the purpose of arriving at rational conclusions about some problems or perplexity in the light of data bearing upon such problem or perplexity. In the light of Dewey's point of view, problem-solving method is therefore a process of raising a problem in the minds of the pupils with the aim to stimulate reflective thinking in arriving at a rational solution of the problem. The Problem-Method uses two well-known general teaching procedures, the inductive and the deductive. If the problem calls for a general law, formula, principle, definition, or generalization, the procedure is deductive. These two procedure of problem-solving are adaptable to a variety of learning situations.

The steps in Problem-Method involving inductive procedure are the following:

1. **Stating and Defining the Problem.** It is the duty of the teacher in this step to help the pupils formulate and define the problem. The pupils must keep the problem in mind and must know the objective of the problem or problems.

2. **Collecting, Tabulating, and Organizing the Materials.** In this step the pupils seek and examine data, ready to

modify or discard the hypothesis in the light of more complete data.

3. **Verification.** This refers to the final check-up of the conclusion to test its validity and reliability.

4. **Formulating the Hypothesis.** This refers to the tentative formulation of possible suggestion or generalization. This is mainly a responsibility of the pupils who have analyzed the situation and may recall certain general principles related to the problems.

5. **Drawing a Tentative Conclusion.** This refers to the tentative formulation of a general conclusion based upon the data collected, tabulated, and organized.

The steps in the Problem-Method involving deductive procedure are the following:

1. **Realizing the Presence of the Principle, Rule, Law, or Generalization.** In this step the pupils are required to keep the general rule or principle in mind.

2. **Inspection.** This refers to the breaking up of the rule or principle into parts for examination analysis.

3. **Verification.** In this step the conclusion is applied to different situations to test its validity.

4. **Inference.** The pupils deduce the hypothesis or formulate the conclusion in this step.

In the use of this method the following points must be taken into consideration:

1. In using the Problem-Method, the subject-matter must be organized on a problem basis. The teacher must always be conscious of the practical value of this procedure. The materials, such as references necessary for the solution of the problem, must be placed at the disposal of the pupils. The teacher must

bear in mind that only problems which stimulate thinking and reasoning are educative. The steps in problem-solving should be followed consistently.

2. The problem should be set up and formulated by the pupils. The teacher should be alert to select problems based only on the interests that are legitimate, fairly permanent, and of efficient group appeal. They should be within the experiences and understanding of the pupils and those which they fell are important. They should be of permanent value to the pupils in life.

3. The problems should not be too broad in their scope. Many such problems make the pupils lose interest long before a solution is reached. In such circumstances; the big problems should be divided into smaller related problems, and each smaller problem should be solved independently of the larger problem. Later, all the minor problems should be reviewed as the basis for the solution of the larger problem.

4. The teacher must help the pupils define the problem clearly and to keep it in mind. The teacher must endeavor to make the members of the class conscious of the purpose and value of the problem at hand.

5. The principle of cause and effect should be emphasized in the use of this procedure. The development of reflective thinking is the fundamental aim of this method. The problem should involve both thinking and reasoning. Facts should be learned as part of a reasoning situation and should not be for mere memory work.

6. The teacher must assist the pupils to recall as may related facts or ideas as possible and to formulate hypothesis or to recall general rule or principles that may be applied. The teacher must be alert in guiding the discussion into worthwhile channels. In addition to this direction and guidance of the pupil's activities, the teacher must be ready, through the mastery of the subject-matter, to supply additional information bearing on the problem.

7. The teacher must keep in mind that problem-method involves a complex act, or a series of acts, that varies with the nature and scope of the problem. This means that no teacher can assume that careful direction in one or two problem-solving situations is adequate for all problem-solving needs. The problem-solving activities must be directed and guided in a variety of situations.

8. The teacher must guide or train the pupils to evaluate carefully each suggested conclusions and being systematic in the consideration of the evaluation. After the mass of material is collected, it must be organized so that the entire class may profit from group efforts. The pupils may resort to the teacher for verification.

Conclusion. Method is the key to teaching and learning. Its an important parameter of quality teaching, in brief we may say that method of teaching refers to the arrangement of the ways or procedure. Through which aim of the content and subject can achieved. A method is not merely a device adopted for communicating certain items of information to students. It links the teacher and his pupils into an organic relationship with the constant mutual interaction. Good methods of teaching should aim at realising all the objectives cognitive affective besided the various specific objectives.

REFRENCES

Anderson, R.C. ***et al*** **(Edu.)**—Current Reasearch in Instruction (Prentice Hall).

Association for Programmed Learning and Education—Technology, U.K., (Aspects of Education Technology Vol—I-III.)

Bloom B.S. (Ed.)—Taxonomy of Education Objectives Classficiation of Education and Goal, Handbook of Cognitive Domain, New York, Longmans, 1965.

Copper H.E.—Aids to Teaching and Learning (Pergamon Press).

Govt. of India—National Policy on Education 1986 M.H.R.D. (Edu.), New Delhi.

Govt. of India—Report of the Secondary Education Commission, New Delhi, 1952-53.

Kochhar, S.K.—Methods & Techniques of Teaching Sterling Publishers Pvt. Ltd., New Delhi, 1978.

Lowman—Mastering the Techniques of Teaching Prentice-Hall of India, 1987, New Delhi.

Mohanty J.—Dynamics of Higher Education, Deep & Deep Publication, New Delhi, 1992.

Sharma R.C.—Modern Science Teaching, Dhanpat Rai & Sons, New Delhi.

Sharma G.D & Ahmed, S.R. (Retd.)—Methodologies of Teachings in Colleges, Sterling Publishers, New Delhi, 1989.

Vedanayogam—Teaching Technology for College Teachers, Sterling Publications Pvt. Ltd., New Delhi 1989.

❐

6

Development of Interpersonal Skill

6. Introduction

The students most likely to call the instructor by his or her first name or to accept social invitations are the ones who already feel relatively comfortable, not those who are most in need of special attention. Many students find the novelty of calling their instructor "Bill" or "Betsy" refreshing for a while, but, like the honeymoon period near the beginning of a course, this comfort is superficial and is no quick substitute for a real relationship developed over time. As Kenneth Eble observes in The Craft of Teaching the best strategy for developing rapport "may be no more formal than providing excuses and opportunities for easy talk." One-to-one interactions with students in the second half of a course are likely to be more meaningful than those that occur earlier. The subtleties of a college teacher's behaviour toward a class throughout the term do more to produce an optimal class atmosphere than sweeping structural changes at the beginning.

The techniques presented here were collected from books on college teaching and observations of outstanding teachers. They are organized into groups of techniques dealing with

(1) fostering personal relationships with students,

(2) obtaining regular feedback from them,

(3) motivating students to work through effective classroom leadership,

(4) showing special attention to certain types of students, and

(5) handling miscellaneous interpersonal issues.

6.1 Personal Relationships with Students

The easiest way to begin forming personal relationships with students is to learn their names. Nothing so impresses students as a college teacher who makes a serious effort to get to know them as individuals. Any instructor can learn to match up to 50 student names with faces in the first few classes if he or she approaches the task with a positive attitude and commitment. With practice, some may be able to learn up to 100. Learning each student's name is so effective at promoting rapport because it begins personal contact immediately but does not seem forced, rushed, or intrusive. When we meet a new colleague, we learn his or her name as the first step in forming a working relationship; so it should be between college teacher and student. The following paragraphs describe a name-learning strategy that has been successful for many instructors. Other general techniques for improving memory can be used but, like the system advocated here, any method will require effort to be effective.

Begin by introducing yourself on the first day of class. Then hand out index cards and ask the students to write the usual information about themselves (plus whatever else you could like to know) on the cards. Be sure to ask them to indicate what theory would like to be called. Then, ask them to add anything else they wish you, the instructor, to know. This asks the students to reply to your personal introduction to all of them by making individual introductions of themselves. The instruction "Add whatever you wish," politely pressures them to divulge a bit of themselves. Most students will add nothing, but a few will dutifully list other courses they have had in the subject or their extracurricular activities; a few will attempt to show off their wit or political attitudes, demonstrating what interesting persons they are.

It helps to have reviewed the names on a pre-registration list beforehand, even though these lists are never completely accurate. Certain first names are common, so make a mental note of how many Bob's, Ram's, Shyam's, Mohan's, Laxman's, and so forth are in the class. Consulting "face books" (annuals or other directories with student pictures) beforehand will make learning the names a little easier, but it is ineffective to attempt to learn all the names in this way before the first group meeting. After asking students to pass in their cards (grouping them by rows makes things a bit easier), read off each student's name and move near enough to the appropriate row to be able to see that student's face distinctly. You need make no effort to learn last names at this time; first names will suffice for calling on students in class and beginning a personal relationship. You will learn last names almost automatically when you grade and record the first exams or papers. Note on the card other information about each student if needed, but concentrate on looking directly at the students' faces, forming a visual image of each face while silently saying the matching first name over and over. Then go on to the next card, and so forth. After every three or four students, make a quick mental note of the first names you have just learned, and ask again for any that you cannot recall. Practice the whole row once more before moving on to the next one.

When you have gone through the whole class, set the cards aside, begin at the first row, and attempt to call each student's first name. Students do not expect an instructor to be able to do this immediately, so you have nothing to lose. Even if you have forgotten over half the names, continue on through the entire class. Tell the students that learning their names is difficult but important and that you are going to keep practicing for a while during each class until you learn them all.

As soon after the first class meeting as you can, go through the cards again, saying each first name silently and attempting to picture the face that goes with it. Repeat this process once more later in the day and once each day thereafter until the class meets next. Give yourself a final refresher just before going to the second class, but do not be disconcerted if you can remember only a few of the faces with confidence. At the beginning of the second class, look at each face and try to call each student's first name. Though this is easier than trying to imagine the faces from the names, no more than 50 percent accuracy is normal. Once again, try to remain calm when you must ask for a student's name. In dismissing the second class, call each student's name again.

Continue going through the students' names at the beginning and end of each class and picturing the faces from the cards each day until you can say every name correctly the first time. By the third or fourth class meeting it is usually no longer necessary to call every student's name; you can scan the room before class and call only those about which you are not completely confident. In addition to these steps, use students' names as much as possible when calling on them in class, answering questions after class, or meeting them on campus. This helps to solidify initial learning, and you will rarely forget the names during the rest of the semester.

This no doubt seems like a lot of time to spend on such a modest goal and instructors who pursue it report that it does require effort and commitment, especially at first. Most find that their memory for names improves over successive semesters, however, and that the resulting rapport is well worth the investment. Learning names is the most important single thing a college teacher can do to communicate to students that he or she values them as individuals.

Another way to develop rapport with students is to come to class five to ten minutes early, especially before the initial class meetings. This conditions students to expect to start on time and also provides opportunities to chat informally with them before class or for them to approach you about their concerns. Similarly, staying after class accomplishes educational as well as interpersonal objectives by allowing in-depth discussions of the content just presented. Most students will not come up after class, however, whereas before class you have a chance to contact the students who are unlikely to approach you afterward. Announced office hours are a traditional way of communicating accessibility to students, though only a minority will use them, and it is rare for a student to come by during the early weeks of the term. Because students expect college teachers to post office hours and want to know that they can come by without an appointment, it is very important to do this. Being available over a large number of hours does not increase the personal interest that students perceive, however; two or three hours per week is usually sufficient.

In addition to being available during regular office hours, offer to schedule meetings at other times as well. Students will take your interest in being accessible to them for questions or discussions more seriously if your home telephone number is listed on the course syllabus and you encourage them to call you in the evening and on weekends ("But never after 10:30 at night!"). Few students will call, but all will view the invitation as a serious indication of your commitment to communicate with them. The accessibility you offer will take little time in actuality and will be more than repaid by the positive attitudes you will create in the class as a whole.

6.2 Soliciting Feedback from Students

Interpersonal relationships require a dialogue, a two-way communication, so any teaching method that encourages students to communicate will help to form personal bonds. Instructors are more likely to know when to clarify content or give emotional support if students feel free to raise their concerns. Some students need little encouragement, but active solicitation of feedback from all students will help to form and improve relationships with those who are less comfortable or who avoid contact. One effective method of encouraging student communication is to begin the third week of class by handing out index cards and asking students to ask a question about you or the content or make a personal comment-anything they want to say about you, the course, or the subject. Stress that they are free to question or comment anonymously but that you will write a personal reply if they sign their names. Circulate more cards than students, and point out they can send in two cards (signed and unsigned) if they wish. Offering this opportunity for personal communication with great latitude in the ways that students may choose to comply (including not at all) says implicitly that you care what they think but respect their privacy. This method makes it very easy for students to say what is on their minds. By writing personal notes in reply you will complete the communication circle, strengthening the personal relationship.

Student questions and comments are commonly divided about equally between substantive topics and personal subjects. When you answer their content questions, you obviously aid their learning. When a student comments on your style of presentation ("You mumble at the end of phrases" or "You jingle your keys in your pocket and it's distracting"), paying attention to the comment may improve your teaching. Even if students write "I can't think of anything at this time," they are still relating to you. Most will ask important questions and will greatly appreciate the notes you write in reply. Using this technique to actively solicit comments from each student (including the quieter ones) in a non-demanding way provides useful feedback on your teaching and establishes the personal relationships with a class from which satisfaction and motivation spring.

6.3 Indirect Classroom Leadership

Some instructors believe that being liked by students and being firmly in charge are mutually exclusive-that students do not like teachers who control them, assign them challenging work, and evaluate it rigorously. Not only is it possible for college teachers to demand a great deal from students and still have positive interpersonal relationships with them, it is necessary for students to view teachers as being in control for the students to be maximally satisfied with their leadership. The key here is the choice of methods. As we shall see, indirect methods are almost always superior to direct or autocratic ones.

Does indirect control mean indicating that students should not worry about grades or exams and should learn only what they see as relevant? Not at all. Such a laissez-faire policy of classroom management fails to recognize that all students need to master challenges and compete with peers and that students differ in the style of leadership to which they respond best. The section after this one details ways in which students with different emotional needs and styles of dealing with authority can be optimally motivated by varying the teacher's interpersonal approach. Indirect methods are ideal for such individualization. The key to using indirect methods is to select words carefully when attempting to control students, suggesting and implying rather than ordering or directing openly. Indirect control is similar to the covert control exercised by the hypnotist or Zen master in that a college teacher lays verbal traps that control students' choices of behaviour while giving the illusion of personal freedom.

One another way to control students indirectly is to give a rational justification for assignments. If students see the work asked of them as consistent with their own goals, they are less likely to respond to it simply as a frustrating task imposed by an educational authority. There are many sound reasons for a college teacher to formulate course objectives, not the least of which is that sharing objectives with students makes the more likely to see requirements as something they want to do rather than as something the instructor says they must do. Giving students choices whenever possible also increases their feeling of freedom in the classroom. This does not mean taking the first few class meetings to formulate course objectives or agree on assignments in order to enhance the group's ownership of the course. It means giving students choices about a few decisions of much smaller consequence, such as whether to have an exam on a Monday or a Friday or whether to schedule a film during class or in the evening. Giving students choices between options that are consistent with the instructor's objectives and the available time tells them that their preferences are recognized and will be considered whenever possible; thus, interpersonal rapport is also enhanced.

6.4 Treating Students Individually

The following suggestions about ways to do this should not be taken as sure formulas for achieving rapport and optimal motivation. Rather, they are illustrations of techniques that a college teacher can use to individualize his or her approach to certain students. Such individualization, far from being unfair or producing negative effects by "unequal" treatment, helps all students work up to their academic potential in a course.

(1) Mann's Student Types. The student categories described below are based on Mann's research. Though some of Mann's labels ("hero" or "sniper," for example) may seem disparaging, they are retained and used here because they are easily remembered and aptly capture the key emotional concerns of each group. No lack of respect toward any students is intended.

The typical compliant student is notably teacher dependent, conventional, and highly task oriented. Unlike other types, these students are comfortable with being dependent and are content simply to learn what the instructor wants them to know. Compliants speak in class most often to agree with the instructor or ask for clarification. They rarely pose problems or question the teacher's control. They are in class simply to understand the material. They often prefer lecture to discussion classes. Because they always do what is asked, compliant students usually do moderately well on exams, but they are unlikely to show much independence or creativity. As might be expected, the percentage of compliants (10 percent in Mann's sample) is greater among freshmen and steadily decreases with age.

College teachers can help compliant students become more independent by initially accepting their dependency. Once the students come to believe that the instructor accepts them,' the instructor can ask them to show more independence.

Anxious-dependent students are very common (26 percent of the Mann sample) and can be spotted early by their excessive concern about grades. Like compliant types, anxious-dependents want to learn exactly what the teacher wants them to know- but these fear that they will miss something. They are likely to ask the teacher to repeat definitions so they can get them word for word. Compliant students generally trust teachers and assume that the grades they receive are justified. In contrast, anxious-dependent students distrust teachers and expect trick questions or unfair grading practices.

Anxious-dependent types frequently hold low opinions of their own work, an evaluation not entirely unfounded; their verbal SAT scores were the lowest of the eight types studied by Mann. It is perhaps this self-doubt that leads them to make a great show of their academic effort. These students commonly come to exams looking frazzled and stay until the last possible moment, rechecking their answers or adding "just one more sentence" here and there. Because of their excessive anxiety and relatively limited abilities, their work is frequently unimaginative, mediocre, or erratic. It may be packed full of memorized details and definitions but be lacking in conceptual complexity.

Anxious-dependent students have a penchant for black and white distinctions, for simple right or wrong answers; a college teacher who expands their range of options aids their intellectual growth. Rejecting their questions or refusing to acknowledge their concerns simply raises their anxiety further and increases their need for specifics from the teacher.

Discouraged workers, Mann's third category, make comments in class that communicate a depressed and fatalistic attitude toward themselves and their education. Like compliants and anxious-dependents, discouraged workers see themselves as having little control over their learning. Some may have worked so hard to earn high grades in the past that they no longer find learning pleasurable; they have burned out. Often they are older students coming back to school after a stint in the military or work force who find it hard to regain their youthful enthusiasm. Some have jobs or families and are more likely to be physically tired and preoccupied than the typical "college kid." Any of these circumstances can dampen curiosity and lead to joyless learning.

Recognizing that certain students are chronically discouraged or resigned calls for a special effort to pick up their spirits. Written compliments on their best work (admittedly a difficult task if they have done poorly) are good, but face-to-face conversations are even better. The instructor should look for some excuse to engage them in small talk before class or ask them to stop by for a conference during office hours.

Independent students take what instructors have to offer and pursue their own goals in equal measure. They are comfortable, (perhaps even detached or aloof) in doing what is asked of them, usually prefer seminar to lecture classes, and do not talk when asked to formulate their own thinking about a topic. The majority of independent students are high participators, make friends with instructors easily, and identify with them to some extent, much as many graduate students relate to their professors. They are ideal, mature students, the ones a teacher can count on to discuss and to perform at a consistently high level. In Mann's population, 12 per cent of the students were in the independent group and, not surprisingly, they were more frequently juniors or seniors. Independent students rarely present problems for teachers, but, if the quality of instruction is poor, they are most likely to be selected as spokesmen for the group's grievances.

Heroes resemble independents in their identification with the teacher and their preference for independent or creative work. They lack the detachment of the independents, however, and seem anxious to make the teacher notice immediately what great students and interesting people they are. Most critically, heroes routinely fail to deliver on their initial promise. They are the erratic, optimistic underachievers who initially excite an instructor with their intensity and grand plans for independent projects, only to disappoint later with poor execution. Heroes would very much like to be the independent, creative students they see themselves as being, but some underlying hostility toward authority figures or inability to maintain their commitment to a goal prevents them from playing this role to the end. Heroes make certain that the teacher notices them very early. They frequently stop by after the first class to let the instructor know how interested they are in the subject and how much firsthand knowledge of it they already have from previous reading or work experience. Their initial comments in class may impress the instructor and raise hopes that he or she has run across an unusually outstanding student. Heroes love discussion; they can be annoyingly argumentative, never admitting that they have lost a debate. Reflection on their comments, however, usually reveals that they have not done the assigned reading and are simply showing off previous knowledge or posing tangential questions that occur to them in class.

Heroes promise much but usually deliver little. This is particularly sad because they are usually quite capable students with very high expectations for themselves. Their failure to live up to their potential often results from a fear that they might not be able to live up to their heroic ideal even if they try their best. Because they typically make friends with the instructor right off, they can be enticed to perform more consistently by skillful handling. Still, they are unlikely to work up to their intellectual potential until their impulsive temperament is stabilized by increased maturity. Though most heroes have poor academic records in spite of their high SATs, so-called late bloomers in this group sometimes settle down during their junior and senior years and receive better grades. Heroes occasionally drop out of school to work for a year or two and return as more mature and better students with high graduate or professional aspirations. Heroes typically have high, even grandiose expectations for themselves, and many are capable of outstanding careers if they lower their expectations slightly and resolve their ambivalence about authority and achievement.

Giving heroes the independence they claim to desire almost never improves their performance; it reinforces the special attitude they hold about themselves without making them responsible for living up to it. It is better to encourage heroes to channel their energies into meeting the more structured requirements of the course first. For example, instead of letting them select a term paper topic more ambitious than that assigned to the whole class, the wise teacher will suggest that they use their special skills or insights to produce a tightly reasoned, well written, polished paper on the common topic.

Heroes are more likely to produce good work if given such special handling. To be successful in motivating heroes, a college teacher must maintain a good relationship with them over the term. Heroes are very prone to withdraw their initial investment in the course and put their energies elsewhere. If heroes believe that an instructor expects great things of them, they are more likely to live up to their own billing—but only if the instructor keeps close tabs on them and applies persistent, soft control.

A sniper is a hero who is hostile toward college teachers, unlikely to approach them, and filled with cynicism. Like heroes, snipers (9 per cent in Mann's group) have very high expectations and positive images of themselves, but they have little hope that the world will recognize their worth or give them a fair chance to demonstrate it. Their hostility seems untempered by positive feelings. They are habitual rebels who sit as far from the instructor as possible and often comment with cutting remarks. Some also show their rebellion by wearing unusual or provocative clothing to class.

As with anxious-dependents, the instructor's first task -in forming positive relationships with snipers is to control anger toward them. Their hostile comments often should simply be ignored. Ignoring snipers does not break through their hostility to form a relationship likely to lead to work or change on their part, however. A more fruitful, but more difficult, approach is to respond enthusiastically to the snipers' comments, emphasizing what is positive and ignoring what is hostile. For example, suppose a sniper criticizes a nineteenth-century political leader for having racist, sexist, or elitist attitudes. The instructor might say in response: "That's an interesting point, and it raises an important dilemma for the historian: How can we look at distant events through the eyes of the people of that era, rather than coloring them with contemporary values? We will discuss historical methods again in a few weeks. For now, let me say that I very much sympathize with your concerns and I suggest that all of us try to imagine why this leader did what he did given the way that he and many others of his time viewed the world." This response relates the student's hostile comment to a critical issue in the field without rejecting the student. By expressing sympathy with the student's concern and suggesting that the whole class try to learn from it, the instructor also recognizes the student as a valuable class member.

A smiling offensive-eagerly seeking them out-does not generally work well with snipers, especially early in the term. Approaching snipers makes them more uncomfortable, so they become more hostile in order to distance themselves from the instructor. A better strategy is to praise their class comments as much as possible, make lengthy and careful notes on their exams or papers, and wait vigilantly for chances to start personal conversations with them later in the course. By that time they can sometimes tolerate short conversations of a personal nature, but even then they will seek out the instructor only rarely. As the Mann study showed, snipers do respect authority, and they will become even more hostile toward a college teacher they see as weak. The snipers' hostility stems from discomfort with authority figures and protects them from close contact with them, but such students may actually desire closeness and welcome someone who makes contact without scaring them away.

Attention-seeking students (11 per cent in Mann's group) enjoy coming to class mostly to socialize with other students or the professor. Like heroes, they are fond of discussion; they love to talk. For them, social needs predominate over intellectual ones.

They are pleasant to have in class, and many will form close personal relationships with an instructor. Attention-seeking students are capable of good work if it is made clear that they must work well in order to be well thought of by the instructor or other students. These students like to organize group review sessions or class parties. Thus, they fill a useful role in class as what is known in group dynamics literature' as "social-emotional leaders". Attention-seekers are no less intelligent than other students, just less intellectual.

An instructor should give them ample attention with no strings attached at first to assure them that he or she thinks well of them. Then the teacher should reduce the level of attention and show it mainly for their academic work, especially good work. This strategy effectively motivates most socially oriented students to take intellectual content more seriously while maintaining their interpersonal engagement.

In the classes studied by Mann, silent students (20 per cent) made so few comments that they could not be classified into one of the other seven mathematical clusters. Mann observed classes with heavy discussion formats, in which not speaking was a more revealing characteristic than it might have been in larger classes. Given this context, it is not surprising that Mann's silent students proved to be similar to each other in other ways as well. For example, their personal questionnaires and teacher evaluations revealed that they were acutely aware of the way the instructor behaved toward them. Of all the types, these students most wanted a close relationship and were most afraid that the instructor did not think highly of them and their academic work. Silent students respond to this fear with silence rather than hostility.

The easiest mistake a college teacher can make with silent students is to ignore them, for they will not attract attention or pose problems. To guard against this, a good teacher goes through the class roster every few weeks, noting how each student has been behaving in recent meetings. Any students who have not made comments or approached the teacher individually by the end of the first third of the semester should be earmarked for special attention. Smiling warmly at them, walking to their part of the room before class, and making eye contact with them during lectures and discussions can help to bring them out. Silent students are often receptive to the direct suggestion' that they come by during office hours to get acquainted. It is preferable to let them approach first, but if they have not done so well into the term, it is appropriate for the instructor to take the initiative.

(2) Students with Unusual Academic Abilities. It is especially important for college teachers to form personal relationships with students at the extremes of academic ability. Identifying such students is rarely easy, but the level of complexity and abstract thinking displayed in class, comments and on exams provides useful clues. Especially bright students—the truly gifted, not merely the high-achieving "grinds"—are vulnerable to boredom and apt to slack off if they fail to find a class intellectually challenging. Besides offering stimulating lectures, instructors should actively cultivate personal relationships with these students and encourage them to think independently or creatively about the subject. They will resent extra make-work assignments, but they may welcome recognition of their talent and encouragement to read advanced works on their own. Some instructors invite very bright students to come by regularly to discuss their independent reading or ideas on the common work.

It is equally important to pay special attention to the student who finds college work extremely challenging or even overwhelming. Such students almost always work hard at their studies, and they are not likely to be helped by admonitions to work harder. Specific guidance on ways to study and organize material is more likely to support their struggle. The instructor should recognize their difficulty and empathize with their fear of flunking out of school but reassure them that doing well in college is not the only important thing in the world. He or she should teach these students as much as they can learn and support their efforts to survive this demanding enterprise. For some students, eventual failure may provide the needed understanding that higher education, or at least some aspects of it, is not for them. In sum, college teachers should treat different kinds of students differently in terms of the interpersonal strategies used to form personal relationships with them, even though all students are assigned the same work and graded using identical criteria.

(3) Students Under Special Stress. Some students enter classrooms under considerably more pressure than others. Though few college teachers advocate assigning less work to such students or grading their work differently, these students do require special understanding if they are to perform maximally. Regardless of the source of extra stress the students are experiencing, the instructor's strategy should be the same. Recognize the added stress they are under and communicate empathy with it. The teacher should not reduce requirements for these students because they are likely to be insulted by such an action. Forming a good relationship with them, being a willing listener without dwelling on their specific condition or asking less of them, is normally all the teacher needs to do.

Which students are under unusual stress? In the following a list proposed by Barnes-McConnell. Students with chronic physical handicaps or diseases are obviously overcoming a greater number of obstacles to attend college. At some point early in the semester the instructor may ask if these students will need special consideration in connection with examinations, laboratory work, or field trips. Students under treatment for emotional problems also may need an especially understanding relationship, though it is important not to reinforce their symptoms by offering to exempt them from requirements.

Other high-stress groups to consider are identifiable minorities in class or on campus. Students of minority sexes, races, or religions greatly appreciate an instructor who acknowledges them as individuals. They are not likely to enjoy being called upon in class to speak for their group. Even students who choose to emphasize their minority identity by class comments also wish to be seen as capable of contributing ideas about other issues. Most minority studets want simply to be treated like other students.

(4) Individual Meetings with Students. Even in small classes, most students will not drop by during office hours or call on the telephone. When one does, the way the instructor reacts will determine whether the student finds the venture satisfying or feels frustrated, even punished, for risking a one-to-one encounter. To begin with, an instructor should always be present during his or her posted office hours. Dropping by a professor's office is rarely a casual action for a student. To prepare oneself to appear "between 1:30 and 2:30 on Wednesdays or Fridays" and find the door locked or standing open with no sign of the instructor or explanatory note is disappointing, if not anger-provoking.

Nonverbal communications to students in the office are even more important than those in class. Offices are seen by students as very much "teacher territory," and entering them often stimulates authority conflicts. Consequently, it is imperative at least to seem eager to see a student, even if one is preoccupied with a research project or must leave for a committee meeting in fifteen minutes. Some instructors act impatient or irritated by a visiting student's interruption. One such person I observed was fully aware of this behavior and remarked that he used it "to make the students more independent and keep them from bothering me too much." Instructors may fear that students will take inappropriate advantage of their time, but if they wish to maintain high interpersonal rapport with students, college teachers must be skillful in the ways they limit accessibility to themselves.

What are some things to consider when meeting with a student when ample time is available? Two aspects of the instructor's behavior are especially important: whether the instructor relates to the student as superior to subordinate or as adult to adult, and whether the instructor assumes that the student's chief purpose in coming is revealed in the first topics he or she brings up.

College teachers may unknowingly emphasize their power over students during office meetings. A common way of doing this is by appearing unconcerned when students drop by to see them. Some teachers avoid eye contact as a student stands at the door or enters. Some provide a place for students to sit that is distant from them or across a large and imposing desk. Answering phone calls or responding to colleagues in the hall as if the student were not there also tells a student that he or she is not considered important. To de-emphasize status differences, some instructors stand when students enter their offices, show them to a seat, offer to take their coats, or practice other common courtesies of our culture. Others find such actions too formal and prefer to behave more casually. Any courteous style that is personally comfortable for the instructor is likely to be effective. A conference in the atmosphere created by such behavior facilitates the development of a person-to-person relationship by downplaying the hierarchical relationship between student and teacher.

Reasons that prompt students to visit a teacher vary immensely. Many students are concerned about their performance on exams or papers, Occasionally students drop by in anticipation of doing poorly, but more usually they come after graded work has been returned.

Other students may visit for a variety of reasons. For example, compliant students may come by to have the teacher check a term paper outline, independents or heroes may come to share some insight they have had about the subject or a proposed project, and attention-seekers may want to chat or reveal personal things about themselves. By their choice of ostensible reason for coming, by the confidence or anxiety they show, and by the dependence or independence they assume, students will reveal what they expect from the instructor in a given meeting.

How can a teacher best handle these hidden agendas in student conferences? It is best to be accepting and egalitarian and also not to assume that a student's first statement about why he or she has come is a sufficient reason for the call. If the teacher waits patiently and lets a student talk or ask questions freely, he or she may be able to guess the student's underlying concern or interpersonal strategy. Then the teacher can respond in a way that both affirms the legitimacy of the student's desire and gently pressures him or her toward a more independent and assured attitude.

A teacher should not let an emotional response to a student's remarks dictate his or her behavior. The instructor who becomes angry or defensive about grading practices when a student questions a grade does not foster a relationship that is conducive to good work nor aid the student's subsequent study. Those who calmly listen to the student's complaint; indicate that they can see why the student might feel that way, and then reread the answers or paper in question communicate to the student that his or her concerns are taken seriously-even if the grade is allowed to stand as originally given. It is important that a teacher not feel guilty about a student's failure or identify to excess with a hardworking student's desire for an "A."

Students may on occasion raise topics of immense personal concern with their college teachers. For example, they may express the fear they are going crazy or will kill themselves, or they may describe troubling conflicts with roommates, friends, or family members. Troublesome eating or sexual behaviour also are commonly revealed. Students talk about their troubles only to instructors they like and trust, so a teacher should be complimented if a student brings a personal concern to him or her. A college teacher needs no special training or professional skills to listen to what are usually transiently troubling problems. The teacher should encourage students to talk about what is bothering them, but only on one or, at the most, two occasions.

An instructor should encourage students to speak with a professional counselor if their problems are interfering seriously with their academic functionIng, if they want to change their behaviour or improve a conflicted relationship, or if their health or lives are in danger from suicidal impulses, drug or alcohol difficulties, or physical abuse by another. In order to deal with such problems a student needs to form a specific counseling relationship. Even instructors who are trained as therapists or counselors should avoid becoming involved in recurring counseling sessions with their own students. If counseling sessions are to be helpful, the counseling relationship must be clearly defined by both participants as existing only for that purpose, and the evaluative role of a college teacher rules out completely the possibility of formal counseling.

(5) Teaching Ethics. College teachers are responsible for controlling the considerable power they have over students and ensuring that it is used only to achieve educational objectives. Not surprisingly, written ethical codes for college teachers do exist. For example, the American Psychological Association (APA) has proposed ethical guidelines for its members. Most APA guidelines are designed to protect students from various forms of abuse or exploitation. For example, instructors are admonished not to require students to reveal personal information that might be used selfishly by the instructors as research data (although having students collect or generate data in order to teach research methods or content is appropriate). The deciding question should be, "Does the activity (laboratory or library research, field observations) fulfill educational objectives for the students?" This group advocates giving disquieting information to students in order to stimulate them to think about both sides of complex issues, but it urges college teachers to respect students as persons and avoid being excessively shocking or provocative.

All students are prone, and some students especially so, to react to college teachers—even youthful graduate instructors—as symbols of important persons in their lives, notably their parents. Though no teacher-student relationship is likely to have the intensity of a psychotherapeutic transference relationship, romance between instructor and student is no more likely to be mutual or rationally chosen than it is between therapist and patient. The difference in power is simply too great for a truly mutual relationship to develop. The student is responding to the instructor more as a powerful symbol than as an individual, and the instructor is likely to be using the less powerful student to meet a variety of selfish needs such as distraction, denial of aging, or affirmation of attractiveness.

An instructor implicitly or explicitly requesting sex for a grade would be rightly damned in anyone's ethical code, but as Eble notes, this is much less common than romantic involvement between generally willing, but discrepantly powerful, participants. The most common type of attachment is the onesided one in which a student develops a crush on a professor or has frequent sexual fantasies about him or her. If an instructor suspects that a student has such romantic feelings, he or she should try to limit individual contacts with that student and discourage a more involved relationship.

Certainly, lasting and satisfying relationships have been formed between individuals who originally met as student and teacher. However, even if an instructor believes that he or she has found in a student a potential life partner, the worst possible time to begin the relationship is when the student is enrolled in that teacher's class. Both should wait until the end of the professional teacher-student relationship before exploring the personal relationship further. Each person will then be in a position to respond freely as an adult. Some colleges have explicit rules against faculty members dating undergraduate students under any circumstances, but administrators and colleagues generally would judge a relationship begun after a class is over less harshly than they would judge one begun during class.

(6) Teacher Tolerance of Youthful Behaviour. Between the ages of eighteen and twenty-one, most men and women complete the process of separation from their families that was begun in their early teens. The open struggles with parents during early adolescence result in increased physical freedom, but it is the private skirmishes of late adolescence that free individuals from the emotional vulnerability of childhood. Relationships with other adults during this period (teachers, military officers, supervisors) provide a useful setting in which to learn how to relate to important others as an adult.

Outstanding teachers have often expressed the sentiment that to be a great classroom instructor one must genuinely like college-age students and identify with their interests, both serious and foolish. Appreciating the emotional tasks facing college students puts their sometimes inappropriate, immature, or even self-destructive behavior into a perspective that makes it more tolerable. Remembering personal excesses when one was a similar age can curb tendencies to judge students too quickly. An instructor who likes college students and accepts their interests will find enjoyable the time he or she is required to spend with them and value even more the greater time needed to have a significant impact on their lives.

The suggestions presented here are based on the position that common emotional reactions will appear in college classrooms regardless of what the instructor does. Instructors familiar with these phenomena, aware of their own expectancies and contributions to them, and skilled at communicating will be able to individualize their approach to students so as to avoid stimulating negative emotions and to promote warm and work-conducive relationships with all. Knowing what emotional phenomena are likely to occur in the classroom over a term also prevents dissatisfaction resulting from incorrectly labeling transient behaviour as permanent. Because most college teachers enjoy classes more when they have personal relationships with students, interpersonally skillful teaching improves the quality of instruction that students receive because a satisfied instructor is more motivated to do his or her best.

Conclusion. It is very essential education should develop interpersonal skills. The informal ways are very important to know the background of the student their weakness and strengthen etc. Interpersonal relationship helps to understand learning difficulty of the pupils. Its basicaly depends on dialogue through which teacher encourage students for better learning and get feedback also. An instructor who likes his or her students accepts their interests will find enjoyable time he or she is required to spend with them and value even more the greater time needed to have a significant impact on their lives.

REFRENCES

Apter Michal J.—Educational Technology, Macmillan London, 1968.

D, Ceccoo, J.,—The Psychology of Learning and Instruction, Prentice Hall, New Jersey, 1968.

Deway, John—Democracy and Education, Macmillan, New-York, 1963.

Dienzeide, Henri—Educational Technology and Development of Education IEY, 1970.

Dutt, Suritee—Learning Process, NCERT, New Delhi, 1960.

Gogne R.M.—The Conditions of Learning, New York, Halt Rinchart & Winston, 1965.

Kumar, Krishna—Raj Samaj or Shiksha—Rajkumar Publication.

❒

7

Programmed Instruction

7. Introduction

Before beginning to explaining Programmed Instruction, let us first see the differences between Teaching, Instruction and Programmed Instruction. According to Edgar Dale, " 'Teaching' is a broad, vague, ill-defined term and 'Instruction' is a purposeful orderly, controlled sequencing of experiences to reach a specified goal." All instruction involves teaching, but all teaching cannot be instruction. Programmed instruction is a sub-head under instruction and represents a more rigorous attempt to develop a mastery over specified goals to secure "insured" learning. Programmed Instruction involves controlled, carefully specified and skilfully arranged learning experiences. They are self-instructional and self-corrective.

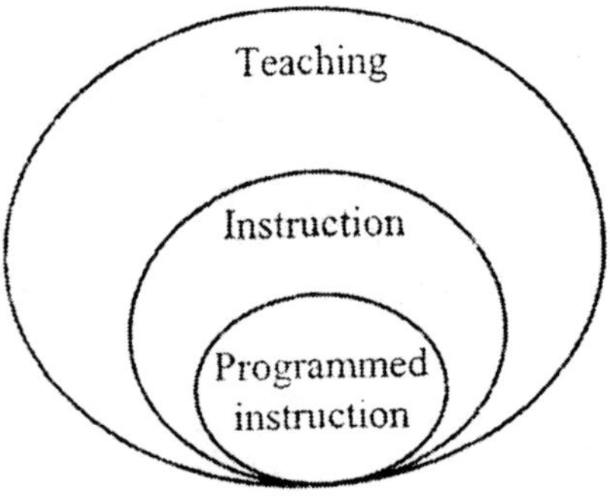

The fundamental idea of programmed self-instructional materials was described in 1912, by Edward L. Throndike in these words: "If by a miracle of mechanical ingenuity, a book could be so arranged that only to him who had done what was directed on page one, would page two become visible and so on, much that now requires personal instruction could be managed by print." Programmed instruction is a technique of self-instruction in which all of the instructional load is carried by teaching machines or programmed tests. Programmed Instruction is a new path towards automation and individualised instruction.

7.1 Major Characteristics of Programmed Instruction

1. The subject-matter is broken down into small steps called frames and arranged sequentially.
2. The content and sequence of the frames are subjected to actual try out with students and are revised on the basis of data gathered by the programmer.
3. Each student programmes at his own pace without any threat of being exposed to any humiliation in a heterogeneous class.
4. Frequent response is required of the student.
5. There is immediate confirmation of right answers or correction of wrong answers given out by the student.

7.2 Need for Programmed Instruction

The present era is passing through a period of a silent revolution in the field of education. 'Knowledge explosion' and 'population explosion' are the two factors that are trying to change the web of life. They mean large quantum of knowledge to be imparted to large population which in turn leads to the spiralling problem of opening more schools and empolying more teachers. In these circumstances what is needed is an 'education explosion'. Technology or automation is the only solution to solve all these problems. Programmed instruction is an innovative step in this direction towards automation and individualisation of instruction. Programmed learning is an application of principles of behavioural sciences and technology in the field of education.

It emerged from the efforts of American psychologists during the present century. Significant contributions have been made to the theory of programming by Sidney L. Pressey, Robert M. Gagne, Robert Mager and B.F. Skinner.

7.3 Contributions of Pressey

Sidney L. Pressey, a psychologist of Ohio State University, is credited with developing, in 1920, a self-teaching machine called 'Drum Tutor' which could teach as well as test. The machine presented a series of questions to the students until the student responded correctly. When the particular criterion was reached, the item was skipped. When the question was set, the student selected his response from the multiple choice alternatives by pressing one of the keys corresponding to the answer. When all the items in the lesson were learned, the machine stopped and hundred per cent mastery of the lesson was taken for granted. Pressey's type of machine was a testing machine and not a teaching machine. This adjunct auto-instructional programming had the advantages of fitting conveniently with all the instructional materials. After teaching the subject-matter in any one of the conventional methods, this self-testing machine can be effectively used as a diagnostic tester.

Pressey described the period as the coming of "industrial revolution" in education. In an era of economic depression marked by rising unemployment. Pressey talked of saving material and labour and hence his remarks were not well-received by educators. Pressey received recognition he sought for his work only in 1950.

7.4 Robert Mager

Mager developed a new concept known as "Learner Controlled Instruction" which is a kind of Socratic dialogue in reverse, where the learner led the instructor. The main theme of the learner controlled instruction is that the learner is one of the best sources of information about himself. The task of the instructor is responsive rather than directive. The instructor remains silent until the learner stimulates him with questions that suggest the needed illustrations, demonstrations or some other help.

Mager conducted studies to find out whether the learner-generated sequence was more efficient than the instructor-generated sequence. It was concluded that learner-controlled instruction was very effective. The programmer develops a unique programme for each learner. It is wrong to claim that learner-controlled instruction is a panacea; it simply reminds one that the learner deserves consideration. The attempt to impose order on learning is futile. In programming sequence, the observation of learner's behaviour should begin early, followed by the determination of objectives before proceeding to write the frames. Mager's studies also emphasise that the experience of the learner can possibly be used as basis for further understanding.

Mager is also remembered for his stress on the formulation of instructional objectives in a clear and specific manner before proceeding to organise instruction. Such objectives are at the bottom of programming too. Mager states, "once an instructor decides he will teach his students something, several kinds of activity are necessary on his part if he is to succeed. The first among these is to decide upon the goals he intends to reach at the end of his course or programme. All other activities stem from the selection of objectives and goals. A statement of instructional objectives is a collection of words describing one of our educational intents." The objective clearly specifies the terminal behaviour of the learner at the end of instruction. Description of such a terminal behaviour will include identifying and naming the overall behaviour act, defining the important conditions under which the behaviour is to occur and defining the criterion of acceptable performance. Though some educationists have criticised the spelling out of such specific behavioural objectives of instruction, research conclusions say that such objectives are useful and almost never harmful. They give direction to teaching and help in curriculum development and also provide guidance for evaluation.

7.5 Advantages of Programmed Instruction

1. The student is continually active when he is using a programme. In other methods of teaching he is active only sometimes and practically nil in a lecture.

2. Programmed instruction is basically individual instruction. Every student proceeds at his own pace. In a conventional class, the teacher attends to only children of average abilities with the consequence that the intelligent get bored and the dull have no extra help. But programme instruction helps the dull with extra information where it is needed and no stigma is attached to the making of mistakes. At the same time, it does not hold up the progress of a fast learner as he goes along and completes the task at his own pace of learning.

3. Immediate reinforcement helps a child to know whether his answer is right or wrong. In normal class feedback takes a long time.

4. A programme is planned and prepared much more carefully than a teacher would do for a conventional teaching programme. Mostly programmes are written by experts in the field.

5. Each programme has to prove itself to be effective during the process of validation and must be re-written as many times as is necessary. If proper learning does not take place, it is only due to the fault of the programme and not of the learner. This positive attitude is quite distinct from what we normally witness in normal class situations where there is always the tendency to blame the pupils rather than the teacher when there are failures in examinations.

6. A programme is not a human being and hance can be used at any time of the day. Programmed materials or

teaching machines are never tried and never lose their temper or patience. Hence programmed materials are very useful in the field of non-formal education.

7.6 Limitations of Programmed Instruction

The following are the limitations of programmed instruction:

1. Programmed learning does not eliminate competition or grades as often claimed.

2. Mere manipulation of machine is not rewarding to children as Skinner seems to think. Once the novelty wears off and if, at the start, too many errors appear the pupils loses interest and motivation. Later reinforcements often do not accelerate learning.

3. Programmed instruction restricts the learner's freedom of choice resulting in cramping of his imagination and initiative.

4. The teacher-pupil contact which is so vital for development of human personality and relationship is completely lost.

5. Operant conditioning is found successful only with some pupils, in some cases and not in all. Programmed instruction ignores or makes inadequate provisions for variables like cognitive variables, personality variables and motivational variables.

6. In language learning, speech is equally important as development of reading and comprehension skills. But there is no scope for providing this experience.

7.7 Styles of Programming

Modes of preparation of programmes are known as styles of programming. The advancement in the field of science and engineering have affected it in many ways. Various styles of programming have emerged. In 1950's B.F. Skinner developed a style which is known as Linear Programming. It was followed by another model namely 'Branching' given by Normal A. Crowder. In 1962 T.F. Gilbert developed a new system of programmed instruction which is known as Mathetics.

These Styles are:

(1) Linear of Extrinsic Programming.

(2) Branching or Intrinsic Programming.

(3) Mathetics.

(i) Linear Programming. B.F. Skinner was the chief originator of this style. He was concerned with shaping and conditioning of behaviour. His view point was that every creature can be guided to a desired behaviour by means of a series of carefully structured small steps on the condition that each correct step is immediately reinforced by some kind of reward. For complex behaviour, each response becomes the stimulus for the next response.

A linear programme is called a straight line programme as the learner starts from his 'initial behaviour' to the 'terminal behaviour' in a straight line. The learner proceeds from one frame to the other till he completes the programme. Subject matter is broken down into very small steps and each step is presented in a proper sequence. The responses of the pupils are immediately reinforced in the succeeding frames. In each frame a small amount of information is provided. The pupils then will be required to make an active response, positive reinforcement or feedback is given and cuse or prompts are provided that increase the probability of correct responses and eliminate the chances of errors.

It is called 'Extrinsic' because the learner has no choice of his own in following the path of learning. It is decided by the programmer extrinsically.

In this style of programming following steps are taken:

(a) The subject matter is presented in small steps or frame.

(b) The student is required to make response to one frame at a time and receive immediate confirmation (feedback) to his answer before proceeding to the next frame.

(c) There is self-pacing among different learners.

(d) The learner compares the constructed answer with the correct answer provided immediately there after.

Format of linear Programme is as follows:

Frame 1................

Response...............

Frame 2................

Response...............

Frame 3................

Response...............

Frame 1 → Frame 2 → Frame 3 → Frame 4

Entry Behaviour—path of learning—Terminal Behaviour.

The response is made within the instructional sequence. The correct answer is found by the side of the next or succeeding frame. The answer is carried over until the learner is ready to proceed to this item.

The author of linear programme tried to make each successive step small enough to avoid student error. If the student does error, he is merely exposed to the desired answer and no other action is taken to correct his response. As the steps are small, a linear programme typically moves slowly in progressive manner towards its goal.

Skip Linear. This is the same as the basic method but at certain points in the programme, the learner is given a test question(s). If his response is correct he goes further to another part of the programme, skipping or jumping a few frames. If 'not' he goes through the normal sequence in order to obtain further piece of information.

Characteristics of Linear Programming

Characteristics of Linear Programming are as follows:

(a) Linear Programme is a single track programme or straight line programme.

(b) It consists of small steps.

(c) In it the responses of the learner get immediate reinforcement.

(d) In this programme one can learn according to one's own speed.

(e) In this programme every learner follows the same path.

(f) Learner has to respond actively to each frame.

(g) In it programmer controls the response of the learner.

(ii) Branching Programming. Branching Programming was developed by Norman A. Crowder. It is an improvement over linear programming. In this progarmming the student proceeds to the next frame, until he makes an error. The error branches him to supplementary material designed to give him remedial instruction. This can be achieved by giving the students some information, and asking a multiple choice question and then providing a different response for each answer chosen. Thus, the students proceed through a programme along different routes or branches. This type of programme is called branching programme.

Branching programming is represented as follows:

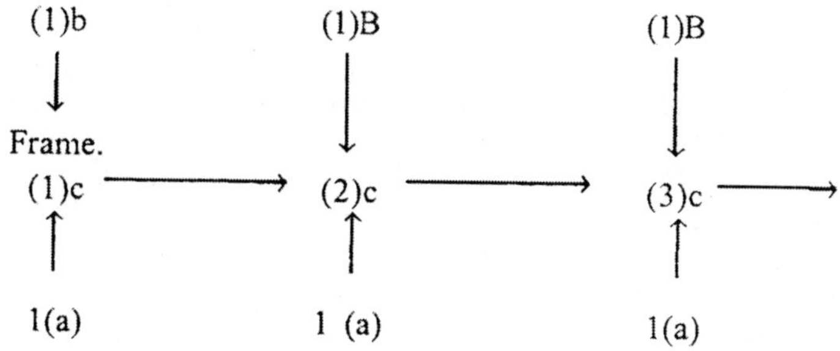

For response three alternative a,b,c have been given at the first frame. It the learner selects 1(c) alternative he can go straight but if he goes for (1a) or (1b) he has to follow the instructions, only then he can move onwards.

Here the learner is independent to choose any alternative that is why if is also called intrinsic programming. Here all the learners do not follow the same path.

In other words we can say that in this style each frame is of bigger size and contains two or three choices. This programming employs multiple choice type of questions. The student is required to choose the one right answer out of the choices. If the student selects the correct answer, he is taken to the next frame in the main teaching sequence. If this response if wrong, he is taken to a remedial frame where his mistake is explained. The topic under consideration is further explained with the help of examples. After remedial work he is directed to the original frame for making new attempt. According to the alternative selected, the pupil is asked to proceed to a particular page.

Assumptions of Branching Programme

This programme is based on the following assumptions:

(a) Multiple choice items help more in the learning process.

(b) The learner learns better if matter is presented in totality.

(c) It is based on the possibility of detecting and correcting errors.

(d) By his ability the learner controls the exact sequence.

Characteristics/Merits of Branching Programming

(a) It is helpful in the development of the power of discrimination.

(b) It helps in practising creativity.

(c) It gives training in problem solving.

(d) The students come to know about their mistakes.

(e) Big size of frame reduces unnecessary repetition and responding.

(f) The large size of frames maintain the interest of the students. The programmer may further enrich his style an expand his ideas.

(g) The programmed material in this style may be employed in the form of programmed test or teaching machines.

(iii) Mathetics Programming. Thomas Gilbert originated this concept in 1962. The word 'Mathetics' has been derived from the Greek word 'Mathein' which means to learn. Mathetics is defined as, "The systematic application of reinforcement theory to the analysis and construction of complex represenıories which represent the mastery of subject matter.

'Gilbert's main interest lies in building a system that guarantees effective teaching. For this purpose he has used only those aspects of reinforcement theory which he found suitable for building the technique of teaching.

It is eclectice in nature and unique in application. It analyses the deficiencies and tries to make it up. As a technique of teaching, it may be applied to any subject but it is more suitable for teaching of skills. It is a complete training system that gives the programmer—

A guide for determining what to teach.

A basis for making teaching strategy decisions.

A detailed procedure for constructing a programme.

It uses backward chaining as a method of teaching. It is also known as retrogressive chaining. In this programming an exercise is the technical unit of learning instead of a frame of linear type.

In this programming the pupil learns the last step first, then he goes to the next one before it and thus to the introductory step. This system where the tasks are connected from the last to the first is called chaining.

There are three steps in designing a mathetics programme.

(a) Demonstration.

(b) Prompt.

(c) Release.

Example of Mathetics Programme

1. To find the square of any two digit number ending in 5.

(i) Multiply the first digit number by the next higher consecutive number.

(ii) Write 25 to the right of result (No. Response required). Programme.

Page 2

2. To find the square of 35.

(i) Multiply first digit (3) by the next consecutive number (4), 3 × 4 =12.

(ii) Write 25 to the right of the result 12 = 1225 (no response required.)

Programme 3

3. To find the square of 55.

(i) Multiply the first digit (5) by the next higher consecutive number.

(ii) Write . . 25. . .to the right of the result.

(iii) The square of 55 is . . . .

Ans. Write 25, 6×5 = 30

The square of 55 is 3025.

Merits/Features of Mathetics Programming

1. It is a complete training system that guides the trainer to describe mastery of skills and knowledge to be acquired.
2. It clearly identifies the task operations involved and gives the student exercises to perform those operations.
3. It is prescriptive rather than descriptive process.
4. It is a job-oriented technique.
5. It is a scientific teachnique of programme construction and is the systematic application of concepts and rules.
6. It uses the principle of motivation in task analysis.
7. It emphasises on the student success, mastery, learning which means that the student is constantly motivated and reinforced by the consequences of mastering the knowledge.

7.8 Development Phase of Programme Writing

The writing of the programme involves the following steps:

Writing the Draft Frames. The progammer should have a clear idea about the programme to be taught to the pupils. First he analyses the subject matter and then the frames are writien in a sequence. Easy and simple frames should be placed in the beginning and complex frames should follow later.

To help learners to proceed correctly and with minimum error rate from one frame to the next, programmer has to make use of priming and prompting. In priming, information is poured into the minds of the learners for facilitating active responding, whereas in prompting, some help in the form of an additional stimulus is provided.

Sequencing of Frames

For sequencing, the frames are to be arranged in a systematic order (remembering the logical and phychological principles) to lead a learner from his entry behaviour to terminal behaviour. Three approaches are followed for sequencing frames which are as follows:

(a) **Matrix Approach.** A matrix is prepared in the shape of table; on one axis, the major concpets and sub-concepts are placed and to the other axis, the frames of the programme that lead to the behavioural changes in learner, are placed.

(b) **Rule Approach.** In this approach the frames which present the rules are placed earlier in sequence followed by frames that illustrate examples. This approach is followed by deductive reasoning logic for sequencing frames.

(c) **Egrule Approach.** In this approach frames representing examples are placed earlier followed by frames that depict the rule. This approach is followed by inductive reasoning logic for sequencing frames.

Editing of the Programme

The draft of the programme developed in the form of frames is subjected to a thorough review and editing process.

(i) Editing is done at the following levels.

(ii) For technical accuracy, editing and to remove inaccuracies of the programme, help of the subject expert should be taken.

(iii) With respect to designing and sequencing of frames, style and format of programming help of the educational technology expert should to taken.

(iv) Assistance is taken of some language experts to remove inaccuracies in language especially with respect to spelling, grammer and punctuation etc.

Evaluative Phase

This is the last phase of the development of programmed instruction material, where activities are undertaken to test effectiveness of the programme and in the light of results proper modifications and improvements are brought about. The activities undertaken in this phase are as follows:

Individual Try-out. In the individual try-out, the programme is administered on a few learners one at a time. In practice the learner is presented with the material of the frames one by one and asked to write down his responses on a separate sheet of paper and then tally them with the correct responses written on the back page of the frames. Here the informal face to face contact with a single learner at a time provides a valuable opportunity to the programmer to study the reactions of the learner regarding the difficulties faced and inadequacies of the programme. Thus, the draft of the programme is improved on the basis of the result of the individual try-out.

Small Group Try-out. The modified draft is next try-out on a small group of learners. Again each learner is provided with a sheet of paper to record his responses and suggestions for modification. Time taken in completing the programme is also carefully noted. Pre-tesat and post-test are conducted. The differences in the attainment scores of pre-test and post-test ar employed to ascertain the effectiveness of the programme.

Field Try-out. On the basis of the finding to a small group try-out, the programmer does a field try-out in order to test the validity of the programmed instructional material in real setting. It differs from the above two try-outs in that the field try-out is undertaken by teachers with real students in a school. Otherwise, the method of try-out is similar. Pre-test and post-test are administered to the students and the scores are analysed to determine effectiveness of the programme. Suggestions and responses of students to each frame are noted and incorporated to improve the programmed material.

Validation of the Programme

Finally, the programme has to be validated in the natural conditions of its use. Following tools are helpful in validating a programme.

(a) Criterion Test. This test helps to determine the extent to which objectives have been realized.

(b) Gain Ratio. The effectiveness of a programme can properly be measured with the help of a concept known as gain ratio. It is defined as the ratio between the amount learned and the amount that could possibly be learned. The gain ratio can be computed with the help of the following formule :

$$\text{Gain Ratio} = \frac{\text{Mean of (Post - test scores minus Pre - test Scores)}}{\text{Mean of (Total scores of Post - test minus Pre - test scores)}}.$$

Conclusion. Present era is a era of information and technology. The world is comming more closer. We need every thing which is easier and useful. Through Programme Instructional Learning would be refined and simple. It is basicaly individual instruction according to the Learning Compentancy & Capacity of the child. Its planned and careful activity in a New Fath towards automation and individualised instruction.

REFERENCES

Alanc *et. al*—Educational Technology J. Wiley & Sons, London.

Mohanty J. (1992)—Educational Technology, Deep & Deep Publication, Rajouri Gardan, New Delhi.

Philips J.S. & Rock Well DM (*ed*) 1976—Instructional Media & Technology—A professional resource.

Richmond W.B. (*ed*) 1970—The Concept of Educaticnal Technology. A Dialogue with yourself Weidenfeld and Nicolson-5 London.

❐

8

Guidance and Counselling

8. Introduction

In order to understand the meaning of guidance, it is to be accepted that the focal point of guidance is 'an individual, not his problem'. From this point of view, before starting guidance, the potentialities and abilities of the individual are studied. Then that individual is made capable of solving his problems. This is known as an act of guidance. In this way, guidance is a process of all-round development. Hence, we can say that the guidance is that process which makes an individual aware of those methods for knowing his natural powers.

Jones, Stefflre and Stewart have defined guidance as "the help given by one person to another in making choices and adjustments and in solving problems."

"Guidance is a continuous process of helping the individual to develop to the maximum of his capacity in the direction, most beneficial to himself and to society."

Guidance is not a direction. It is also not imposition of one's ideas on others. Guidance is not making decision for others. Decision should be made by an individual himself. To carry over the bruden of an individual is also not guidance. In such situations, to what we can call guidance? Keeping in view these ideas, the definition suggested by Crow and Crow bears very comprehensive meaning:

> "Guidance is assistance made available by competent counsellor to an individual of any age to help him direct

his life, develop his own point of view, make his own decisions and carry his own burden."

In the context of dynamic interpersonal relationships, Carter V. Good has said in Dictionary of Education (1959), while defining guidance, "Guidance is a process of dynamic interpersonal relationships designed to influence the attitudes and subsequent behaviour of person."

Knapp has given the definition of guidance as "Learning about the individual student, helping to understand himself, effect changes in him and his environment which will help him to grow and develop as much as possible."

G.E. Smith, by considering the group of various services for helping an individual, has defined guidance as, "the process consists of a group of services to individuals to assist them in securing the knowledge and skills needed in making adequate choices, plans and interpretations essential to satisfactory in varieties of areas.

"Guidance is a help to the students in making the best possible adjustment to the situations in the educational institutions and in the home and at the same time facilitates the development of all aspects of the personality."

According to Skinner, "Guidance is a process of helping young persons learn to adjust to self, to others and to circumstances."

8.1 Nature of Guidance

We familiarize ourselves with the following characteristics after analyzing the various definitions of guidance. This analysis also throws light on the nature of guidance.

(1) **As a Process.** Guidance does not occupy independent place. The chief aim of this process is to assist in the development of an individual keeping in view the social needs.

(2) **A Continuous Process.** Guidance is a process. Here, it is important to point out that the process of guidance never ceases. It remains dynamic. In this process, an individual understands himself, learns to use maximum his own capacities, interests and other abilities. He continues his struggle for adjustment in different situations. He develops his capacity of decision-making. Hence, we see that it is a non-stop process.

(3) **Related with Life.** The process of guidance is related to life. This guidance contributes formally or informally to life because life experiences both formal and informal occasions. A person gets informal guidance from his friends and relatives while formal guidance is sought from organised school guidance services and other organised guidance services.

(4) **Development of Capacities.** During the process of guidance the individual is assisted in such a way that he makes himself enabled to develop his capacities maximum from all angles. Hence, guidance stresses the complete development of possibilities present in an individual. An individual becomes familiar with his real image. Hence, guidance is helpful in self-realization.

(5) **Individual Assistance.** Guidance is accepted as individualized help. Through guidance an individuals personal development is provided a direction and not to a group. Hence, it is process of individualized assistance.

(6) **Wide Scope of Guidance.** The scope of guidance is too wide. Any needy person can be guided. This can include the persons of different age, different interests, various characteristics and persons of different nature. Hence, we cannot draw boundaries around the process of guidance.

(7) **Task of Trained Persons.** Providing guidance is not the function of all persons because various techniques

and skills are to be used in it. Everybody does not possess the knowledge of the same. For this task, trained persons psychologists and counsellors are required. Hence, guidance is a skill-involved process.

(8) **Helpful in Adjustment.** Guidance helps th person in his adjustment in different situations. This process allows to learn to adjust with different types of problems. In this way, the main characteristic of the nature of the guidance is to provide new energy to the demoralized person by adjusting himself in the problematic situation through the process of guidance.

(9) **Helpful in Developing the Ability of Self-Guidance.** The nature of guidance also includes the characteristic of developing self-guidance in a person with the help of guidance process. This enables him in achieving self-dependence by searching out the solution of problems of life.

(10) **Helpful in Preparing for Future.** The process of guidance is helpful in preparing a person for his future. Hence, a person can succeed in preparing himself for future activities. In this way, guidance is a well-wisher of an individual's future.

(11) **No Imposition of One's View Point.** It is also the main characteristic of guidance not to impose one's view-point on others. It depends upon the wish of an individual how he acquiries benefit by accepting the decision of the guidance worker. If he wishes, he may deny to accept such decisions of the guidance workers. Hence, it is not a process of imposing the decisions.

8.2 Objectives of Guidance

Guidance process is purposeful process. Without determining the objectives, this process cannot be completed or concluded. Due to the variations in the scope, guidance has a variety of objectives. If we start guidance process without any objective it cannot be concluded because various sub-processes involved in the guidance cannot be given any direction and these activities ramain meaningless.

Objectives of guidance change at each level of education. Every stage of education enjoys different objective of guidance. For example, the functions and objectives of guidance at primary level will be different from those of middle stage. Similary, objectives of guidance at high school or higher secondary stage will be different from those of middle stage:

(1) Objectives of Guidance at Primary Stage. Every activity at primary stage includes guidance. At primary stage, there is need to pay special attention towards the health of the children. At this stage there is great need to coordinate the functions of a teacher, guidance worker, school, staff members of medical service and school social service workers. All these persons help in learning properly essential skills for primary education, for acquiring basic knowledge, for adapting according to the social traditions and for developing proper attitude towards school activities. These too are the objectives of guidance at this stage.

When a child leaves home and enters into the school environment, he has to make many coordinations. School environment is very comprehensive for a child. In school, the child comes in contact with various types of persons, children and teachers. Also, he lacks security in the school and he becomes very fearful, hesitating and remains suppressed in the school. Those children are more in difficulty who are fully dependent on their parents.

Primary stage ranges upto fifth class. During this period, children make their place in the school. Gradually they get themselves established in the school and they consider themselves an honourable member of the school. When these children cross over from primary stage to higher stage, they feel suffocated.

Behaviours of primary stage sometimes look like a joke. The traditions of new school, rules, administration, curriculum etc., are all new. In such situations, the guidance worker plans the guidance programme in order to prepare the children of primary stage, for next higher school stage, such as arranging the visits of primary stage children to high schools, inviting high school teachers to primary schools, explaining the procedure for getting admission to high schools after leaving the primary schools, making them familiar with the curriculum of high schools etc.

In nut-shell we can say that the following are the objectives of guidance at the primary school stage:

(a) To coordinate all the activities of all the workers such as a teacher, medical service staff members, school social-workers and the activities of a person providing guidance etc.

(b) To assist developing higher attitude towards school activities.

(c) To assist children in developing their physical and emotional stability.

(d) To assist children adapting according to the school traditions and rules-regulations of the school.

(e) Objective of finding out problems regarding adjustment in the school and to control them.

(f) Objectives of making children ready for crossing over from primary school to next higher stage.

(g) Objective of making children self-dependent.

(h) Objective of creating the feeling of cooperation in the children.

(i) Objective of supplying various informations to children regarding higher stage such as curriculum of next higher classes and distribution of booklets regarding various school functions among the children and their parents.

(2) Objectives of Guidance at Secondary Stage. The child leaves primary stage and enters secondary stage. At this stage the scope of guidance becomes more comprehensive as compared to the scope of guidance at primary stage. At this stage, guidance becomes more important as a result of multiple reasons. At this stage, teachers too teach according to the subjects. Therefore, all the children cannot contact all the teachers. At high and higher secondary schools, only subject specialists teach. At these stages, personal, social and vocational problems of the children come into light and solution of these problems is necessary. In order to achieve this objective, a comprehensive and organized guidance service is continuously required.

In this way, we see the following are the objectives of guidance at secondary and higher secondary stages:

(i) ***Objective of Familiarizing with New School Life.*** A child is not familiar with the life of new school when he leaves the primary school and enters to a new higher school. He has to face a number of problems regarding admission. Also, it may become difficult for him to coordinate with new classmates and new friends. Hence, the objective of guidance service existing in the school should be to eliminate such problems of the pupils.

(ii) ***Objectives of Helping in Selecting the Subject.*** After reaching at this higher level, the selection of subject becomes necessary. In this task, the pupil may face difficulty. He is unable to understand in which subject he is competent and which subject he should not opt. The selection of subjects has become very difficult task due to the variety of subjects. Hence, the objective of guidance should be to understand this type of problem and the same should be solved.

(iii) ***Objective of Fulfilling the Needs, related to Students Health.*** The objectives of guidance service existing in the school is to take care of needs related to the health of the children and to inform timely the relevant persons regarding those health deficiencies so that the necessary action can be taken.

(iv) ***Objective of Co-curricular Activities.*** Co-curricular activities are being considered very important for the physical development of the children, such as debates, sports, cultural activities, programmes of social service etc. Hence, the important objective of guidance services is to guide the children for such activities so that their physical development may be given proper direction.

(v) ***Objective of Maintaining the Records.*** In schools it is important to maintain the records regarding the development of the pupils, education, psychological development, cultural activities, because the entire guidance programme is to be conducted on the basis of these records. Hence, the objective of guidance programme workers should be to maintain such record so that the counsellor may feel convenience during counselling.

(vi) ***Objective of Emotional and Individual Needs.*** When an individual enters adolescence, an individual experiences emotional and personal needs. Therefore, the objective of guidance services should be to solve the problems related to such needs.

(vii) ***Objective of Creating Environment.*** According to Crow and Crow, the creation of academic environment in accordance with the adolescent stage is very essential so that the pupils may be motivated in order to acquire higher education and they may be helped in selecting the subject according to abilities.

(viii) ***Objective of Cooperation.*** In solving the problems of the children, cooperation plays an important role. This cooperation is desirable in guidance at all levels. The objective of guidance services should be to create a feeling of cooperation among all the workers involved in this service. This cooperation acts as a substantial base for guidance at the next higher level.

(3) Objectives at College and University Stage. When a child enters the college he becomes a complete young man and his personality acquires has own pattern. Some of them have clear objectives. Some start feeling their responsibilities. They are also very serious in their studies because they know the meaning of success and failure. But there are some persons who fail to understand what the college education means. They come to college without knowing what they can do. After securing admission to the college they face multiple difficulties. They consider their studies meaningless. That is why they go to college without any objective.

In such situations, the objective of college guidance programme is that the needs of such students should be looked into immediately who are unable to make progress in the college affairs and who can use their telent in their activities on providing proper educational facilities.

In college, the objective of guidance service should also be to help the pupils in selecting the subject so that they can acquire specialization because such specializations help the pupils in their future vocational plans.

Similarly other objectives of guidance service include organized programmes of tutorials and providing help to the pupils for making progress by studying the books existing in the library. It would be very meaningful if the students are made aware of objectives, nature and scope of college educations before its commencement in the college. According to other objectives of guidance service, the pupils should be informed regarding the various facilities existing in the college such as library facilities. If such is not informed, it would lead towards the wastage of pupil's time.

In this way, we see that there is no much difference between the functions and guidance objectives of high, higher secondary and college stage. Hence, the guidance objectives at college and university stage can also be presented in the following manner:

(i) To make available informations regarding admissions to college and university.

(ii) To provide informations regarding co-curricular activities in the college and university.

(iii) To help pupils selecting subjects so that they may achieve their future programme and objectives.

(iv) To arrange for testing the pupils.

(v) The help the children eliminating their financial difficulties.

(vi) To provide vocational informations to the pupils so that they may take decision regarding their future.

(vii) To make aware the pupils regarding the existing hostel facilities so that the problems of their boarding and lodging can be removed.

The objectives of guidance can also be expressed as follows:

(a) Objectives from pupils' point of view.

(b) From institution's point of view.

8.3 Counselling—Its Meaning & Definitions

The scholars have exhibited variations in their view-points regarding defining the term "counselling". One major cause of these variations is—occurrence of historical changes in the perceptions of the persons. Inspite of this, there was a lot of variation in the philosophy of experts.

According to **Wrenn** (1951), "Counselling is a dynamic and purposeful relationship between the people in which procedures vary with the nature of the students' need, but in which there is always mutual participation by the counsellor and the student with the focus upon self-classification and self-determination by the students."

According to **Shostorm and Brammer** (1952), "Counselling is a purposeful reciprocal relationship between two people in which one a trained person, helps the other to change himself or his environment."

Ruth Strang, emphasizing mutual relationshps of persons, has said, "Counselling is a face-to-face relationship in which growth takes place in the counsellor as well as the counsellee."

Wolberg (1954), has considered counselling as a form of interview. He has defined it as, "Counselling is a form a interviewing in which the client is helped to understand himself more completely in order to correct an environment or adjustment difficulty."

Myers has written as, "Counselling means a relationship between two persons in which one person provides special assistance to the other."

Rogers says about counselling that, "Counselling does not mean providing a service by means of which specific problem of an individual may be solved. The process should help the counsellee in gaining claer insight into the problem and in achieving the self-confidence."

Considering counselling as a problem-solving effort, Hamrin and Erickson have said that, "Counselling is an attempt made by the counsellee to think through and solve the problem that confronts him. It is an experiment in cooperative thinking, who two individuals (the counsellor and the counsellee) srtike to solve a problem."

Considering counselling as a mutual learning process, Willy and Andrew have said, "Counselling is a mutual learning process involving two individuals—one seeking help and the other a professionally trained person helping the first to orient and direct himself towards a goal which leads to his maximum development and growth in his environment."

8.4 Characteristics of Counselling

The following facts become distinct about counselling after studying and analysing the above mentioned definitions:

1. Counselling is a conversation with some one regarding some problem.
2. Normally, not always, one of the two persons possesses facts or experiences or abilities which the other lacks.
3. In the process of counselling, the problem is made clear through discussion. The counsellor explores the problem and its importance through his skilful questioning.
4. Counselling helps the pupil in making selections and following those selections.
5. Counsellor draws out the facts from the pupils through counselling process.
6. Counselling is an assistance to the persons in their behaviour related problems in which their emotions and motivations are main.
7. Counselling involves interactions in which the counsellor accepts the responsibility of positive contribution in the development of other person's personality.
8. He also informs the pupils certain facts.
9. Counselling is a vital part of the entire guidance programme.
10. Counselling is only one aspect of guidance.
11. Counsellor guides the pupils to establish contacts with various factors in the counselling process. He explains

the importance of those facts which the pupils consider unimportant.

12. Counselling is a learning oriented process.
13. Counselling is democratic. It lays down the democratic system. The client can behave as he wishes.
14. Counselling is a face to face relationship with a person. This relationship is between a counsellor and a client.
15. Counselling is a professional service.
16. Best counselling is in the form of the decision made by the counsellee.
17. Counselling is possible in humorous and cooperative environment only.
18. Counselling is problem-oriented.
19. Counselling is based on the appropriateness of counsellor's prediction.
20. Counselling is completely based on self-guidance.

8.5 Basic Principles of Counselling Process

According to Mc Daniel and Shaftal, the counselling process is based on some basic principles:

(i) **Principle of Acceptance.** According to this principle, each client must the accepted as an individual and dealt with as such. The counsellor should give, due regard to the rights of the client.

(ii) **Principle of Permissiveness.** Counselling is such a relationship which develops optimism and the environment shapes according to the person. All the thoughts accept the relative relationship of counselling.

(iii) **Principle of Respect for the Individual.** All the schools of thoughts of counselling advocate for the respect of the individual *i.e.*, respecting an individual's feelings must be an integral part of counselling process.

(iv) **Principle of Learning.** All the assumptions of counselling accept the presence of learning-elements in the counselling process.

(v) **Principle of Thinking with the Individual.** Counselling emphasizes thinking with the individual. It is essential to differentiate think for whom? And 'why to think'? It is the role of the counsellor the think about all the forces around the client to join client's thought—process and to work collectively with the client regarding his problem.

(vi) **Principle of Consistency with Ideals of Democracy.** All the principles are associated with ideals of democracy. The ideals of democracy desire to accept a person and want to respect the rights of others. The process of counselling is based upon the ideals of a person's respect. It is a process with accepts individual differences.

Directive or Counsellor-Centred or Prescriptive Counselling. Counseller-centred counselling revolves around the counsellor. He tries to establish good relations through the friendship and assistance. In this, the counsellor is very active and he expresses his ideas and attitudes independently. He evaluates the expressions of the client. According to this view-point the counselling leads the interview. In this, the counsellor asks a series of standardized questions. Each question carries a short answer. The counsellor does not allow the development of client's expression and feelings. He leads as an expert, evaluates and gives suggestion or advice.

The chief advocate of this school is E.G. Williamson of the University of Minnesota. Hence, according to this school of thought, the counsellor owns entire responsibility of solving client's problem. In this procedure, the counsellor explores the problem and defines it, diagnoses it and tell about the remedy of the problem.

8.6 Basic Assumptions of Directive Counselling

According to Andrews and Willy, the following can be the basic assumptions of directive counselling:

(i) **Counselling as an Intellectual Process.** Any client's intellectual capability is not destroyed as a result of his mal-adjustment. Hence, counselling is primarily an intellectual process. It stresses upon the intellectual aspects of a person instead of his emotional aspects of the personality.

(ii) **Counselling Objectives as Problem Solving Situation.** The objectives of counselling are achieved through problem solving situation.

(iii) **Competency in Giving Advice.** The counsellor possesses the best training experience and informations. He is more competent to provide an advice to solve the problem.

(iv) **Client's Incapability of Solving the Process.** The counsellor assumes that the client does not possess the capability for solving the problem always.

Hence, we observe that the direct and explanatory methods are suggested. In such a counselling focus should be on the problem instead of the person and the client should cooperate in the entire process. The client is to act under the counsellor, not along with him.

8.7 Steps in Directive Counselling

Williamson has described the following six steps of directive counselling:

(i) Analysis. In this steps, data and informations are collected regarding the situation or the client which can be used in the counselling process as a valid and reliable base. For this counselling step, the following tools are used:

(a) Cumulative records.

(b) Interview.

(c) Time distribution form.

(d) Autobiography.

(e) Anecdotal record.

(f) Psychological tests.

For the integration of entire data, case-history method is used. It includes family-history, recreational interests and habits etc.

(ii) Diagnosis. Diagnosis consists of the interpretations of the data in terms of the problems indicated and assets and liabilities, the strengths and weaknesses of the students.

Diagnosis has the following main three stepes:

(a) Identification of Problem.

(b) Discovering the cuase.

(c) Prognosis.

(iii) Synthesis. Williamson has defined synthesis as—"The process of summarizing and organizing of the data from the analysis in such a manner as to reveal the student's assets, liabilities, adjustments and mal-adjustments."

(iv) Prognosis. This step can be a part of diagnosis and can be a separate step too. It depends upon the available specfic information. Where the result of the problem or knowledge of the situation occurs then the prognosis becomes the part of the diagnosis. Both, prognosis and diagnosis are cooperative processes in between the counsellor and the client.

(v) Counselling or Treatment. It is that step when the counsellor helps the client. In this, various questions are answered. Client answers these questions for himself, such as, How I can make changes in self? What can be its alternate? If such goes on, how the progress will occur in future?

(vi) Follow-up. In this step, the evaluation of the effectiveness of the counselling procedure is done and in this, it is observed what the client could achieve through counselling?

ADVANTAGES OF DIRECTIVE COUNSELLING

1. This method is useful from the time-consumption viewpoint. It saves a lot of time.
2. In this type of counselling, there is more focus on the problem and less on the person.
3. Counselling focuses more on the intellectual aspect of the person than his emotional aspect of the personality.
4. In this process, the counsellor becomes readily available to help the client which makes the client very happy.
5. The counsellor can look the client directly.

DISADVANTAGES OF DIRECTIVE COUNSELLING

1. In this process the client is more dependent. He is also unable to solve the new problems of mal-adjustment.
2. As the client is never independent of the counsellor, it is not an effective and best guidance.
3. Unless and until a person does not develop some attitudes through experiences he cannot make any decision himself. This type of guidance always lacks such experience and development of attitudes.
4. There is scarcity of informations regarding the pupil which creates the possibility of wrong counselling.

5. The counsellor fails in saving the client to commit the mistakes in future.

Non-Directive or Client Centred or Permissive Counselling. The main advocate of non-directive or client-centred or premissive counselling is Carl R. Rogers. This principle was developed in many years. Hence, various areas got included in such type of counselling such as, the development of personality, group leadership, education and learning, creativity, interpersonal relations and the nature of an entirely active person. This theory was developed in between 1930 and 1940. This theory believes that the sufficient means of solving a person's problem are present within the person himself. The function of the counsellor is to provide such an environment in which the client is independent to grow so that he may become what he likes to become. This school of thought gives importance to the emotional aspects of vocational and emotional problems and disapproves the diagnostic information as a part of counselling process.

The client-centred counselling revolves around the client. In this, the client is encouraged to leadin conversation and to express his own attitudes, feelings and ideas. The counsellor mostly remains passive. He never interferes the client's ideas, thoughts, feeling, flow of expressions. The counsellor helps the client in completing his conversation, basically the counsellor makes his efforts to develop rapport and mutual feeling of confidence in both the parties.

In this approach, open-end questions are asked. These questions are loosely structured. In the answers of these questions, the person projects his own personality. The main concern of the counsellor is with the summarization of emotional contents told by the client.

When the client is answering, he should be encouraged to speak in detail through proper methods. The client feels that the counsellor really respects the client's ideas. He gets the impression from the types of questions which a counsellor asks from the client and the interviewer is taking interest in the client. The counsellor does not ask the questions merely to explore the facts. In the non-directive counselling, every person has the right to be independent as a specialist psychologist. In such type of counselling, diagnostic instruments are used either infrequently or completely not used.

8.8 Basic Assumptions of Non-Directive Counselling

1. Tendency Towards Actualization. In the earlier writings of Rogers, it was emphasized that the person's or client's growth and developmental capacity is that person's characteristic on which the methods of counselling and psychotherapy depend. Even after so many years, his this opinion got strength that a persons' inherent tendency includes growth, adjustment, socialization; freedom etc. This directional tendency is termed as 'Actualizing Tendency' these days.

2. Belief in the Dignity of Man. Rogers believes in the dignity of the man. He considers the person capable of taking decisions and he accepts his right to do so.

3. Man is Trustworthy—Rogers considers the person basically good and reliable. He also knows that the person behaves in an unreliable manner too. A person is born with some urges which must be controlled if healthy personality development is desired.

4. Man is Wiser than His Intellect. When some organization is functioning independently and effectively, then the 'awareness' is a very small part or component of the entire process. When the organization feels some difficulty in its system of functioning, this awareness becomes more sharpened and focussed.

Snyder has also mentioned the following assumptions of non-directive counselling:

(i) The client has right to select the goals of his life.

(ii) Emotional disturbance inhibits a person's proper adjustment intially.

(iii) If the client is given an opportunity, he will select those goals which may possibly provide him great happiness.

(iv) In the counselling situation, one should reach very quickly at a point from where the client may be able to start functioning independently.

(I) STEPS IN NON-DIRECTIVE COUNSELLING

Carl Rogers has given the following steps of this non-directive counselling:

1. Defining the Problematic Situation. First of all the counsellor should define the problematic situation.

2. Development of Insight. The counsellor goes on thinking regarding the client's new feelings along with the development of client's insight and he goes on classifying all those new feelings.

3. Free Expression of Feelings. After the first step, the client is made aware of the fact that he can express his feelings freely and the counsellor approves this.

4. Termination of Counselling Situation. The counsellor looks for a point where he can terminate the counselling situation after all the above steps. According to this school of thought, either the client or the counsellor can suggest for such termination of counselling situation.

5. Classification of Positive and Negative Feelings. After the free expression of feelings by the client, the counsellor identifies his negative and positive feelings and he classifies them.

(II) CHARACTERISTICS OF NON-DIRECTIVE COUNSELLING

1. It is a client-centred counselling.

2. It is based on the principle that a person has so much capacity and drive that he can grow and develop so that he may face the situations in reality.

3. In this school of thought, the counsellor is passive to the maximum.
4. In this type of counselling, there is closeness betwen the picture of the self-drawn by the client and a desirable or an ideal picture of his own.
5. Its use reduces psychological tensions.
6. In this type of counselling, defensiveness falls down.
7. Through this counselling his psychological adjustment improves.
8. Client's behaviour is considered more matured emotionally.
9. A person is accepted in his originality and he is free to express his any attitude.
10. In his research Axlines has shown that the reading improvement speeds up as a result of client-centred play way-methods in the primary schools even if special reading instructions are not given.
11. This school of thought is just reverse to that of directive counselling.
12. In this counselling, the entire responsibility is of client or the person.

(III) DIS-ADVANTAGES OF NON-DIRECTIVE COUNSELLING

1. This counselling is not so deep like psycho-analysis.
2. This counselling has a drawback of lack of permission for flexibility to the counsellor.
3. The client is allowed for the free expression of his present attitudes but it is not attempted to explain why these attitudes occur? There is no research regarding the past, no suggestion, no attempt of re-education.

4. The client cannot depend on his resources, decisions and intellect.

5. It is a time-consuming process. Once the client strats his conversation, he does not cease to speak. This makes the other's turn for seeking counselling impossible.

6. This client-centred theory suffers the basic defect that it does not care how the behaviour is affected by the stimulus-situation and the nature of the environment.

7. Many counselling situations do not arise successfully in this client-centred counselling.

8. Sometimes, due to the counsellor's passiveness, the client hasitates in expressing his feelings.

9. All the problems cannot be solved orally or verbally or by talks only.

10. It is not possible in all the schools because the counsellor has to attend many pupils.

(IV) ADVANTAGES OF NON-DIRECTIVE COUNSELLING

1. The development of the problem-solving ability in the client through this school of thought is definite.

2. Being client-centred school of thought, other unwanted activities and tasts can be avoided.

3. This school of thought shifts the person from his unconscious state of mind to the conscious state of mind and releases tension.

4. This type of counselling leaves its impressions for a longer period.

8.9 Basic Considerations For Organizing School Guidance Service

In order to organize school guidance services, certain principles should essentially be followed. Jones has insisted not to separate guidance from the normal school life. According to him, this can be focussed in some specific part of the subject. It cannot be restricted to the office of the counsellor or a headmaster. Jones has assigned the responsibility of providing guidance to every teacher. In this exercise, co-operation of all is desirable. Hence, for organizing school guidance service, application of certain principles is must.

Humphery and Traxler, in their book entitled 'Guidance Services,' have mentioned some basic things for organizing school guidance service, which are as follows:

Defining the Objectives Clearly. The objectives of entire guidance programme should be clearly defined at the time of organizing school guidance service. While defining these objectives, the school ideals and needs of the pupils must be kept in mind.

Defining the Tasks. All the activities to be performed through the guidance programme must be enlisted beforehand.

Defining the Powers. The workers should be made aware of their powers just like their duties.

Allocation of Duties. The success of the guidance programme depends upon the allocation of duties to the persons involved in this job in advance so that every person should have a clear idea what he is to perform. The allocation of these duties should be according to the abilities of the persons or workers.

Defining the Relations. The relations of employees working in the guidance programme, whether full-time or part-time, must be defined clearly. Inspite of this, their relations should be defined in accordance with their guidance responsibilities with other employees.

Simplicity. The organization of school guidance service should not be of complicated nature. The framework of its structure should remain simple as far as it is possible, because every person will start taking interest in such a simple framework of the organization.

8.10 Nature of Guidance Organization

It is proper to decide about the structure of school guidance service prior to its beginning such as number of its employees, finance, size etc. The basis of its composition should be the objectives of the institute, financial resources and the number of students in the school etc.

Crow and Crow, in his book, has also suggested the following points to keep in mind before executing the plan of guidance programme:

(i) First of all it should be decided the number of persons to be involved in executing the guidance programme and the time required for the same.

(ii) How much increase in the workers' strength is required.

(iii) Is the building and the space are enough for conducting the various activities of guidance?

(iv) Do the parents too show interest in the guidance related planned programme and will they cooperate in this programme?

(v) Which teachers are available to provide various proposed services?

(vi) Are the teachers and other employees available in the school capable of devoting expected time and energy in the guidance programme?

(vii) What is the viewpoint of schools and the society regarding the expansion of guidance services?

(viii) Do the employees exhibit interest in the programme? If yes, to what extent?

(ix) To what extent other community agencies can be associated with the guidance programme?

(x) In which experience areas the pupils are required to serve?

(xi) How the pupils can be motivated to understand for themselves the value of the guidance programme?

(xii) Would the provision of finance in the school budget be possible?

8.11 Forms of Organisation of Guidance Services

The following can be the forms of organisation of guidance services:

1. The Centralised Form. The guidance work should be performed by the experts because the teachers are not trained in this guidance job.

The teachers cannot provide properly any assistance to the pupils who need the same to solve their problems. the central form of the guidance programme means conducting and controlling most of the guidance activities from the central guidance office. All the teachers also perform their duties according to the supervision of Central Guidance Bureau and its orders.

2. Decentralized Form. The decentralized form of the guidance means providing guidance as a responsibility of the teachers. The teacher remains in close contact with the pupils of his class. He understands the needs and problems properly of his pupils. Due to this reason the teacher can help the pupils in a better way. Some people also believe that if a separate department is opened for guidance in the school, the teacher will not show any interest in guidance work and also he will not consider guidance as his responsibility. Hence, it would be better if the responsibility of guidance work in schools lies with the teachers.

3. Mixed Form. The centralised and decentralised form of the guidance have their own merits and demerits. No form of guidance is practically possible independently. Hence, some experts express their views that the form of guidance programme should be mixed one. The mixed form means—guidance provided by the teachers and experts collectively. Crow and Crow also said, supporting the mixed form, that the school guidance programme includes the coordinated services of administrators, teachers, employees and social institutions etc. There are certain jobs in guidance programme which the teachers can do better, such as, collection of informations related to the pupils. There are certain jobs which can be done better with the help of experts.

The designs or forms of school guidance service organization can also be described in the following terminology:

(i) The Line Organisation.

(ii) The Staff Organisation.

(iii) Mixed Line and Staff Organisation.

In the line organisation, the employees are arranged in an order with regard to their duties or rights. The top position occupies by the administrative officer *i.e.*, head of the administration. There other assistant officers and the officers and employees working under them come in the sequence. Being head, the administrative officers supervises and examines the performance of other officers and employees.

The administrative officer controls both the line and staff organisation. The staff members deputed in certain areas have their definite responsibilities. The specialist employees play a special role in the process of guidance management and policy making even they work under the administrative officer.

The mixed form of line and staff organisation is known as 'line-staff mixed organisation'. Such organisations have the elements of both types of organisations. The provision of such form of the organisation is possible only in big institutions and occurs there.

PERSONS WORKING IN SCHOOL GUIDANCE SERVICES AND THEIR FUNCTIONS

As it has already been made clear that the guidance job is a specific task. To run this programme in schools, a specific category of staff members and officers is required. In the school guidance service organisation, the participation of the following persons is mainly involved:

1. Headmaster.
2. Class Teachers.
3. School Psychologist.
4. Counsellor.
5. School Doctor.
6. School Activities Coordinator.
7. Placement Officer.
8. School Psychoanalyst.
9. School Social Worker.
10. Child Welfare Worker.

8.12 Characteristics of Well-Organised Guidance Programmes

The following should be the characteristics of a well-organized guidance programme:

1. Child Centredness. The main characteristic of guidance programme should be its child centredness *i.e.*, the organisation of guidance services should be in accordance with the needs, interests of the children and objectives.

2. Specialisation. The role of specialists is very important in the organization of guidance services. Hence, for the success of guidance service, the presence of specialists in the guidance service is essential, such as the counsellor, psychologist, psycho-analyst, social worker of the school, doctor etc.

3. Budgetary Provisions. Budgetary provisions are also necessary to make the guidance service better. Budgetary provisions are made before starting the programme.

4. Continuity. Continuity of each guidance service is very essential. Continuity of problems occurs in the life of each person. Therefore, the continuity of these services is needed.

5. Proper Information and Record. The superiority of the services also depends upon the proper information and record. The guidance service should be used to collect the informations about educational and vocational needs and tests and to record them.

6. Cooperation. The characteristic of a good guidance service organisation is that it should seek the cooperation of the parents. The guidance service can be made better by seeking the interest and cooperation of each staff member.

7. Guidance for All. The principle of guidance for all is followed in a good guidance service. In a democratic country each pupil has a right to get guidance. In school, all the pupils should be provided with guidance.

8. Coordination. There should be another characteristic of guidance service that it should maintain coordination between all the associate agencies and the community for the guidance of youth for a longer period.

9. Confidential. It is very important to maintain confidentiality of the collected informations for the guidance in guidance service so that the confidence of the pupils on the guidance workers may be maintained. After winning the confidence of the pupils, true informations about them can be collected. Only the counsellor should have access to the confidential informations.

10. Opportunity for Final Decision to the Client. In a good guidance programme, the opportunity for final decision should be provided to the client. There should be no compulsion on them.

11. Selection of Guidance Workers. For a good guidance programme, the guidance workers should be selected on the basis of their abilities, training and experiences. It is not possible to perform all the duties related to guidance by the teacher alone. Hence, for specific duties in guidance, persons with special abilities in guidance are needed to be appointed.

12. Sufficient Time for Guidance. The guidance workers should be allotted sufficient time to provide successful guidance in the guidance service, such as time for testing and time for counselling. In time-table too, the sufficient time should be allotted for guidance.

13. Use of Various Methods. It is not possible to apply a single method for collecting informations meant for guidance. Also, it is not proper to use single method for the same purpose. Only one method cannot collect reliable informations. It is essential to apply various methods on one person at the different occasions and in different situations. It increases the reliability of the programme.

14. Simplicity. If the guidance programme is simple, it will be interesting and successful. In such simple programmes, all the persons show more interest.

15. Finding Solution. The utility of guidance service increases when it is organised for finding the causes of the problems. These problems should not be allowed to arise and preparation should be made to solve them if the same arise.

16. Responsibilities According to Abilities. A good guidance organisation is that where all the persons are assigned their responsibilities according to their abilities and capacities. If they are not assigned the responsibilities according to their abilities, then the success of the entire guidance programme cannot be expected. However, the client can experience some harm.

17. Providing Opportunities for Acquiring Abilities. The opportunities should be provided to the guidance of workers and other persons associated with such programme to increase their abilities. It is essential because new methods are innovated in the field of guidance every year and old methods are modified and improved. Every year new tests are constructed. The guidance worker should be given an opportunity to remain in-touch with all these modifications or changes.

Hence, we see that the above characteristics are responsible for the success of guidance service in an organisation.

8.13 Educational Guidance

The most important type of the various types of guidance is educational guidance. Educational guidance is directly concerned with the pupil. In the student life, educational guidance is very important. The chief aim of educational guidance is to develop the ability of coordinating with the school environment in the pupils and to create necessary awareness and sensitivity so that they may select themselves proper learning objectives, devices and situations. If we study and analyse Indian conditions, then we shall find the educational guidance is more needed in Indian conditions. Therefore, guidance is considered an integral part of education because educational guidance is viewed in the context of child's growth.

According to Jones, educational guidance is concerned with that assistance to be provided to the pupils which is expected for their adjustments in the schools, selection of curricula and school-life.

Four Main Functions of Educational Guidance

(i) To plan education according to the capacity, interest and resources of the pupil.

(ii) To be helpful for necessary progress in educational programme.

(iii) To collect information regarding the future possibilities of the pupils.

(iv) To fulfil the needs of the pupils.

Myers has also described educational guidance as a process of creating favourable conditions for the pupil's development or education. From this point of view, educational guidance is required at each level during the pupil's education. For example, educational guidance at primary level, secondary level, at higher secondary level and at college level. Psychological research has also proved that the educational guidance must be given to the pupils at each level. In order to study educational guidance, we shall have to go through its various aspects. Various aspects of educational guidance have been described in detail in the next units.

8.14 Vocational Guidance

Vocational guidance is not a mere technical process by which a person can be fitted in some vocation. Also he is not born for some vocation. The persons having normal intelligence can be adjusted in various vocations. In vocational guidance, a person is evaluated with regard to his capacities, capabilities and the changed conditions in the vocational areas and needs. In the vocational guidance the help is included in order to solve various problems related to the selection of a vocation, which is provided keeping in view the expected capabilities.

According to Super too, the main aim of vocational guidance is to enable a person for coordination with his vocation, he can use his energies properly and can develop the society financially by the existing facilities.

Crow and Crow have also given the objectives of vocational guidance. The process of vocational guidance is organised by keeping in view these objectives. In the process of vocational guidance, vocational charts, vocational information booklets, talks can provide information to the pupils relating to the vocations.

In nut-shell, we can say that vocational guidance helps the persons to adjust in the various vocations. The function of guidance is not only to help in selecting the proper vocation, but also to help in placement and progress. If all the persons possess same powers and abilities, then no guidance is required for various guidance processes. Hence, in all the vocations, same abilities are not required. Every vocation has its own needs. Persons are selected who are fit for those vocations. Hence, vocational guidance is needed. Therefore, vocational guidance is:

(i) a process.

(ii) must for selection of a vocation or adjustment in a vocation.

(iii) to know the necessary features of various vocations and abilities.

(iv) a process of introducing with various vocations.

A detailed description of vocational guidance has been given in other unit.

8.15 Personal Guidance

Personal guidance includes personal-psychological or emotional relationships which a person develops himself. Paterson has included social, emotional and leisure time guidance in personal guidance. In fact, the problems regarding health, emotional adjustment, social adjustment and leisure and recreational problems are included in personal guidance for solution. Under social adjustment, an individual's economic problems are included. The aspects of the life's character and spiritual fields can also be included in the personal guidance. In other words, the problems which cannot be included in educational and vocational guidance, we can include them in personal guidance.

In this way, the main aim of personal guidance is to establish balance between the individual's mental, social and physical aspects, because it is often seen that a person sometimes is surrounded by abnormal behaviours and social demerits even though they possess educational competencies and satisfactory progress in the professional areas. Such persons lead neglected life among their families, neighbourers and members of the community. Due to lack of balanced personalities in the families and neighbourhood and due to vague identification of mental and emotional deficiencies, the resultant conditions do not allow the person to imagine a peaceful and progressive life. In such conditions, personal guidance can prove helpful in solving such problems.

Hence, the solution of the following types of problems is possible in personal guidance:

(i) Problems related to the health and physical development.

(ii) Problems related to emotional behaviour.

(iii) Problems related to home and family relationships.

(iv) Problems related to religion, morals, ideals and values.

(v) Economic Problems.

(vi) Problems related to sex, courtship and marriage.

(vii) Problems related to social relationships.

The vocational guidance is a long continuous process which begins in the school and is needed throughout the working life of the individual. It is aimed at wise use by person of priceless native capacity and the results of costly training provided by the school for the good for the individual and the society.

According to the National Vocational Guidance Association of America 1973, "The vocational guidance is the process of assisting the individual to choose an occupation, prepare for it, enter upon and progress in it. It is concerned primarily with helping individuals make decisions and choices involved in planning a future, and building a career decision and choices necessary in effecting satisfactory vocational adjustment."

The general conference of the International Labour Organisation in 1949, described Vocational Guidance "as assistance given to an individual in solving problems related to occupational choice and progress with due regard for the individual's characteristics and their relation to occupational opportunity."

8.16 Scope of Vocational Guidance

The scope of vocational guidance may be understood better, perhaps, by a consideration of the general activities which comprise it. These are as follows:

(a) **Analysis of the Individual.** Without extensive knowledge about the individual desirous of getting vocational guidance, it would be impossible to effect his matching with the vocation. Competent men do this appraisal through various tests.

(b) **Occupational Information.** Next to the analysis of the individual is the collection and dissemination of information about an occupation. This is done by career talks, career conferences, visits to factories, establishing career corners, career clubs, career news-letters etc. Then only we shall be able to match the individual with the job.

(c) **Counselling.** Counselling is a technique of guidance—any type of guidance. Herein we give individual help to students.

(d) **Community Occupation Surveys and Follow-up Studies.** Most of us find jobs in the immediate neighbourhood. Other than national occupational information, vocational information should be focussed upon local conditions. Community occupational surveys and follow-up study of school-leavers wilol provide data on local training and employment conditions, labour turnover and job opportunities. This is to be done by a vocational guidance worker.

(e) **Group Activities.** Much of the work of self-appraisal and occupational study is handled most efficiently through group approach. Group activities in vocational guidance be done by the properly educated and trained teachers. These activities stress the methodology of vocational selection, preparation, job-getting and advancement. They provide occupational motivation and infor-mation through field trips, career conferences etc.

(f) **Placement.** This is the last and most important activity of vocational guidance. It cannot be left to chance. Herein the school places the individual in a job vocation and watches his progress.

8.17 Need of Vocational Guidance

According to Myers, vocational guidance is needed because:

1. If an individual stays in wrong profeesion for along time, he suffers economically. There is financial loss.
2. If an individual stays in a wrong profession, he suffers from a psychic loss. The individual is not happy. He is frustrated. His family life is affected.

3. There are a large number of personal and social values of vocational guidance. Leaving aside financial considerations, the worker's happiness, his personal development, his value as a social unit and contribution to human welfare are all involved. Right vocational guidance helps us achieve that.

4. It is needed from the point of view of health of the workers. If the profession is such where health of workers breaks down, production suffers and morale of workers goes down.

5. Vocational guidance provides many economic advantages to the employers. Their labour problems are less because these workers enjoy job satisfaction.

6. Human potentialities are utilised to the maximum with the help of vocational guidance. We are then truly benefited by it.

Conclusion. In the new pattern of Education system, where education has to meet the objective of total development of personality and all the domain which is motive and cognative all. It must to have give knowledge of all the aspects and skills to the learner. Keep this aim today curriculum includes social science, life sciences, mathematics, SUPW, language, arts, music and other co-curricular activities. But this multiplicity of subjects creating problems. It has been observed that neither are all the students interested in all the subjects nor do they possess the ability to grasp them. The failure to learn can cause emotional disturbance in terms of the damage. It does to the child self image often it creats stigma. The Guidance and Counselling work is very important and necessary in todays world. The guidance and Councelling plays effective role to enable the children to learn the new subjects ensure satisfactory progress and success. Proper guidance and training to the students enable them to conduct themselves properly in colleges and universities and in future in family and self life too.

REFERENCES

Arbnekle, Dugald A.—Counselling Philosophy Theory and Practice, Bostan Allyan & Bacon Inc, 1965.

Beck, Carlton E—Philosophical Foundations of Guidance, Engle Wood Clills, New Jersey, Printice Hall, 1964.

Jones, A. J.—Vocational Guidance and Education Columbus. Ohio Marrili Publising Co., 1970.

Murphy G.—"The Culture and Context of Guidance" Personal and Guidance Journal 1955.

Zinzberg Eli.—Occupational Choice, New-York, Columbia University Press, 1966.

❐

9

Computer in Education

9. Introduction

The computer is known as electronic brain. It is a speedy electronic device which is designed to accept and store.data information instructions to process the same automatically to produce result according to the given programme.

The term computer is the origin from the Latin language word computer. It is a calculating device. The letters of computer have same specific meaning—C-Calculate, O-Operate, M-Memorige, P-Print, U-Update, T-Tabulate, E-Edit and R-Response.

It is an electronic device which organizes and controls the data. The computer analysed the data in short time accurately.

A computer is considered as a machine which performed number of operations.

9.1 Development of Computer

It all started with ABAUS in 3500 B.C. After that John Napier's bone or cardbon, multiplication calculator came in the early 17th century.

Blasie Pascal's adding machine (1642) and Gottfered Wilhelm von Leibnitz's calculate (1694) were the mechanical devices used for computing. In 1833 came Babbage's Analytic engine, concept of which was similar to that of modern computer. It was used to process data on a set of precise instructions to produce information. It had a STORE (To store data and intermediate results) A MILL (Just like ALU for calculations), A CONTROL to supervise that machine performs the required operations in correct sequence, an input device pass into machine both data and instructions. An output deyice to display results.

Charles Babege devoted 40 years of his to invent a computer. He developed a model of machine to work for human programmes. He had very limited resources, even electricity was not available. After fifty years of his death, an Amierican Scientist Herman Hollereth could fulfil his dream. He was working in census depth. He introduced transitor in the place of bulb in computer in 1948, He also reduced the size of computer J.L. Kilvi designed a Small size successful computer 1985.

Then it was an era of digital computers. Harvard Mark I. Eniac. Edva Manchester Mark I. Edsac were the computer to follow the band of digital computer.

9.2 Stages of Computer Development

If we judge according to the time frame and electronic components used for the growth of computer industry we will get different generations of computers. Study the follows paragraphs to know about the different generations.

First Generation. Around 1946 computer used vacuum tubes with filaments which required heating to be functional. Size of computer was very large and power consumption was high. Also programming capability was low, Eniac, Edvace, Edsac, Univac-I examples of these type of computer.

Second Generation. Around 1955, a device called transistor replaced the by electronic tubes in first generation computer. Transistors don't have filaments and have high Operating speed. Manufacturing cost was low and also size of computers got reduced. If 1620, IBM 1401, CDC 3600 are examples of these types.

Third Generation. These were introduced in 1964 and used Integrated Circuits (ICs) so commonly known as chips. Size of computer further get reduced. IBM 360. Honeyell 200. vax 750 few examples.

Fourth Generation. Near about 1975, Large Scale Integrated Circuits (LSIC) built on single chip called micro-processors replaced the ICs. Later very large scale integration of recuits (VLSIC) replaced LSICs. These, computers are very powerful and also small in size. The PCs you see belong to his generation .

Fifth Generation. These computer are still in development stage and will be using a concept of Artificial Intelligence (AI) which will allow computer to make its decision Since fifth generation computer are going to use Artificial Intelligence (AI), let us have an idea about the AI.

Artificial Intelligence. When the concept of artificial intelligence will come into practices, computer will be called intelligent machines instead of dumb machines. They will learn from their mistakes and try different approaches to reach the solution. (How about computer analysing its past mistakes and swerating not to repeat those?)

Natural Language Programme and Expert systems are being developed in AI to facilitate a work for the human beings.

Natural Language Programmes. These programmes allow users give computer programme commands in English or any her language. Then they translate the commands into machine language so that computer can understand it. Like if you have a record of all school students in a computer and you ask computer show students with marks more than % in first unit or something like this, it will display all an requested records.

Expert Systems. These systems have a huge amount of data and rules stored in them so that a human being can used the expertise of this system to make his own decisions. As a user inputs the data or queries, an expert system gives possible to diagnose diseases and like in medical field there are diagnostic expert systems available to diagnose diseases and recommend medications by analysing data of diseases and treatment stored in the package.

9.3 Types of Computers

We can classify the computers according to their performance and functioning. The following information is about computer.

We can divide computers in four category based on their performances:

1. **Super Computers.** Super computers are the most powerful computers and are used for problems requiring complex analysis and calculation like weather forecasting, reartive models for the action and reaction of millions of atoms during a nuclear chain reaction. Examples are Cry Ymp. Cray 2. Nec Sx-3 and Param from India.
2. **Mainframe Computers.** These type of computers are generally used in organizations where many terminals are connected to it to handle huge volume of input output and storage. These are huge computers. Occupy lot of space and are generally placed separate air-conditioned office. Examples are EDC, ICL and IBM 300 servers.
3. **Micro Computers.** These are often termed as PC (Personal Computers and) becoming more powerful day to day to reduce the gap between micro and higher. These are available in DESLTOP (sits on floor), TOWER (stands on flor) & LAPT (Which you can carry anywhere) models.
4. **Mini Computers.** These are general purpose computer of size and capacity between micro computers and mainframe and mostly used as servers to serve multiple users in Local Area Network (LAN) or in UNIX environment Examples are IBM 9375. DIGITAL II.

9.4 Main Characteristics of Computers

It was like an extension of a calculator, where you input instructions a data and it calculates the complex results with hundred percent of accuracy. But 600 percent of use is now in not so calculative fields like office automation, DTP (Desk Top Publishing) designing and multimedia application. The following are the main characteristics of computer.

(1) Speed. It is right that computer calculate, compare, search data etc. But what's the big deal? You can also do it. Can not you add 67 + 23 or put a series of numbers in a sequence. Of course, yes but not as fast as a computer can do. A computer has a tremendous speed to work on huge amount of data to produce 100% accurate results. For us a second is very fast but for a computer a second is a very long period. It works in Milli, Micro, Nano and Picoseconds.

A computer has electronic circuits and all operations are performed in the form of electric signals which travel at incredible speed. This is the cause of its high speed.

(2) Accuracy. Above all, computer is a 100 percent accurate machine irrespective of amount of data given to it and its great speed.

It does not have an mechanical part (gear, pulley, handles etc.) which can wear with time and malfunction. It is all electronic circuits which perform mllllions of instructions in a second to give us accurate result. In case of wrong results delivered, staight way we should check for erroneous data or wrong instructions. (if you are expecting the result 5 and giving data and instructions like 10–4 or 10 ÷ 5, there is no use losing your temperon the computer.) It works on the principle GIGO *i.e.* GARBAGE IN GARABAGE OUT meaning if your will input quality data or instructions, You are bound to get wrong results.

3. Storage and Retrieval. We human beings have a limited memory. We can remember few names or telephone numbers.

Even if we store this kind of enormous data on papers or diaries, it will be very difficult to store these papers and search any particular from, whenever needed. But with the help of computer we can store any amount of records of an organisation in a sorted way and get any details in seconds out of huge numbers of the stored records.

4. Automation. It is a great advantage that you give all the instructions in the form of a programme to computer. Once it starts executing the programme, no human intervention is required. Suppose you want to find the greatest among ten numbers. Just make a programme and given logic in the form of computer instructions to solve the problem. Now to execute the programme, just input the required data and get results. Data can also be stored in a separate. He so that the programme automatically picks it and performs the necessary operations on it.

5. Versatility. Nothing can be more versatile than a computer. It is a mathematical a statistician, a designer, all architect and a lot more. It is present in your car, watch come out washing machine etc. It is in banks, shops, schools, offices, hospitals, police station, airports. Research centres and almost in every profession.

9.5 Uses of A Computer

A computer is used in all human life. It has revolutionized all phases of human activities. The most important areas have been given as follow:

(1) **Routine Job Handling.** The routine classical and stano type jobs-calculating and formality bits, salories, updating stocks, tax return, reservations records and information.

(2) **Traffic Control.** Controlling traffic, traffic lights. Television cameras are used to maintain traffic light routine.

(3) **Electronic Office.** All type information are stored, manipulated and utilized in the electronic form. A

document is sent to different place with Fax, internet and e-mailed.

(5) **Industrial Application.** It plays an important role in production controls. It bringing efficiency in trade and industry.

(5) **Telephones.** With help computerised telephone through salellites STD and 1ST services have been introduced. It maintains the record of calls and does the beilling for you.

(6) **Electronic Money.** Automatic Teller Machine (ATM) in very common in banks. You can deposit and with draw money with the help of ATM.

(7) **Medicine.** There is wide use in medical science e.g. ECG, CAT scan, Ultra Sound. The proper and accounts diagnosis is done with the help of computer.

(8) **Space Science:** The satellites are controlling the space with the help of computer. The informations are collected by using the computer from the space satlites. (9)**Trade.** In every type of trade computer is used successfully. It is used in Banks, Stock Exchanges to control stocks and accounts.

(10) **Scientific Research.** In every science, the research work become economical from time energy, money point of new. A large data is analysed very quickely.

(11) **Communications.** The computer is used for sending message *e.g.* telepriter, fax, e-mail, internet. The import and export work is done on internet.

(12) **Publications.** The composing work is speedily and economical with the help of computer. The designing work is also done by computer. The quality is maintend in publication by computer.

(13) **Film Industry.** It has influenced film industry such as Animation, titling etc. The multi-media approach is used in film productions with the help of computer. The cartoon films are developed by computer.

(14) **Education.** The computer is widely used in the field of education. An independent study field of computer sciene has developed which is very popular these day. At every stage computer education is compulsory. The distance education is using computer for instructional purpose as multimedia approach. The computer makes teacher learning process effective by involving audio and visual sense of learners.

9.6 Computer in Education

On of the most significant forces, influencing change in education in the present century, is the emergence of highly advanced communication technologies. The distance education system being and innovation in itself, is continuously influenced by these technological reforms. The distance education institutions in some developed countries have grown very much dependent on these technological advances. The media, have become almost an indispensable part of the whole education system in those countries.

The fundamental premise of distance education is the assumption that is has to provide individuals 'access' to the learning attained in should not be inferior in any sense to the learning attained in a traditional institution. A knowledge about recent technological developments will help becoming critricaly aware of the new opportunities for increasing accessibility to education and maintaining the quality of education. Due to various constrains, at present developing countries like India are unable to benefit fully from these technological advances. But by becoming aware of the opportunities that are available, Indian educators can feel more confident that there are technologies that can help them to improve the quality of education and to increase the accessibility of education to masses. The following are the other non-print Media of Education—*(1)* Computer as Non-print and Print Media *(2)* Videodisc and *(3)* Videotex.

Computer as Non-print and Print Media

Computer is an important technology used in distance education. During the past decade, the computer has become one of the most widely used aid to education instruction in the developed countries, chiefly because of its interactive capabilities.

A longer list of its advantages-besides its interactive capabilites—can be drawn to prove that the computer is an asset to distance learning. A computer can record, analyse and react to students responses, it can store and manipulate information on an extensive scale, can control and manage a wide variety of learning materias, it can simultaneously cope with the learning requirements of many individuals. In addition, it can by itself, offer instruction of learners. It can, moreover, through its electronic circuit, accurately make a myriad of decision necessary to the planning and implementation of an individualised programme of instruction on a mass basis in almost no time.

Technical Description of Computer

A computer is an electronic device that accepts data, performs operations on that data in sequence (decided by a programme) and outputs the results. Computers are termed according to their size and thus we come across terms like mainframe computers, mini-computers and micro-computers. Besides size, specifications of the electronic devices (that differ from computer to computer) are also used to identify computer-types. The specification includes details about the amount and type of storage, the capabilities of the central processing unit, and the type and the nature of the peripheral equipment (such as discstorage) that can be connected to the computer. The advent of micro computers in the 1970s at comparatively cheaper price made the accessible to many people and made the possibility of using them for educational purpose a reality. The basic micro computer system consists of an input device (*e.g.*, the keyboard), the central processing unit of the computer and storage devices (*e.g.*, cassette tape player; floppy disc device) and the output device (*e.g.*, and IV) display unit, or a monitor and/or printing terminals. The actual equipment of the computer system is called the hardware, while the term software refers to the instructions or the programmes that the computer carries out.

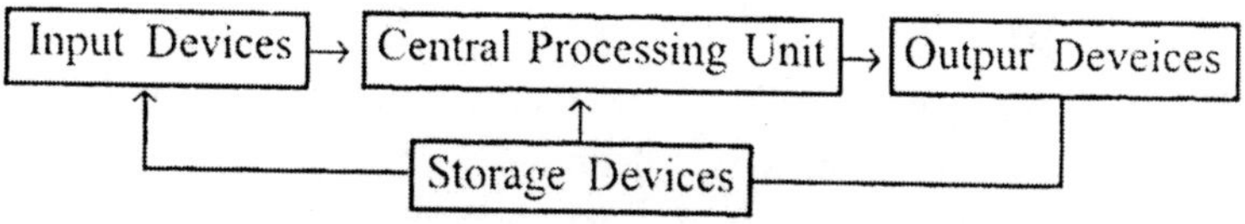

The input unit, usually a keyboard, (or cassette recorder or discdevice) is to send data and instructions to the central processing unit. The central processing unit performs the calculation and manipulates the data according to the instructions given to it. Storage devices are arts of the central processing unit. Their function involves the storage of tall related information and data. The output unit enables the user to receive data and instructions from the central processing unit. Normally, a television screen displays the work that the computer has done. A printer can also be used if a hard copy is required.

Application of Computer

While observing groups of students working with the computer, you would notice that students enthusiastically participate in the learning programme. The computer's novelty, the challenge involved in the programme, the wonderful display of tasks-all help in creating and sustaining their motivation. Learning with the computer is never dull and monotonous.

The programme called CODEBREAKER is a programme which keeps asking questions and the students supply the answers. In pedagogic terms this question answer sequence provides an opportunity for useful interaction which is essential for successful learning.

The programme called YELLOW RIVER KINGDOM is a problem solving activity. The computer displays a vast kingdom with a lot of resources. Can one imagine creating such a difficult situation in the classroom without a computer ? The Computer is capable of stimulating such complicated situations for the purpose of teaching learning. It can be stimulated dangerous situations such as a bring forest or division of atom.

A programme called VARIETEXT is a part of the text with blanks for the students to fill in for each blank four alternatives appear on after another and student has to choose the most appropriate one. Wherever necessary, the student can get the computer to display the correct words. This instant feedback is apart of the programme and no other technological instrument can be faster than the computer in providing such instant feedback.

These pedagogic qualities of the computer can be summed up as follows:

(1) Motive the learners,

(2) Interacts with the learners,

(3) Stimulates situations which are difficult and dangerous, and

(4) Provides instant feedback.

Such a powerful instrument has several uses in the field of education where technological media are a basic necessity. There is education instruction in the world which does not make use of media such as radio and T.V. Regular, though in a small scale, radio broadcasts and T.V telecasts are a part of education courses in India too.

In this technological atmosphere, the use of computers cannot be a far-fetched idea. We have successful examples in countries like Britain, Canada, Netherlands and Germany where computer are used on a large scale by the education institutions.

Some of the major advantages of using computers in education are given under:

(1) Computer brings flexibility and individuality to the study process.

(2) It reduces the isolation of distance learners.

(3) Computer-based study materials are cost-effective when produced on a large scale.

(4) It stimulates students to experiment, design and create solutions to the problems,

The increasing availability of micro-computer in the developed countries offered major new opportunities for distance education. The computer has various applications for distance learning. It can be used as a teaching medium, a learning tool, a manager of learning or as an aid to educational administration.

Administrative Applications of Computers

(a) budgeting and monitoring of finances

(b) keeping students records

(c) maintaining statistics

(d) mailing of score

(e) monitoring materials production register and so on

(f) student billing

(g) preparation of payroll, bills and date ledger

Instructional Situations of Computer Application

(i) pretesting of students knowledge on enrolement,

(ii) monitoring students progress,

(iii) planning and printing individualised programmes, and

(iv) compiling test and scores etc. A number of such data files can be stored in the computer.

Other contributions of computers are word processing to aid course development and data processing to aid administration. In addition, electronic mail is also used to communicate, change and exchange and exchange materials. The course term can also use computers for conferencing, establishing a communication channel among multiple writers and other professionals.

'On-line' and 'Off-line' Computers

Computer can be used in distance learning two modes—local mode and transmitted mode—local mode or 'off-line' computer stands on its own as an independent system helping the learner to work on his own. In transmitted mode, one computer is connected to another computer which is 'on-line' and then the operation depends upon communication between these devices. By inter-connecting the computers, a complex learning network can be which could link all distance learners with their teachers and with a central institution.

9.7 Advantages of Computer

The computer applications described above have certain remarkable advantages over the traditional 'print' medium of instruction. These advantages can be briefly pointed out in the form of the following hints:

(1) the novelty of working with a computer raises the learner motivation;

(2) colour, music and animated graphics can addrealism and appeal to drilling exercises, laboratory activities, stimulations etc.

(3) high-speed personalised responses to learner actions yield a high rate of reinforcement;

(4) step, can present a more positive and effective climate, especially for slow learner;

(5) memory capacity allows student's past performance to be recorded and used in planning the subsequent steps;

(6) the teacher's span of control's enlarged, as more information is put easily at the teacher's disposal, helping to keep control close to; and

(7) the record keeping ability of the computer makes individualised instructional feasible individual prescriptions can be prepared for all students (particularly main streamed special students) and their progress can be monitored.

9.8 Scope of Computer

Certain characteristics of computer-interaction can make computers well suited for distance learning. The features listed below make the prospects of computer-use look more promising:

(1) Access to experts and respected peers,

(2) One-to-one and one-many communications,

(3) Active learner participation,

(4) Self-direction-control over stop or start, time, pace and place of learning or communication activity,

(5) Linking of new learning to concerte on-the-job problems,

(6) Follow up, feedback and implementation support from peers or experts.

9.9 Limitations of Computer

In spite of the advantages and the promising prospects, computers do differ from some disadvantages too. Some of the major limitations are:

(i) Despite the dramatic reduction in cost of computer and computer use, computerised instruction is still relatively expensive. Careful consideration must be given to the costs and benefits of computers in education. Maintenance can also be a problem especially if the equipment is subjected to heavy use.

(ii) The design and production of computer specifically for instructional purposes has lagged being design and production for other purposes.

(iii) There is a lack of high quality direct-instruction master for use with computers, especially for the micro-computers. There use with computers, especially for the micro-computers. There is also a compatibility problem-often the software developed for one computer system cannot be used with another. The ease with which the software-especially cassettes can be duplicate without permission has inhibited commercial publishers and private entrepreneurs from producing and marketing instructional software.

9.10 Computer Use in India

Computers have been put to a widespread use for educational purpose in the advanced countries. Especially with the advent of the relatively cheap micro-computer, the technology has become more popular with the instruction (CAI) has already been used in Canada and at the Open University in Britain to provide diagnostic feedback remedial help; and revision aids in 1986.

The projects in the area of Remedial English. In India education is a new phenomenon but we have made a begining in using computers in our school system.

Computer Literacy and Studies in School

The project was initiated in India in 1983-84 by the Ministry of Human Resource Development in collaboration with the Department of Electronics. The main objectives of the CLASS project was to demystify computers and acquaint the students and teacher with the computer application and it potential as a learning medium.

CLASS was launched in 248 selected secondary and higher secondary schools representing all geographical areas. Preferential termtent in selection was given to Government schools with limited resources and whose student population that came largely from the lower socio-economic status. Later on, 501 more schools were added in the project. It is proposed to include another 500 schools in the year 1987-88.

The software and hardware components for the project were obtained for the united kingdom.

Since the inception of the project, 3180 teacher have been trained at 10 resource centres.

After conduction a study in 250 schools, the Space Applications Centre, Ahmedabad has claimed that the task of demystification of high technology and creation of computer climatic had been achieved. NCERT also noted that the programmed had generated a great interest among the students and the teacher.

By 1990, the NCERT hopes to have spread its CLASS programme, to nearly 14000 higher secondary schools in the country.

Internet System

The internet system in our country is the recent development. It has the great scope and possibilities. Internet services are being introduced through developing web-site. In India, thousand intercom companies are registered.

The internet system is based on network of the channels connecting computers at national and international levels. The message is passed on in printed and typed form on the monitor of a computer which is connected to network of the channels. The message can be obtained in printed form.

The contribution of internet system in education is the, convergence of various technologies. The basis of internet is also know 'National Informations Infrastructure'. The various network of channel are connected to a computer. It is known as host computer. The computers are known as Provider which send the massage or required information. The computers are connected to simple telephone lines.

The quality of education can be maintained by using interest system. The latest knowled~e of subject matter can be obtained for classroom teaching. The services of Cyber Caffe can be used for best educational material. The student can acquire the lastest development in his area of interests.

In our country Indira Gandhi Open University (IGNOU) and Indian Institute of Technology (IIT) have introduced internet programme of education. The Internet system has overcome the barriers of time, place, social and economic in learning process. The internet system has provided the following facilities:

(1) E-mail (Electronic Mail). E-mail is mode of communication of informations or message. The network of channel connected two computers for sending message immediately. The message can be sent by a computer it can be sent on other distant computer where it is wanted. In this system digital information is remitted through telephone line in the form of on-line, form one computer to for distance computer. It requires the e-mail address for such communication. The message can be read or can also be printed with the help of printer. Now it is used in industry, commerce occupations and education. It is economical than fax, telex, STD and speed post.

(2) E-Com. (Electronic Commerce). E-com, is a new system is our consumers marketing. Under this system sale and purchase of communities is done in the same way. In our country the E-com facility is in the beginning stage, but it has reached more 500 crores rupees business. E-com facility is provided by the following companies Annual, ICICI and National Stock Exchange. The investment laws have not been formulated in our country. It is the reason that this facility of E-com could not developed in our country. The Central Government India is taking some solid steps in the development E-com facility.

The main source of E-com is electronic data exchange. Under this system the data are converted and transmted through internet system. In the E-com facility custmer chooses the commodity to purchase on website. Then he has to fill up a farm on available computer. He has to provide the following information:

(a) His credit card number,

(b) Payable amount, and

(c) Name of the firm for purchasing commodity.

The customer has to deposit the required money in firm or transfer the amount. He can issue a cheque by his digital signature. The facility is available in the countries where digital signatures have been legalized.

9.11 Videodisc as Non-Print Media

Vidodisc is comparatively a newer medium that has widened the scope of use of the television set.

Vidodisc players are available in two models:

(i) consumer model, and

(ii) educational industrial model.

The consumer model is basically a playback medium and is mostly used in homes. The educational/industrial model more versatile, it can prone interaction individualised instruction. Sometimes, it is rendered more capable by means of a built-in microp rocessor. Videodisc can record materials from a variety of media, including film slides, audio and printed text. This makes rich the opportunities for individualised instruction for students learning at a distance.

Technology of Videodisc

A videodisc system is made up of a videodisc (on which the information is stored), a videodisc player and television set. Videodisc is used as information storage medium. A videodisc rotates on the turn-table of the videodisc player at a high speed and is read by a stylus or laser. Microscopic pits, of varying length and density, contain information on the disc. The pits are in tracks or gross. The information read room these pits is displayed on a regular television set.

Application of Videodisc

There are two major types of videodisc system:

(1) Capacitance Videodisc. Capacitance is a technical term for the electrical charge that can be collected on a plate. It may very player, which other. Thus, when the stylus rides over the disc (which contains the pits convered with a plastic coating to even out the surface), the distance between the disc and the stylus varies, causing changes in capacitance to occur. These changes are translated into the video and audio signals which are displayed by the television set.

(2) Optical Videodisc. The optical videodisc is more useful than the capacitance videodisc. The potential of the optical videodisc lies in its enormous storage capacity and optical disc can store 108,000 tracks (54,000 on each side). Each of the 54,000 frames on a side is addressable With a five-digit number and can be randomly accessed in 5 seconds or lets. The entire Encyclopaedia Britannica could be stored on a single videodisc with room to spare.

In addition to the information stored onto the disc, there are two channels of accessible audio, the accessibility to the dual audio channels allows for use of a second language, *i.e.* for the use of one language with the content oriented for a audience of a different linguistic background. It can allow for the addition of stereo sound too.

The videodisc system is capable of fast forward, fast revers, slow motion and stop frame movement. Individual images can be displayed indefinitely in freeze frame mode without a wear on the disc since there is no mechanical contact. But sound cannot be used in the freese frame mode.

Intelligent Videodisc

The intelligent videodisc system (videodisc connected with computer) which is particularly useful for education consists of a videodisc player under the direct control of a computer. This system permits interactive instruction for individualised learning. The videodisc is used simply as a storage medium for both still frames and video. The external computer programme may be used interactively to compare a student's response with a programmed correct response and can automatically move to a preassigned number of material depending on the response. Thus by combining two powerful technologies the computer and the television, the videodisc can offer mere individualised and interactive instruction for learners.

Advantages of Videodisc

Use of videodisc is inexpensive, when the discs are mass produced. Besides, the discs require little storage room. These two factors make it possible together extensive library of courses on small discs, the discs also provide easy accessibility and retrieval of the material of our choice.

The videodisc can be used to increase learner productivity through:

(1) More information in attractive presentation modes,

(2) Facility for repetition to achieve mastery,

(3) Immediate access (forward and revers) to different parts of the disc,

(4) Higher motivation through simulations of actual events in living colours,

(5) Provision for immediate 'feedback',

(6) Automatic frame stop, and

(7) Provision for students.

Limitations of Videodisc

However, we have to bear in mind that the information on disc is permanently catched into the surface of the disc. One cannot record new material into a finished disc as one can with a videotape. Therefore, videodisc suits best for such subject areas that do not require continual upgrading. Further, in order to minimise the unit costs of the disc a large production run is required therefore, course material meant for small groups will be too costly to present by means of videodiscs.

9.12 Videotex as Non-Print Media

Video is a system for providing an interactive information retrieval service. This particular technological development is one further step of the 'information revolution' which many industrialised countries are new experiencing. There are three videotex items prevalent today: British (Prestal), French (Antiopc) and Candian (Telidon).

Videotex allows the home television to function like a computer terminal that retrieves text information and graphics from a remote data. Thus, these technologies bring in the 'Power into home at a reasonable cost.

Technology of Videotex

The basic videotex system consists of keypad or key board, a TV display unit, a decoder, a telecommunication link and a central co.mputer co.ntaining a data base. Videotex uses television and telephone in order to provide access to the computerised information. The keypad, a small frame with number-buttons on it, is used to request pages of required information from a remote computer.

The television is connected to the computer by telephone and it is adapted by means of a decoder to display the recordings on videotex when it is played. Thus the home television set is turned into a terminal. As a television set is already present in most of the homes of developed countries, this device premises a wide range of social and educational utility.

The decoder can be wired directly into the television set during the manufacturing process or can be fitted on externally at a later stage. The decoder allows a TV set to display text and graphics from digital transmitted down the telephone line and to transmit back to information entered through keypad. A modem (modulator-de-modulator) ables the computer and the decoder to communicate in digital form ever telephone lines designed for the speech.

(2) Application and Advantages of Videotex

Most videotex applications are currently at initial phases. A number of applications for videotex have been tested much as work game teaching a second language, instruction to deaf etc. In distance education videotex can be used for the transmission and to way interaction on general or a specific information courses.

A videotex system is very useful in disseminating general information about courses and programmes available in raising the level of awareness of potential learners about educational opportunities available.

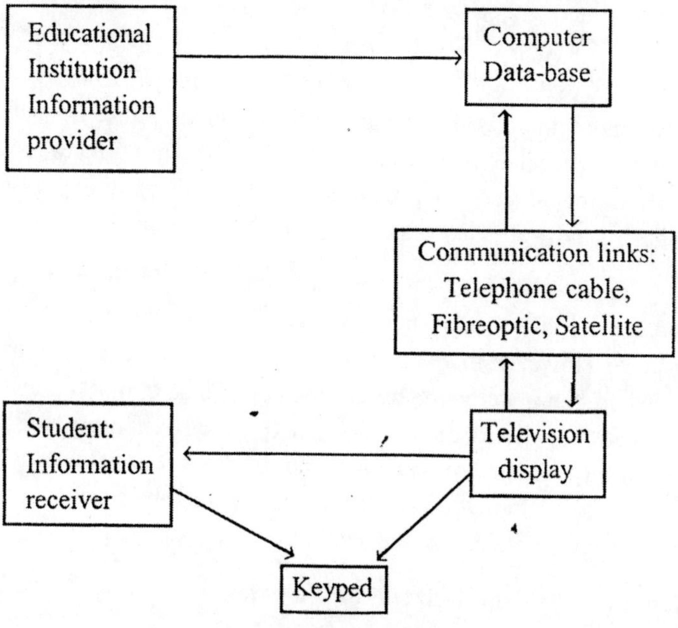

The Videotex System

The system with a substantial database can be very helpful to learners in remote areas as they could have access to the kind and the volume of information currently available to learners in areas with large libraries.

Videotex offers advantages over other time-bound communication media like radio, television of telephone because it is free from a time schedule. If a keyboard could be added to the user terminal, a videotex can offer computer-assisted instruction also two-way interaction between the teacher and the taught is also possible with alphanumeric keyboard (*i.e.*, a keyboard with number-buttons). This interaction resembles an electronic main, and learner can address questions to the tutor and receive immediate feedback. It is definitely faster than the post and has an advantage over telephone because this kind of interaction does not have to wait for a mutually covenant time for discussion. In the long run it may also prove to be cost-effective.

Limitations of Videotex

However, while the videotex system provides graphic capabilities, there is no provision for including audio. So videotex would work better if it is used as a part of a multi-media system in providing instructional material. As it is still at an experimental stage, its cost-effectiveness could not be determined.

Thus videotex system provide means for delivering instructional material to those individuals who have chose to learn at a distance. However, there are, at present few instructional programmes which are being delivered by this method. To date, most educational applications of videotex and teletext (a system using a similar technology as that of videotex and is discussed below) systems have as their information base a catalogue listing the courses available or services provided by the institution,

Teletex a System Related to Videotex

There are two system that deliver words and graphics to a modified television set-one, videotex which uses the telephone to connect the user to the data base; two the broadcast version known as teletext in which pages of . information are broadcast in cycle (usually 400 pages) and when the requested page comes up in the cycle, it is 'grabbed, and displayed on the screen.

With the vidotex about of material available for retrieval is limited only by the storage of the host computer. This is in contrast to the teletex, which has limit on the amount of material that can be transmitted.

Teletex Application in India

The teletext service in India was formally inaugurated by the doordarshan, Delhi on 14 November, 1985. It is known as 'INTEXT (meaning Indian teletex). Teletext uses the medium of television for transmitting information. The data are organized into pages, which contain text and graphic symbols six colours can be used in creating these graphics. The information is poled and transmitted on a few pre-determined lines in vertical 'blanking' interval of television signals. The information is in the form of magazines each of which contains about 100 pages. The details of contents of the magazine are given on the first page.

The news items, sports events, financial trends, timings of arrival and departure of important trains, weather forecast, city engagements, AIR and TV programmes to be telecast, etc., are given through teletext service. The information is collected through for hot-lines connecting teletext information room to:

(i) the meteorological department,

(ii) the northern railway central enquirey,

(iii) the Indian Airlines enquiry (for international arrivals), and

(iv) the Air traffic control (for interactional arrivals).

The using of the existing television broadcast, additional information can be transmitted in the form of teletex service.

Efforts are being made to provide the teletext service on a large scale. In addition, work has been undertaken to develop necessary software for creating pages with characters from different Indian languages. Non-effort has so far been made to use teletex service for educational purpose. In advanced countries also the educational application of telextex has been largely on experimental basis so far.

9.13 Scope of Non-Print Media

As the videodisc/videotex are relatively new media, the opportunities of these media to serve distance education are yet to be fully realised. The greatest advantage of the videdisc is its dense storage capacity. The interactive medium can provide educators with a highly effective delivery system for learning at a distance. The use of videotex is still at an experimental stage but it is believed that videotex system (such as Telidon, used in Canada) can be an educational medium in their own right with a potenital to deliver educational material to any participant in the system, at any time and in any location.

Although the use of new technology in the Indian context raises certain issues for educators to reflect upon, it also presents them with new opportunites for overcoming barriers of distance and time. Inspite of the media boom in the field of distance education because of the availability and accessibility of the technological instruments and their great potentiality, it is unfortunate that very few institutions in the world use them to a large extent. Printed material seems to be the main stay of education institutions. Some Australian institutions use audio cassettes with the printed materials, telematics, etc., some European institutions use video cassettes; the Open University in Pakistan uses several media successfully. Students enrolling on their computer courses are sent a micro computer each for their use at home on a loan basis. Some of the distance education institutions in India use radio and TV for their courses. The Indira Gandhi National Open University is pioneering the use of computers in home study. More and more institutions should start using computers for non-instructional purpose to begin with so that more and more people are educated about the use of computers.

India, as we know, is one of the leading manufactures of computers in the world. Computer process are coming down (pre-budget-estimate). The Government is also coming forward to help educational institutions with computers. Why don't the education institution make use of the apparently and provide the benefits of the wonder matching for their students? Let us hope that more and more institutions take on the computer in future.

Conclusion. The most remarkable development that has changed the world since the invention of the printing press and the postal communication is the computer. If a teacher walks parallel to technology and tries to develop software technology will be a boon to education.

The Computer Assisted Instruction (CAI) is a revolution or an innovation in the field of Educational Technology. The Computer Assisting Instruction (CAI) can taken the problems related to education easily and effectively. The NPE (1986) also put great emphasis on computer education. The Computer helps teachers and learners both. It has very significant role in the total education system of the country.

REFRENCES

Criswell, EL (1989)—The Design of Computer Based Instruction, Macmillan Publication, New York USA.

Dean, C, and Whitlock, Q 1988—J. Handbook of Computer Based Technology Kogan Page, London.

Gunter, MA Ester—T.H. and Senwab—J. H. (1990)—Instruction—A Model Approach Allyan & Bocon, Bostan.

Kulkarni, S.S. (1996)—Introduction to Education Technology—A system approach to micro level Education, Oxford and IBH Publishing Co., New Delhi.

Ministry of HRD Govt. of India (1986)—National Policy on Education.

Sampath, K. ***et al***—Introduction to Educational Technology (1981) Sterling Publishers, New Delhi.

❒

10

Hardware and Software in Teaching

10. Hardware in Teaching

Hardware is that part of educational technology which refers to tools and instruments. With the advancement of science, we find that the process of teaching-learning has been gradually mechanized through the use of teaching machines, languages laboratory, television, radio, computer, epidiascope, slide, projector, over head projector and opaque projector etc. All these sources are involved in hardware. Hardware approach has physical science and applied engineering as its basis.

Characteristics of Hardware in Teaching

(a) Hardwares are generally electronic and mostly depend on mechanical system.

(b) New techniques and research is being done of evaluating the effect of hardware

(c) The outcome of hardware is direct and immediate because they can be seen in concrete form.

(d) Hardware are media of communication. Some commercial agencies are manufacturing hardware from business point of view.

10.1 Need and Importance of Hardware

The proper use of hardware helps in maintaining the tempo of motivation and attention in the process of teaching and learning.

By using hardware, subject matter becomes clear and simple.

The proper handling of hardware contributes to the economy of time, resources and energy of teacher and students.

Educational Hardware are as follows:

(i) Overhead Projectors

By the name of the equipment itself it would be evident that in overhead transparency projector, the projected image is obtained behind and over the head of the instructor. The OHP reflects images coming from a powerful light that shines through a transparency on a screen by means of a tilted highly polished mirror and lens assembly.

The screen image is brilliant enough to be seen even in a lighted room. The projector area ranges from 3" ×3" to 10" ×10".

Normally overhead projectors are composed of a projection lamp to act as a source of light condensing lenses to concentrate all the light into usable beam, a polished mirror and lens assemblys and a blower for cooling the system.

(ii) Epidiascope

Epidiascope as the name suggests is the combination of episcope and diascope. With its help a picture, chart, map, diagram photograph or printing material can be projected in an enlarged size. For showing these materials there is no need of any slide, they can be shown on the screen as it is. When it is used to project an opaque object it works like an episcope and when it is used to project slides then it works as a diascope. Thus, it serves both as a diascope and as an episcope and therefore it is rightly called epidiascope. In epidiascope different types of pictures as well as slides can be presented on the screen, where as in diascope only slides can be projected. Plane mirror, projection lens and horizontal straight line projection with a lamp are essential requirements for epidiascope. A plane mirror is placed at an angle of 45° over the object. It reflects the light so that it passes through the projection lens forming a magnified image on the screen.

(iii) Utility of Epidiascope

Use of epidiascope makes teaching learning process more interesting, easy and impressive. Small pictures can be enlarged with its help. This instrument helps in enlarging those pictures which can not easily be enlarged by artists. Written lesson, map, cartoons, posters, diagrams and photographs can easily be shown to the students in the class with the help of epidiascope. A model of good handwriting can also be shown with its help to encourage the students to improve their handwriting. General mistakes committed by the students can be shown with its help to enable the students to make corrections. Teacher can explain the difficulties of the students simultaneously while showing the picture with the help of projector. Students become more attentive, active and disciplined in the class. Use of this instrument in teaching learning process makes teaching and learning more interesting and effective as students derive more pleasure in learning by seeing pictures. It also makes teacher active as he has to plan and prepare in advance all that he has to show in the class.

(iv) Radio

Radio is considered to be an improtant media for effective education. It is a powerful audio aid. It was invented by Marconi in 1895. It is considered to be the most effective means to impart education to the masses. Its popularity as a means to education is fast increasing in both developing and the developed countries. Invention of radio has brought about a great revolution in the world of educations. Radio helps the students to listen to the lesson. It was the only popular means to impart education in schools and colleges in different countries of the world before the invention of television. It holds fascinating opportunities for the world of education. In this era of constant change it has opened a new vista of an instructional media to alleviate the difficulties and problems of critical shortage of school facilities for ever growing school population. It is of great help to poor countries of the world in the field of education where school going population is large and where there is acute shortage of qualified teachers, well equipped laboratories and other necessary infrastructure for growth of education. It can reduce the mounting cost of education in underdeveloped countries.

(v) Tape-Recorder

Tape-recorder is an important audio-aid. The invention of tape recorder has brought about a revolution in the teaching-learning process. Its main function is recording and reproducing of the sound. Microphone, amplifier and reproducer are its three parts. It is an instrument which is used to record speeches, songs, music etc. and which may be played back at any time and any number of times. Teaching with tape recorder is extention of a teacher work. Talks and leactures of great educationists of the world can be recorded permanently. Different types of errors especially related to language can be recorded with its help. If the tape recorder is handled properly and carefully, the matter recorded on it can be repeated 100 times. The same lesson can be heard again and again in the class. Children feel happy when they listen to their own voice and feel encouraged. Tape recorders are available in all sizes and it is not at all difficult to handle them.

(vi) Educational Utility of Tape Recorder

1. Like radio programme we need not fix time for tape recorded programme and no change is required in the time table of school. Tape record as a teaching device can be used any time and any where.

2. It helps in supplimenting the educational output of radio and television broadcasts and guest lecturers.

3. It can help in preparing recorded educational programmes to be used for instructions in schools and colleges.

4. Tape recorder is helpful in bringing social awareness among people and can be used for canvassing in the elections.

5. It helps students in developing the skill of oratory by practising again and again on it.

6. It is of immense use in developing conversation skill, expression power and techniques of effective dramatization.

7. Educational material related with film strips and slides is recorded in the tape recorder. Thus, it is helpful in preparing commentary, display of slides and filmstrips.

8. Sometimes students can not be taken to real life situations *e.g.*, in Delhi on the occasion of 15th August and 26th January. Students remain deprived of speeches and ideas of the President and other great patriots of the country. Tape recorder can be used in recording the speeches of these great men which can be heard later on by the students. Thus, tape recorder helps in overcoming this shortcoming.

9. The teacher can record talks and lectures related to various subjects like science, maths, religion, music, morality, dance, social-studies, drama, poetry, economics etc., on tape recorder can be presented before the students whenever need arises. Thus, by presenting the recorded talks to the students and by listening to it again and again, the students can enhance their knowledge.

10. Use of tape recorder in teaching learning process gives more emphasis on learning by doing. Students can practice on tape recorder again and again till they become perfect. Thus, tape recorder helps students to learn things by trial and error method.

(vii) Television

Television is the most powerful media which has revolutionised the world. It can reach enormous cross-section of population with simultaneous presentations. It is helping learners and viewers to overcome the social deficiencies and cultural obstacles. It has immense attraction and potentiality in moulding characters, forming attitudes and shaping values.

According to M.J. Apter, "Television is the most powerful medium of mass-communication which has ever existed and it has revolutionised our life in many ways. It appears that the future television is going to have definite positive contribution to make childrens' life in the class-room happy. Television is already being used in schools more and more widely."

Through a television programme the audience not only hear but also see an event happening. Television is both audio and visual media. It is an improvement upon radio broadcast. It is fast becoming an integral part of school education. Invention of television has brought about a great revolution in the world of education. Today, television is considered to be really an important means for effective education. It is a powerful medium of communication through both auditory as well as visual channels. It helps the students to listen to and directly see the lesson on the television screen ensuring teaching learning to be durable and everlasting.

It is rapidly becoming the centre of the audio-visual approach to education. It is an important aid to teachers, supervisors and educational planners. It is utilized for informal and formal education and for distance and correspondence education.

Educational T.V. was first telecasted by AIR in 1960. The regular T.V. service was inaugurated in Delhi on 15th August, 1965. The famous satellite Instructional Television Experiment (SITE) was implemented during the year, 1975-76. The T.V. programmes produced by Doordarshan and Space Application Centre were telecast for primary school children in the day time and for the community during evening hours. Educational Television has been made available in most of the important cities of the country with the help of the satellites. Besides education other subjects like health, family planning, agriculture and technology were provided through educational television programme in six states—Andhra Pradesh, Bihar, Karnataka, M.P., Orissa and Rajasthan.

The Educational Television Programmes were telecast through Indian Nations Satellite (INSAT-1A) during 1982, and then (INSAT-1B) from 1983. More than 200 transmission centres have been set-up throughout the country. Each and every corner of the country is being linked with the television services. For spreading more television programmes National workshops are being organised by NCERT. More T.V. sets are being supplied to primary schools and non-formal centres for better education and awakening.

(viii) Video

The Video helps to increase the educational and entertainment values of Television. It can not only play pre-recorded cassettes, but also record any programme and replay it. Thus, the educational T.V. programme telecast can be recorded and later on shown to the pupils as per requirement. With the help of Video cassette recorders educational and other useful events can be recorded for the teaching purposes. The replay of those programmes in colour makes viewing very interesting and its impact on the viewers leaves a cosiderable impact.

Operation of video cassette recorder is very easy and simple.

It is quite portable and can be moved from on place to another easily.

(a) Knowledge acquired by video is permanent.

(b) It is helpful to the students in providing them the knowledge of social and political conditions of different countries.

(c) It is helpful in developing thinking and reasoning power of the students.

(d) It is equally helpful in educating and entertaining both backward and gifted children.

(e) With the help of video, teacher can remove the doubts of the students side by side, which is not possible in T.V. lesson.

(f) Teacher hold control over video presentation.

(g) Picture can be repeated as many times as one wants.

(h) Video films are easily available on different teaching subjects.

(i) It can be used anytime and anywhere.

(j) We can put the picture on the screen as long as we want.

(k) These days the use of video is on the increase in the education and recreational field due to the expensive use of T.V.

(ix) Computer

The advent of the computer and the educational technology related to it, clearly points to the way to major changes in education that will free the individual both teacher and student, to interact in more human ways than ever before.

The computer is one of the most wonderful inventions that man has made. At present the computer is used in almost all the fields where very complicated functions are to be performed. The computers are guiding the sophisticated rockets and satellites to the moon and to the distant planets. The computers are also guiding the submarines jet engines etc., for safe voyage. Computers are also used in large business concerns offices, banks etc. Now the computers have also entered schools and colleges.

"A computer is an electronic device which stores information on discs or magnetic tape, analyses it and produces information as required from the data on the tape etc". Computer is essentially a device for storing large amounts of information and handling this information in specified ways in extremely short period of time.

"Now education is, at least partly, about information. Sometimes the learning of this information is regarded as an end in itself, at other times it is regarded as the means to more general educational objectives. But even to merely learn information, more must be provided by an educational system than the mere presentation of information. Information must be processed to and from the student in order to provide the right information to fulfil particular needs. The amount of information processed in any educational system, taking into account the needs of all students at all times in all subjects, is enormous; and at its best, the processing of this information must be fast and accurate".

We see that the computer can handle and process enormous amount of information accurately and at tremendous speeds. If we put the computer at the disposal of teacher and pupil we open up the possibility of a revolution in education.

Many teachers oppose the instruction by computer on the assumption that it will make them unemployed. But actually computer cannot replace a teacher, but it will simply release him from some of the chores of information processing. Acutally computer is only an aid to the teacher. That is why now we talk of "Computer Assisted Instruction". The overal control of computer assisted instruction is in the hands of the teacher. It should also be noticed that the computer is not being used to treat all pupils in an identical way.

10.2 The Over Head Projector (OHP)

The name comes from the fact that the projected image is behind and over the head of the speaker. In overhead projection, a transparent visual is placed on a horizontal stage on top of light source. The light passes through this transparency and then is reflected at an angle on to the screen at the back of the speaker. Using OHP is not a new concept. It dates back to World War II when the armed services employed this equiment for teaching recruits.

Design of OHP

Overhead projectors are designed for direct or indirect projection. The projectors designed for direct projection use either Halogen lamps, linear or pea (650W) or in some cases 30 volt locomotive head lamp, worked with a transformer.

The overhead projectors designed on principle of indirect projection use the tubular projection lamps (750 or 1000 W) as in a film projector.

In all the overhead projectors, the lamp enclosure is blower cooled. In some overhead projectors, the blower is kept working till the enclosure cools to normal outside temperature by using thermostat (bimetallic) switches which switch off the blower. In such projectors only the lamp should be switched off and the power supply should be on to enable the blower working.

A fresnel lens is used to form a convering beam of light which illuminates the stage area uniformly and converges to the projection lens. The projection lens is a combination of two lenses with their principal axis at right angles. A surface silver or surface aluminised mirror or very thin flat mirror is serves to rotate the path of light by 90. The lens head could be rotated to form the image at any height. In some projectors, the mirror rotated to do the same function. The screen usually of 1 cm thick joly board or plywood (.5cm) or hardbound (3mm) is painted with non-glossy white paint and fixed to the right side corner near ceiling at an angle of 30-45 degrees to the vertical. This tilting is necessary to prevent keystoning. The OHP should be kept necessarily in a fixed place so the that rotated projection axis meets the screen normally and the teacher does not cast a shadow on the screen.

The general precaution to be observed for use of any projector should be observed when suing the OHP projector. The projector should not be subjected to mechanical vibrations. Provision for voltage fluctuation should be taken care of by using a voltage stabiliser or by having a suitable choke in series. Halogen lamps particularly will not withstand heavy surge in voltage. The lamp should not be touched by hand. OHP should not be kept on continuously for long periods. To use it as one would use a chalkboard is a very costly procedure. The fresnel lens is protected by a glass plate on top. It is necessary to remove dust or dirt on the protecting glass and also from the outside lens surface by flat camel hair brush. Surface silvered or aluminised reflector should not be cleaned.

(xii) Advantages of OHP

1. Large Image. A very large projected image in a minimum of projection distance is obtainable.

2. Flexibility and Versatility. The '"user operated" visualisation may be integrated into the total presentation with complete flexibility. The teacher maintains complete class control and interest in a lesson by turning a switch on or off.

3. Face the Audience. The teacher can always face the class, maintaining eye contact with the pupils. There is no "back and forth" action when using the OHP as in the case of chalkboard.

4. Identity with the User. Whether in a teaching or a presentation situation, the audience sees the visualisation from the same point of view as the communicator. The feeling of oneness with the communicator is created.

5. Lighted Room. This equipment can be used in a well-lighted room which enables the teacher to develop a sort of 'circuit of understanding' by watching the expression of others.

6. Home-made Materials. Effective visuals can be made in a minimum of time and at low cost. Once a transparency is made, it is permanent. It need not be erased as in a chalkboard.

7. Light Weight. The comparative lighter weight to the equipment makes it portable.

(xiii) Method of Using OHP

A tri-acetate film of minimum thickness is available as continuous roll. This roll could be constantly rolled over the illuminated stage. Matter clearly wirtten or continuously created over the surface could be presented on the screen. This method of using the OHP requires the projector to be continuously working during the entire period. This procedure is costly as the lamp has a limited life and the projector may also get very hot in spite of the cooling arrangement. Matter can be permanently written on acetate sheets using quill or ruling pen or rapidomat pen with special Indian ink or acrylic markers with special inks. Temporary, erasable impressions may be created with Chinagraph pencils, also called glass marking pencils (wax pencils), and water colour markers with special inks. These impressions can be removed by wiping with a dry cloth or cotton waste. Acetate sheets may be cleaned with sponge dipped in detergent or soap solution.

Tri-acetate sheets are available in large rolls of 75 cms width which could be cut into sheets of dimensions 20×25 to 25×25 cms. They can be suitably mounted on suitable cardboard mounts. Poster boards make attractive mounts.

(xiv) Specific Uses of OHP

The real advantage of OHP lies in the different uses to which it can be put. Instead of presenting static pictures on the screen, the teacher can develop the diagrams. The teacher, by moving an opaque or coloured pointer on the stage, can very easily focus the attention of the class on the screen, on the required aspect. The teacher can cover the completed visual on the stage and by sliding an opaque cardboard can progressively disclose one item at a time in stages.

One of the most effective ways to teach with overhead projector is using overlays. This is an effective technique for persentation of material in a step-by-step fashion. The information that is to be presented can be broken down into component parts. A transparency is made of each component and then the component transparencies are taped together. The basic transparency is mounted on a frame and three overlays can be hinged to the side of the frame. The series of components are then flipped into place on the stage of the projector as the information is developed in the class. For example, a geography teacher may wish to show a country depicting its rivers, mineral deposits and major cities. The first overlay transparency would have lines representing rivers; the second would depicit only the mineral deposits, and the third overlay would show only the major cities.

Sectional Models. To explain the working of certain machines lift-pump may be made with tinted acrylic sheets cemented by chloroform on a clear acrylic sheet, along with pieces which can be moved in slots or rotated about rivets. This will be highly effective.

Small live aquatic animals may be kept in a flat glass dish and get projected. Leaf profiles, flower petals and details can be projected. Silhouttes of small flat objects may also be projected using sectional models. Even dynamic demonstrations like rotation of a magnetised needle when a magnet is brought near could be shown.

10.3 Motion Picture Projector

Motion picture as an aid to teaching is inferior to direct experience. But in some cases motion picture will be able to provide the expected learning outcome better than even direct experience. The bright image on the screen with the associated sound is more realistic if it is in colour.

Tape-recorders and the mixed re-recording of the final tape done on a third recorder. All recordings should preferably be made during night time, when disturbing sounds will be minimal. When sound a material for use with a particular slide has been recorded, a single short peal from a bell will indicate to the operator of the slide projector that the side being shown should be changed and the next one brought on. Many projectors with automatic slide changing mechanisms are now available and a high frequency sound pulse from the tape acts as a cue for automatic slide change in some of these.

Present day slide projectors are more compact and efficient than those of the past and are fitted with low voltage halogen lamps and utilise a large percentage of light output. The slides produced using a camera with near focussing attachment, are made using 35m.m. perforated film with a picture size of 36mm × 24mm. Slides can be made with black and white film and then coloured or could be made using the costlier colour film. The slides are mounted on cardboard or plastic mounts. For line drawings, black and white film is more suitable than coloured film. From the resulting negative, a positive film print is taken and this positive could be used to get further prints which would display the diagrams clearly as bright lines on dark backgrounds. Such lines of diagrams can also be toned to suitable colours using required dyes (dye toning).

The mounted slides are kept in the required sequence in a linear or circular magazine for use. With non-automatic slide projectors, the operator should change the slide on hearing the cue-bell from the recording in the cassette tape recorder. The same set of slides could be used for instruction in different languages with suitable sound tracks recorded in different languages in spearate cassettes. The recorded sound could be easily changed by recording if needed. The slide-tape sequence, suitably produced can be almost as effective and dynamic as a motion picture and it appeals to the eye and ear of pupils.

10.4 Epidiascope (Still Picture Projector)

Epidiascope is a combination of episcope and diascope. With the epidiascope in the epi-position, flat opaque objects can be projected. In dia-position, slides either 3¼" × 3¼" or 3¼" × 4" can be projected using suitable slide carrier.

In epidiascopes, one 1000 watts lamp or one 500 watts lamp or two 500 watts lamps are used. There is a powerful blower cooling the lamp and directing blast of air on the opaque object to be projected. In spite of the cooling provided, page of any book if exposed for a long time to the intense heat from the lamp or lamps, will become dehydrated brittle and crumble to pieces.

The light that is scattered from the book page is less than 20% and is used to form the image on the screen. Hence in spite of bright light source and wide aperture epi-projection lens, the image formed on the screen will not be bright.

It is not advisable to resort to epi-projection for normal classroom teaching. Episcope can be used to enlarge book diagrams for preparation of charts by the teacher.

For dia projection, total darkening is not necessary. The large slides 3¼" × 3¼" or 3¼" × 4" can be produced by hand drawn or using camera or by retlex printing process. As the light rays are transmitted through the transparent slide, the image appears vary bright on the screen.

The reflecting mirrors in episcope or epidiascope are surface silvered or surface aluminised and should not be touched on the surface. The projection lenses should be kept covered when not in use to prevent dirt and dust settling on the exposed front surface. Proper cleaning of the lenses and perfect alignment of lamps will ensure better and brighter image. The epidiascope should be kept covered when not in use. It is a heavy equipment and it is desirable that shifting the same from place to place is dine carefully. A trolley with castor wheels would be ideal. In some epidiascope, there is provision of a mechanical pointer to point out any specific aspect in the projected object. It will be convenient to have book diagrams either reflex printed or photographed and enlarged. They can be suitably mounted on cardboard and can be projected on the screen, in desired sequence.

Stereo pictures and stereo-slides provide a three dimensional effect to the viewer. The stereo viewer like the 'view-master' takes in a disk with seven matched pairs of scenes taken with a stereo camera. Stereo slides are prepared in pairs from photographs taken with stereo cameras which take 2 pictures simultaneously through 2 lenses that are a few inches a part like the human eyes. Each picture is thus taken from a slightly different angle and when viewed through the 2 eyes at the same time fuse into one giving the impression of depth.

(i) Use of Epidiascope

It is used for making classroom teaching more interesting and effective. In this device slides are not need. The teaching aids such maps, chests, small pictures, graphs, line drawing are directly projected on the seven. The size of small pictures can be magnified or enlarged by the epidiascope.

In the epidiascope slides, transparencies are also used. The OHP requires transparencies of teaching aids. In epidiascope books and original matter or teaching aids are directly projected on the screen. The small pictures and diagrams can not be enlarged by an artist. The enlarge size is easily understandable to the learners. Therefore, the epidiascope is commonly used in classroom presentation. It also makes lesson interesting and effective presentation.

(ii) Precaution in Using Epidiascope

The following precautions should be used by teacher, while using epidiascope in classroom teaching.

(1) Before teaching, the epidiascope and screen should be set in the classroom properly.

(2) It requires the darkroom for projecting teaching aids. The proper arrangement should be made for this purpose.

(3) The size of teaching aids should be according to the size of epidiascope aperture.

(4) The classroom climate should be calm and quite.

(5) The teacher should acquire the place, so that his shadow may not cover the diagram.

(6) The teacher should give his comments side by side while projecting the teaching material.

(7) The teacher should make use of a pointer for indicating the aspects of a diagram or picture.

(iii) Advantages of Epidiascope

With the help of epidiascope, the text books and teaching aids are directly projected in the classroom in large size. Therefore, the epidiascope has greater use in teaching. It has the following major advantages.

(1) In epidiascope slides and transparencies are also used. The teaching aids are directly projected from the text books or other original sources.

(2) It is used for projecting the still pictures in large size on the screen to explain clearly to students.

(3) It is used in dark room as will as in lighted room. Which helps in teacher-taught interaction.

(4) The accurate diagrams and figures of science and geometry are projected in large size in the classroom.

(5) It functions as supporting device in classroom teaching and interaction to provide deep experience.

(6) By this apparatus two dimensional still pictures are projected on the screen. Multi-dimensional models can projected as it is.

(7) The small pictures and small diagrams are projected in large size which are easily understandable to the learner.

(iv) Suggestions and Precautions in Using Epidiascope

In using epidiascope in classroom teaching, the teacher should follow the suggestions and precautions.

(1) Before teaching, proper arrangement should be made for screen and epidiascope.

(2) Teacher should check all the electric connections and functioning of the apparatus.

(3) Teacher should use the pointer for showing the parts of the figure and material. Teacher should stand on right side of the screen.

(4) Teacher should keep an eye over the students as well as on the projected aid.

(5) The epidiascope should be used for important and necessary content. It should be projected side by side on the screen. So that students can feel its necessity.

(6) The teacher should have some technical skill for operating the epidiascope in his teaching. He take help of the technical person.

(7) The size of the projected figure should be according to size of the class. It should remain on the screen upto the end of its presentation.

(8) The teacher should have practice or training for using epidiascope properly in his presentation.

10.5 Motion Pictures Projector

Motion picture as an aid to teaching is inferior to direct experience. In some cases motion picture will be able to provide the expected learning outcome better than even direct experience. The bright image on the screen with the associated sound is more realistic if it is in colour. It provides a vivid, dynamic visual which is remembered longer than any other visual presentation in teaching.

Motion picture films can be classified as entertainment films and educational films. Educational films may be further subdivided into general educational films, and classroom films. Classroom films are on curricular subjects produced for promoting learning in a specific curricular subject. Educational films should be films devoid of anti-social activities, and abnormal behaviour. Some entertainment films can be classified as educational also. Any film can be considered educational if it promotes learning in general in any aspect of knowledge, correct attitude and behaviour.

(v) Advantages of Using Motion Pictures in Teaching

The following are the advantages of motion pictures in teaching:

(1) Motion presents certain meanings involving motion. Action gives impression of reality and promotes better understanding.

(2) Many general topics can be covered and conveniently presented in an easily digestible form and in an interesting way to maintain attention.

(3) Motion pictures compel attention and, as a result, help in permanent retention of observed events.

(4) Fast and slow motion can be shown to occur at normal speed, making analysis and appreciation possible. Slow motion technique is slowing down the action as in the case of a fast working machinery and movement of the limbs and parts of body in sports events and games. Sometimes the slow movement is shown to take place rapidly in the screen by employing fast motion technique. Events like crystal growing, plant growth, flower blossoming, etc., Which occur over days can be made to appear to occur in seconds.

(5) Motion pictures bring the past and the distant to the classroom.

(6) Motion pictures reach a mass audience at a low average cost per person.

(7) Motion pictures present materials that cannot be seen by the human eye and even by the microscope and telescope. Technical animation involving animated drawings can effectively serve to explain things that are too abstract, too large, well as working of machines, processes and movement of in which we do not need hundreds of pictures as in animation.

(vi) General Classification of Motion Picture Films

Educational films can deal with the following classification.

(1) Films about achievement due to advancement of knowledge in technology.

(2) Sports films.

(3) News and information films.

(4) Popular science films.

(5) Travel films bringing the world to the classroom.

(6) Health education films.

(7) Films about working of big institutions, hospitals, etc.

(8) Nature films dealing with flora and fauna.

(9) Films aimed to produce and encourage social awareness and expected behaviour of individuals towards betterment of society.

(10) Films about working of industry.

(11) Historical events.

Films of this nature are produced by the Films Division, Bombay in several languages. These films are available free of hire charges to educational institutions. In addition, classroom films or films on all curricular subjects are available from the Film Library, Department of Teaching Aids, Ring Road, New Delhi to educational institutions. Many foreign embassies like U.S.S.R., German Democratic Republic, National Film Board of Canada, British Council, French Embassy, Netherlands Embassy have very good films which can be shown to advantage in institutions.

(vii) Principle of Motions Picture

The motion film capitalises on the weakness in the human eye which is called the persistence of vision. Any object that is seen by the human eye will remain in the field of vision for a small length of time, *i.e.*, 1/6 second even though the object recedes. Hence, if a series of 16 still pictures are taken in rapid succession, developed and finally projected on the screen as a series of pictures, it will give the viewer a sense of motion. The addition of a sound signal results in a sound motion picture: Normally 24 pictures per second is the norm adopted for sound films and 16 pictures per second is the standard adopted in the case of silent films. A revolving shutter excludes the light during the time required for one frame to move out of the light beam and the next frame to move into it.

(viii) Films of Different Gauges or Size

Motion pictures are made with cellulose acetate which is not highly inflammable and hence are called safety base films. Highly inflammable nitrate base films are not manufactured now. The following is the description of the films made in different widths.

(1) **35 mm Films.** These are available in black and white or colour and have perforations on either side. These are used for production of commercial entertainment films and filmstrips. If used for filmstrips, there will

be 16 frames 'per foot in single frame filmstrip and 8 frames per foot in double frame strip.

(2) **16 mm Films.** 16 mm films are used for production of educational films, in black and white or colour. There are about 40 separate frames or individual pictures in every foot of 16 mm motion picture film. The running time of a 400-ft reel of 16 mm film is approximately 11 minutes. The sound film moves at the rate of 24 frames per second while the silent film moves at the rate of 16 frames per second. Hence the running time for a 400-ft silent reel is more than 15 minutes. Further sound films have perforations only on one side of the film and on the other side there is the sound track. The sound track can—be recorded using variable density of variable area optical techniques. 16 mm films can also be provided with magnetic tape striping on one side for magnetic sound recording. Silent picture films have perforations on both sides.

(3) **8 mm Standard Films.** This film either in black and white or colour with single side perforations is now extensively used in loop cassette projector. 8 mm super film is gradually replacing the 16 mm gauge film for use in educational institutions to impart instruction. There are 72 frames per foot in this type of film.

(4) **8 mm Super Films.** This either in black and white or colour with single side perforations is now extensively used in loop cassette projector. 8 mm super film is gradually replacing the 16 mm gauge film for use in educational institutions to impart instruction. There are 72 frames per foot in this type of film.

(5) **70 mm Films.** 70 mm film with provision for magnetic recording in multiple sound track is used to make high class commercial entertainment movies. Rear projection or using curved aluminium screens makes it possible to

show an adequately bright picture even when there is some extraneous light.

(ix) Motion Picture Projector

There are many different 16 mm motion picture projectors, made by various manufacturers. Each has its distinctive characteristics and advantages but all are similar in principle.

The principle involved in a motion picture projector is this: An object kept in between f and 2f of a convex lens will produce a real enlarged image beyond 2f of the lens on a screen. In the case of motion picture projector, the object is the transparent film. The film unwinds from the feed roll and goes through the picture head where it is illuminated by the light-source and is then projected on the screen kept at a distance by the projection lens. Then the film passes through the sound head to give sound. Here the sound track on the film is illuminated by the exciter lamp and its image is turned into corresponding electric signals by a photo-electric cell assembly. These signals are then amplified by means of an amplifier and fed to the loudspeaker, assembly. The film is finally rewound on the take up spool.

(x) Operations of Motion Picture Projector

Threading. The feed and take up spool arms are fitted in proper posItion. Thee drive belts are fitted. The film is threaded into the projector according to the diagram given in the projector itself. Threading is done using 5' leader in film. The film runs through as follows: from feed spool-sprocket-upper loop-film gate-lower loop-pressure roller-sound drum-sprocket 2-guide roller-take up spool. The perforations in film should be properly engaged by sprocket teeth. Upper and lower loops are necessary since film runs at constant speed at sprockets but in jerks at gate.

Starting and Running

(1) Check threading of film

(2) Switch on amplifier

(3) Switch on projector motor

(4) make sure the blower is operating. A blast of cool air would be felt over the lamp house

(5) Switch on lamp

(6) Focus the picture

(7) Frame the picture, if necessary

(8) Increase the sound volume to required level

(9) Adjust sound quality by operating tone control

(10) While the film is running it is necessary to gently fell the perforations as the film enters the take up spool. This is done to find out it the film is properly spooled without damage.

(11) When end is projected on screen:

 (i) Switch off lamp

 (ii) When the entire film is in take up spool (film reel have 3' trailer) switch off motor

 (iii) Decrease sound volume to zero

 (iv) Switch off amplifier

 (v) Rewind switch is put in rewind position and fjlm is rewound and spooled. Projector is lift for some time to cool then only packed.

Rewinding can be done using a hand rewinder. While using the hand rewinder the film can be checked. Any spoiled portion can be cut off and remaining spliced. Films are spliced using. film splicer and film cement. Using splicer ensures that the distance between perforations is not altered at joint Film cement bottles should not be kept open. The volatile solvent will evaporate and cement will become useless.

Films should always be kept in containers in rewound condition so that they are ready for use.

The following spares should always be kept in stock:

(1) Take up spools—400', 800', 1200 and 1600

(2) Spare spring belts

(3) Exciter lamps

(4) Projector lamps

(5) Cartridge fuses

(6) Oil for lubrication

(7) Film cement

(8) Lens cleaning liquid—cleaning cloth

(9) Camel hair brush for cleaning gate

(10) Film rewinder and splicer.

(xi) Sound Reproduction

Sound recorded in the sound track is converted into sound using photo-electric cell. Light from an exciter lamp is incident on the moving sound track. The light is restricted to a very thin rectangle by a slit. The light, transmitted by sound track is incident on a photo-electric cell. Since sound track transmits different intensities of light, as it moves along, the light incident on the photo-electric cell is varying accordingly. This results in a similar varying current through the photo-electric cell and the resistance in series with it. The potential across the resistance is amplified by using an amplifier. The potential across the resistance is amplified by using an amplifier. The potential across the resistance is amplified by using an amplifier, The output from the amplifier is connected to the loudspeaker which reproduces the sound. Projectors now made have a photo diode and use a solid state amplifier. If no sound is emitted during projection it may be due to the following actors:

(1) Amplifier not switched on

(2) Fused exciter lamp

(3) Exciter lamp not energised

(4) Loudspeaker connections not made

(5) Volume control at zero position.

(xii) Motion Pictures as Aid to Teaching

An instructional film should be shown at the proper time only. For example a film of 'electromagnetic induction' should be shown only when that particular topic is taught. There should be adequate preparation and follow-up work along with the screening of the film, as these induce pupil involvement practically doubling the learning outcomes. The following flow pattern will result in maximum benefit.

(1) **A Felt Need.** It is felt that a film on electromagnetic induction will help considerably to promote full comprehension and understanding in pupils. The film could be used to supplement other media. Perhaps a film on the life of Michael Faraday if shown would inspire the pupils and hence would be appreciated at this time.

(2) **Selection of Suitable Film.** The teacher gets a number of films on the topic and, if possible, preview them to find out the suitability for his needs. He should consider the age group, entering behaviour of the pupils while selecting the proper film. He should find out if the commentary could be understood by the pupils. He decides upon the nature of preparation needed. He also creates good viewing conditions, paying attention to venti-lation, seating arrangement of projector, screen, speaker etc.

(3) **Preparing the Pupils.** Relevant supplementary aids are brought in to motivate the pupils. For example, a dynamo with provision for rotating the armature manually connected to a lamp, a cycle with a dynamo and lamp fitted may be brought to the class. Though these are common objects the pupils evince lot of interest when the lamp glows as a result of the rotation of the armature. Pupils would like to know the 'why' of it and also some details about the inventor.

(4) **Reinforcement.** The film on electromagetic induction is projected on. If the commentary provided is unsuitable or inadequate for the class, the teacher can provide the necessary commentary. After the screening is over, the teacher gets a feed-back by posing questions. Wrong concepts are clarified. The film may be followed by a demonstration experiment to show induced *e.m.f.* When there is relative motion between conductor and magnetic field. All experiments shown on the film are repeated. The pupils get confirmation of what they have seen on the film. There is complete and clear understanding. The students would have also seen application in daily life of the phenomenon of electromagnetic induction.

(5) **Rescreening.** The film is shown again. Often students will learn more if they can see the film again either immediately after discussing it or at the start of the next class period.

(6) **Follow-up.** Consolidation and practical applications of knowledge gained could be by giving assignments, problems involving writing answers on paper or collection of data or further reading or doing practical work. Pupils can also be asked to work on related projects or any related creative activity. It would also be better if the teacher evaluates the film for later use, using a standardised film evaluation record.

> Motion films selected for the specific purpose may be shown to pupils before they launch on field trips. Motion pictures may be shown before a group of pupils embark upon a project. There are quite a lot of motion pictures dealing with problems connected with teacher training and education of retarded and gifted children. Films are only resources; they are seldom complete teaching units in themselves. Their value is like that of all other instructional media; it will depend on how well a teacher uses them in classrooms.

Many research studies have been undertaken on the impact of silent and sound films on the behavioural development of pupils. The results reveal that such films used properly accelerate cognitive learning of pupils and retention is also comparatively enhanced. There is also strong evidence to support the view that motion pictures exert a measurable positive influence on the feelings and attitudes of pupils. Research findings point out that appropriate films used wisely bring about increased student interest in instruction resulting in greater interest in reading.

10.6 Micro Projection

Science teachers want students to make accurate observations and to draw correct conclusions from what they see. Sometimes, live insects and specimens in microscopic slides may have to be viewed by a small group of pupils in a biology class. A microscope can normally be employed for this purpose. While adopting this technique, the teacher can draw the attention of the pupils on any salient feature in the image. But the teacher is not sure whether an individual observes what he says because only one student can observe through a microscope at a time. In such circumstances, micro-projection can be resorted to using simple dissecting microscopes or compound microscopes. Micro-projection is a technique by which the actual microscopic slides or tiny objects can be enlarged and the image of which can be projected on a screen so that it small group can view it. Rear projection will result in a brighter image. Since power of magnification is very high, the illumination used should be very powerful and this may be secured by making the room totally dark.

Powerful illumination will result in heating of the specimen or causing damage to slide. Live organisms can be kept in a liquid medium which will reduce the heat. When dissecting microscope is used, live objects like mosquito larvae, tadpoles etc., can be kept on a watch glass. In the case of insects, it is difficult to keep them in the brightly lit hot area, as the specimen will move to cooler sides. The illumination can be switched off periodically. When a compound microscope is used, a few drops of water may be placed on a microscope slide and micro organisms like paramecium could be projected.

Rear projection screens 20 × 25 cms dimension will be suitable for micro projection. It will be necessary to cut out stray light by suitable shields.

Light from a filmstrip/slide projector suitably condensed using additional lenses will serve as a bright light source.

10.7 Video Tape

Storage of instruction for repetitive use is easily accomplished now with the use of video tapes. They may be played back through monitors in a studio or class-room. Video tape can provide virtually instantaneous reproduction and in that sense, it is superior to films. Video cassettes are also available now-a-days. The user simply attaches the cassette player to his own television set, inserts a cassette and presses a button. The obvious advantage of the cassette is that it is portable and can be used and reused at will.

Suggested Lessons for Instructional Video

Video materials can be used from mass lectures to individualised learning; from primary classes to open university systems. Any subject can be presented in a video format. Many processes and procedures, techniques and skills lend themselves to video presentation, such as the following:

(a) For reproducing rare field trips in Earth Sciences like tectonics, minerology, creation of geysers and natural springs, volcanoes, oil retireval, oceangraphy, paleontology, meteorology.

(b) For demonstrating basic priciples of Physics and Mechanics, like machines, energy, force, gravity, Newtonian laws and the applications of these principles to human development.

(c) For demonstrating a process or procedure using laboratory facilities in Physical Science.

(d) Showing aspects of plant life in Biology, photosynthesis, relation between plant life and animal and human development, ecological aspects.

(e) Demonstrating vocal inflections, lip movements and body gestures in learning foreign languages.

(f) In Physcial Education, the effects of different exercises on the basic anatomy of body, health education, athletic skills, gymnastic demonstrations, games techniques.

Modes of Using Videos

There are many ways that learners can use the videos. The following are some ways for using a 30-minute video programme in learning situations:

(a) The video can be played continuously to a large group in a lecture room as a prelude to discussion and a question-answer session.

(b) The 30-minute video can be played as a series of half-a-dozen shorter 'clips' during the 1-hour-long discussion.

(c) The video can be used in tutorial groups, either played continuously or as a series of clips.

(d) The video can be part of an open learning package, where learner individually or collectively in small groups use it at their own pace.

(e) The video can be given to individual learners supported by handout or workbook material.

Guidelines for Preparing a Video

The following list of guidelines is not a rigid prescriptive 'recipe' but contains only suggestions.

1. **Objective.** For the grade level, subject area and nature of the lesson, keep goals to a minimum. Fomulate the specific behavioural objectives in terms of learning outcomes.

2. **Content Outline.** Determine the content of the lesson by gathering materials and extracting the most important elements.

3. **Audience.** Identify who will use the lesson. Specify age and subject knowledge.

4. **Treatment.** Determine the style or combination of styles, *viz.*, lecture, demonstration, interview, dramatic form, field observations. Decide on the specific visual and aural materials like title, charts, models, sound and music. Video is essentially a visual medium. Narrative should play a supportive role rather than a central role. When planning the sequences to be filmed, think visual at all times. The TV camera makes use of four types of lens, normal, wide angle, telephoto and zoom. A wide angle lens helps to create illusion of objects being further apart. Telephoto lens narrows the angle and compresses distance and creates illusion of objects being closer than they are. The zoom lens changes the focal length from the telephoto to the wide angle usually in the ratio of 4:1.

5. **Review.** To focus attention, a brief review of materials covered may be given, summarising main points at the end, or one review in the middle.

6. **Continuity and Pacing.** While preparing the script, let the sequences be logical. Determine how much time each point should take. Provide variety and pace for difficult points. Avoid emphasis on subpoints at the expense of major ones.

7. **Evaluation.** Evaluation will give information concerning the value of the tape in instructional process. A few questiones can be arranged with reference to achievement of goals, the relevanoy and accuracy of the subject matter, effectiveness of the graphics used, etc.

8. **Instructional Guides.** To clarify materials and methods and reinforce concepts. Instructional guides may be designed to accompany the video cassette.

9. **Validation.** On the basis of the evaluation, the cassette material may suitably be revised, reused, re-evaluated and validated for wider use.

The film projectors in schools have became obsolete as result of the advent of camcorders, video-players and TV sets. The camcorder consists of a camera and a recorder and is very easy to handle. Video tapes are also cheap and can be used over and over again. Hence, it costs very little to practise taking shots with the camcorder. The art of making good videos is learned by trial and error. If zoom facilities are to be used, it is better to use a simple tripod to avoid camera shake. When capturing sounds, it is desirable to use a suitable separate micorphone instead of the built-in microphone in the camcorder.

Three basic types of shots form the bulk of most sequences in cine and video programmes. The long shot provides a general view of the subject taken from a distance so that the subjects is seen in the context of the background. The medium shot provides a closer view of the subject and eliminates most of the background details. The close-up provides a closer view of the subject or a specific part thereof. When the readings of a small meter are to be shown clearly, a close-up shot is used.

10.8 Educational Value of TV

1. Communication by TV is effective because it can bring very good demonstrations and audio-visual materials to the class-room.

2. TV can bring the world to reality of the home and to the class-room.

3. TV permits everyone to look through a microscope at the same time.

4. TV facilitates a school or college to share its best teachers rather than rationing them.

5. TV can save the time and effort of the student and teacher.

6. The concrete nature of TV makes some programmes understandable, appealing to a wide variety of age and educational levels of people.

7. TV can be both instructive and enjoyable.

Limitations of TV

1. TV is one-way communication. It does not stop to answer question. It does not permit class discussion.

2. There is no personal contant with the teacher. The programmes do not adjust well to individual differences.

3. TV encourages a passive form of learning rather than an active seeking. It cannot provide for individual and group activities. It does not provide for laboratory experience.

4. The equipments necessary for TV is costly and complicated. A properly designed studio with controllable lighting facilities and with acoustic proof walls is necessary. It should be maintained by competent staff all the time.

5. TV screen is small in size as compared to projected pictures.

10.9 Audio-Visual Aids of Hardware-Software

Today's education system is not the same as it was in the past and witness lot of changes in it. Even the current education system is fast changing and we expect this system to be entirely different in the years to come as a result of the impact of continuous research in the field of education. The object of teaching is to make teaching learning more effective, permanent and long lasting by focussing the attention of the students at the communication. For realising these objectives, it is essential for the teacher to make use of different types of teaching aids and materials such as models, films, tapes, charts, diagrams, maps, television, radio, projectors, epidias-cope, filmstrips concrete objects and similar other resources. All these materials, instruments and resources are termed as teaching learning aids as they supplement class-room teaching and come to the help of a teacher in making his communication clearer, class-room inter-action healthier and teaching popular and effective.

These aids are also known as audio-visual aids as they influence the auditory and visual senses of the learners and permanently imprint teaching upon the minds of the students. These aids provide real experiences to the learners. It is well understood that a student can better understand, appreciate and preceive by touching, seeing, smelling and directly tasting an object. For example a child can better understand the difference among an orange, an apple and a banana by seeing, touching, smelling and tasting these fruits, thus by applying his senses rather than by simply being told about them. These aids are sort of means which provide real and valuable learning experience to the students. A learner with the help of these aids successfully makes better utilisation of his senses in making learning more permanent, interesting, effective, meaningful and clearly understandable. According to an old saying, 'A thousand hearings are not as good as one seeing.' So strong is the influence of our senses on understanding that according to Joseph J.Weber, "We get 40% experiences from vision, 25% from auditory, 17% from touching, 3% from smelling and rest 15% from other physical experiences. According to Dr. Kenneth B. Hass and Dr. Harry Q Packer, "It is natural that in education, we should appeal to the mind chiefly through the visual and auditory sense organs since it is possible that 85% of our learning begins at those terminal points. "Audio visual aids are being increasingly used at all the stages of education—primary, middle, secondary and higher secondary. In the process of learning, greater is the involvement of senses more permanent and effective is the learning as senses are taken to be the gateway of knowledge. Audio visual aids are better means for drawing the attention of the students towards their studies. By creating attention and arousing curiosity of the students these aids help and prepare the students for teaching learning.

Following points highlight the need of audio-visual aids in teaching-learning process:

1. **To Develop Educational Interest.** These aids motivate the children to learn effectively and thus to acquire permanent knowledge. In this way audio visual aids develop educational interest among the students to attain knowledge about some subject.

2. **To Supplement Direct Experiences.** These aids help in getting direct experiences from real things. Children always get pleasure in getting direct experiences by touching, tasting or seeing a particular object. By using these aids the students give practical shape to their ideas. When a teacher teaches with the help of a model or a

picture about a particular animal and when the child sees the same animal in reality in the zoo, his acquired knowledge about that animal is reinforced and becomes permanent. The direct experiences of the students can be supplemented by showing models and charts in the class. It will also reinforce the knowledge of the students.

3. **Attraction Towards New Things.** Audio-visual aids develop attraction and interest in the process of teaching learning. Children have great attraction towards new things. If the teacher teaches with the help of audio-visual aids, he arouses the interest and attraction of students towards learning new things.

4. **Educational for Life.** It is said 'life is for education and education is for life.' Education makes the life happier and meaningful. An educated man is generally said to be more rational compared to an uneducated man. Thus, these aids become the part and parcel of the life of children and help them in solving various problems related to life.

5. **To Help in Meaningful Experiences.** These aids provide meaningful experiences with the use of more and more senses, which is the foundation of educational process. The senses are gateway to knowledge. When knowledge is imparted to the students with the help of various senses and more the senses are involved, the stronger is the foundation of knowledge.

6. **Direct Experiences.** The knowledge which the students get through direct experiences is everlasting because of involvement of the sense organs like eyes, ears and nose etc. Similarly when a student sees for himself the process of manufacture of various commodities like vanaspati ghee, soap, oil etc., in factories, it gives him direct experiences and his knowledge about manufacturing

process of these commodities which he has acquired from books and teachers, is reinforced and becomes permanent.

7. **To Develop Reasoning and Logical Power.** Use of audio-visual aids develops the imaginative reasoning and logical power of the students. The children become capable of differentiating between effective and ineffective teaching.

8. **For Clarity in Educational Process.** It is here that audio-visual aids play their role to make educational process simpler, clearer and more understandable for students. Some times due to inherent shortcomings of lecture method students feel bore and lose interest in studies. It is here that these aids come to the help of teachers in reviving the interest of students in teaching learning process.

9. **To Make the Students Active.** Use of audio-visual aids makes children more active in learning and motivates them to actively participate in teaching learning process. Such activities as turning of globe, to see seven colours in Newton's disc, to make a picture, to prepare gas in the laboratory, to draw and fill the maps with colours etc., provide ample opportunities to the children to learn by doing.

10. **Useful for Slow and Backward Learners.** The use of audio-visual aids is specially helpful for backward and slow learners in teaching learning process. Due to low level of intellect and understanding some times they fail to understand from books and class-room teaching. But when the same thing is taught by teacher with the help of pictures, charts, models and other aids, it facilitates their learning and helps the students to understand abstract things more clearly.

Thus, it can be concluded that audio-visual aids play dominant role in the process of education. In the present modern scientific age, audio-visual aids are those effective tools in the hands of the teachers which enable him to perform his duty more effectively and efficienty. These aids help him in imparting education properly. Such aids are also very useful in providing direct experiences and in imparting education related to life and profession. These aids motivate the interest, aptitude and capabilities of the learners and by actuating the senses help students to take active part in teaching learning process.

10.10 Main Principles in Using Audio-Visual Aids

Use of audio-visual aids in teaching is increasing day by day. Its use has been recommended in all subjects like science, arts, commerce and other humanities. These aids are of immense help in making lessons and teaching learning simple, clear, interesting and comprehensive. The utility of these aids is relatively greater for younger children and in lower classes. While using these aids we should bear in mind that following principles must be emphasised as suggested by eminent educationist Maurice P. Moffat.

1. Principle of Effectiveness. In the selection of audio-visual aids the principle of effectiveness is very important. It implies that the aids should be chosen carefully so that they prove meaningful, important and effective for understanding the lesson. Selection and effective use of these aids depend upon ability, foresightedness and capability of the teacher.

2. Principle of Selection. The principle of selection implies the need for carefully selecting these aids for use in teaching. The chief aim of their selection should be to achieve the desired and pre-determined objectives of teaching learning. While selecting these aids the teacher should ensure that they are in accordance with the age, mental level of students, interests and objectives of the lesson.

3. Principle of Means. Principle of means implies that these aids should only be taken as means to achieve certain ends. They are neither the ends in themselves nor can they replace the teacher and the books. They serve only as helping aids in the process of teaching learning, use of which makes the lesson and the teaching interesting, easy, clear, understandable and durable, which is the main aim and objective of using aids.

4. Principle of Stimulation. These aids provide direction, motivation and stimulation to the learning process. Audio-visual aids actuate the learners and make them participate in the process of learning by influencing their sense organs and thus help them in remembering the learning for a longer time.

5. Principle of Purposiveness. The teacher always has certain definite purpose in mind while making use of these aids. In other words aids should not be used without purpose. The purpose of using aids should be explained by the teachers to the students beforehand. The objectives of lesson should be predetermined for which these aids are to be used. It will create interest among students and they will actively participate in teaching learning activity. Thus, it will help in making learning process more useful for learners.

Concludingly we can say, while using these audio-visual aids, the efficient teacher should keep in mind and practice above mentioned principles, if he wants to succeed in making his teaching and lesson forceful, meaningful and really effective. These aids act as motivators in the exchange of ideas and view points, which finally make teaching process more interesting and dynamic.

Some Precautions in the Use of Audio Visual Aids

These aids are use only for fulfilling certain aims, objectives and purposes. Efficient and right use of these aids calls for a teacher to be efficient, skilled and trained accordingly. Even an efficient and trained teacher should keep in mind the following precautions in using these aids in teaching learning.

1. These aids should be proposive and educative and should not be allowed to become means of amusement, joke and fun for students.

2. They should be according to grade, age, and mental level of the pupils. Before using these aids it is essential that a teacher should prepare himself mentally to do so and he should have the necessary capacity and ability of using them.

3. The utility of these aids should be according to the needs and objectives of lessons. Some times in some lessons they do not prove useful. Every type of topic being taught in the class does not need to be illustrated by every type of audio-visual aid.

4. Due Emphasis should be placed on the educational value of these aids. They should be true, authentic, accurate and real substitute for the first hand experience.

5. These aids should be used in proper class-room environment ensuring lighting, space and other facilities.

6. They should be capable of providing more and more learning experiences so as to make teaching learning effective. Also, an aid to be effective must be capable of representing whole idea in a concise but comprehensive manner.

7. To make these aids more meaningful, useful and effective in understanding the lesson the teacher should make supplementary comments at the time of using the aids. Mere display of an aid is not sufficient.

8. Before using the aids, the teacher should explain their utility and relevance for the lesson in order to arouse interest, zeal and curiosity of students about these aids and their use in making the lesson effective and clearly understandable. The teacher should be clear in his mind

about the exact point in the lesson which the aid is expected to illuminate and the way it could do it. The teacher should see that audio visual aids are not too numerous and over used.

10.11 History of Computer Development

The need for counting and calculating was felt as early as The Stone Age. The primitives used pebbles to count their cattle and other food stuff. Later, with the production of surplus goods, goods started getting exchanged for rice and other similar commodities, resulting in the Barter System.

Still later, people used to count by putting tally marks on sand or stone. A need for counting became more urgent giving rise to the development of various counting systems and devices.

Abacus. The Chinese developed the Abacus, a manual calculator of sorts. in as early as 3000 BC. In about 1000BC, Greeks and Egyptians improved upon it. The final version, can still be seen being used in Hong Kong and other parts of China.

Leibnitz Machine. In 1964, Gottfried Wilheim Leibnitz improved Pascaline and called it Stepped recliner or Leibnitz machine, it could multiply and divide as well as find square roots.

Pascal's Calculating Machine. In 1642 AD, Blaise Pascal, a young French scientist, developed a mechanical calculating machine, known after his name and called Pascal's Calculating machine. This machine was capable of performing only addition and subtraction. It was also called Palestine.

Analytical Engine. In 1833 AD, Charled Babbage, invented a Difference Engine to generate logarithmic and stromatal tables of numbers upto 6 places. The technique he used was the computations of successive differences. Later he developed, the concept of Analytical Engine, a calculating machine, which still forms the base of all computers. He however, could not complete his work during his lifetime. For his fundamental research he is known as the father of computers.

His work was completed by Lady Augusta Add loveless, daughter of Lord Byron, the English poet. She developed the essential ideas of programming the analytical Engine. For her contribution she is known as the first Computer Programmer.

Hollerith's Machine. Herman Hallerith, an American statistician developed a punch-card machine in 1887 AD. This machine could store the results in the form of punched cards and read them later on. Hollerith formed a company called Tabulating and Calculating? Company of America. It combined with other companies to form what is now known as IBM (International Business Machines Corporation, USA). IBM is among the largest manufacturers of computers in the world.

Mark I. In collaboration with IBM Howard Aiken of Harvard University developed 'Automatic Sequence Controlled Calculator' or Mark I. This was the first commercial computer available in the market. IBM marketed it in 1944. It was the fastest electro-mechanical machine, capable of multiplying in 4 seconds and dividing in 10 seconds. It was a huge structure, 15 meters long, 2.5 meters high and weighing 31 tons, having around 750,000 parts. At the same time came into existence the use of electronics in computers. Computers like ENIAC, EDVAC, and UNIVAC were developed. These were all huge and very expensive machines mainly used for research and development work.

Three Generation Computers. The principle of On Switch and Off Switch, that is the two states represented by 1 and 0, was used here. First, electronic devices, vacuum tubes were used to provide On and Off conditions. This formed the 1st Generation of Computers (1940-52). Then transistors replaced vacuum tubes forming 2nd Generation (1952-64) reducing overall size of components required for the computers. Next were Integrated Circuits or ICs also called the Chips. These were made of a material called silicon. A small silicon chip had hundreds of transistors forming ON (1) or Off (0) conditions in a very small space. This was third generation computers (1965-71).

Around 1972 to Till Data. Several more transistors and other electrical components like capacitors were added on to this IC to make large scale integration (LSI). In fact, a chip had an entire CPU on it and was called a micro processor resulting in smaller size, faster speed and lower cost of operations. Our present day ICs belong to 4th Generation.

Research is going on for increasing the speed of operations, decreasing the size and adding more components on a chip to give human like intelligence to computers.

Kinds of Computers

1. IBM 650. In 1955, this was launched by IBM. It was one of those big computer requiring full room to store with cables running underground to connect the various components of the machine.

This machine actually made the scientist sit back and think of creating new machines, which could work faster and would take less space.

2. Apple PC. In 1977, this computer was developed by two young men in their twenties, named Steve Worzniak and Steve Jobbs. It became vary popular for home and small business use. They formed, Apple Computers the company which manufactured more small computers than any other computer manufacturer of the time. Over the years the company has grown tremendously and has McIntosh brand of computers available throughout the world. Their computers are better than those manufactured by IBM.

3. Personal Computers (PCs). In 1981, the IBM launched its first Personal Computer called IBM-PC, since then, manufacturers other than IBM have also developed PCs which are of the same standard as that of the IBM. While IBM-PC remains the trademark of IBM, the other manufacturers market their small computers as PCs, which are also called IBM-PC compatible machines. PC has become a general term including all kinds of personal computers from IBM and other companies. PC has been improved over the years as per the following development stages:

(i) PC-I. A PC with a single floppy diskette drive. This PC had a 51/4" double sided diskette can could store upto 360 kilobytes of data. It was based on Intel 8088 IC chip. The computer operated at 4.77 Megahertz speed and had a memory of 640KB.

(ii) PC-II. A sort of extension of the PC-I computer mentioned above. Instead of single floppy drive, it had two of them. Rest of the features remained the same.

(iii) PC-XT. Developed in 1982, Personal Computer with extended Technology, had an additional fixed hard disk drive and a floppy disk drive. The microprocessor used was Intel 8088; however, the speed was increased to 8 megahertz. The usual capacity of hard disk was 20 Megabytes.

(iv) PC-AT. Developed in 1984, Personal Computer with Advanced Technology, also had a floppy drive and a hard disk drive in a minimum configuration. It could also have, within the system box, a maximum of 2 floppy drives and 2 had disk drives. The floppy diskette used were of Double sided High Density and could store data upto 1.2 Megabyt. The capacity of a hard disk also increased from 20 to 80 Megabytes and been beyond that. The speed was also increased to 13Mhz (Megahertz) because of use of new Intel 80286 chip. The memory also increased from 640KB to standard of 1 MB but could be increased to 16 MB.

(v) PC-AT/386, 586. Form 1985, through 1997, and beyond, advancements in computer technology has brought about Intel processor chips in market ranging from 80386 to 80585 in such a short span of time. Now a days 80586 chip which is also known as Pinetum is used in the computer system.

AT/386 introduced 1.44MB mini floppy of 3½", which revolutionized floppy system to such an extent that the new computers now do not have 5¼" floppy drives.

Hard disk capacity also went on increasing from 80MB to 1.2GB, in between experimenting with 256MB, 512MB and 800MB etc. Even 1.2 GB is now replaced with 2.1 GB and even 4.3 GB are available presently.

The memory chip which was IBM in case of XT, increased to 4MB, 8MB, 16MB, 32MB and even higher.

Speed of processing also kept on increasing. It was 4.77 Mhz in case of XT and then went on to 50Mhz and then on to 133Mhz and now 200MHz is the standard. PCz with speeds of 400MHz are also available.

(vi) Pentium PC. The optimum machine these days, it has a hard disk of 2.1 GB. The memory is of 32MB. It has one floppy drive of 3½", 1.44MB capacity. The clock speed is 200MHz and is based on latest Intel chip called Pentium.

(vii) Pentium MMX. The new version of Pentium chip which supports the multimedia operations like audio speakers, video card capabilities and has all these features built-in on to the single chip of the system is called Motherboard.

(vii) Pentium II-Processor. A new, more powerful processor has been developed by Intel Corporation. In its competition, Cyirx Corporation, US has produced equivalent micro-processors. K-6 and K-7.

Another American Company—Motrolla has developed another series of micro-processors-68000 series, which are mainly used in the Apple-MacIntosh computers.

(ix) Power PC. There is also consortium of Apple. IBM and Motrolla which manufactures Power PC. Power P/C is supposed to take advantage of all the features of the IBM-PC compatible machines (PCs) and the MacIntosh (ac) machines. Programmes written both or the PC and the Macwill run on the Power PC machines.

10.12 Use of Computer

Progress in the field of science and technology has worked wonders in the different walks of life. The latest advancement is of computers and their successive use for instructional purposes. In the developed countries like U.S.S.R., U.S.A., Canada etc. Computer facility has reached every educational institution. But in our country, its need and importance has been recognised increasingly and efforts are afoot to have it and make use of it in different facets of life. Only in limited institutions, computers are being used for the instructional purposes. Computer can work wonders almost in every field of human activity. Countless number of calculations within a second are possible with the help of a computer.

A Computer is a power-driven machine equipped with key boards, electronic circuit, storage compartments and recording devices for the high speed performance of mathematical operations. It his also a capacity for storing of memorising a large amount of information and producing any of them when called for. We may say that the computer is a box loaded with information. It has its own symbolical language. In order to work on a computer or to derive benefit, we shall have to familiarise ourselves with the language of the computer. So we shall have to feed the computer first. Then it interacts and manipulates the information, translates the answer and types it on a tele-type-writer.

Basic Parts of a Coumputer

There are five important parts of a computer which are briefly explained below:

1. The input equipment of the computer is in the form of key board and cassette recorder. It receives the outside information so that it may work accordingly.

2. The output equipment translates information back into understandable form.

3. The memory part contains all information which has been fed into the computer. It helps in storing information and retaining it. Further it can be used whenever needed.

4. The processing unit is the arithmatic and logic mind of the computer which is responsible for all types of date manipulation and computation work.

5. The control sub-system controls the execution of the programme and co-ordinate all the activities of the sub-system of the computer.

The computer is a hardware machine. The software used in it is in the form of written programme which is prepared by the computer programme writer. The computer works as the programme writer directs it. The computer in itself is not an independent thinking machine.

Computers have their own languages. They are known by different technical names Basic, Logo, Pilot, Cobol etc. We should understand the languages of the computers if we want to communicate with them. Most of the computers make use of binary system, where two digits symbol O and 1 are used for expressing any number.

For Example,

Step I. Number	Computer Language
0	0000
1	0001
2	0010
3	0011
4	0100
5	0101
6	0110

7	0111
8	1000

Step II. Then the operations are given code numbers as given below:

Operations	Code Number
Add	1
Subract	2
Multiply	3
Divide	4
Read a card	5
Square	6
Draw a line	7
Transform	8

Step III. At this stage, the code numbers are transformed in computer language as suggested above in step I.

According to J. Bruchner, there are two systems for computerized instruction:

1. In computer assisted instruction, the student participates with the computer system on a direct basis and the instructional materials are stored in the computer system.
2. Computer managed instructions are used to help the teacher to administer and guide the instructional process but relies on separate hardware and learning materials; the student is usually not on line with the computer system and the processing need not be in real time. Instructional materials are not stored in the computer system.

Advantages

We can use the computer as an effective and indispensable aid in the teaching-learning process. Here below are given a few advantages:

1. It helps the learners in the development of variety of skills. It can also be used for providing drill and practice to the learners.

2. It can serve the role of an inquiry officer. The students put questions and it gives response with the help of answers it has already stored.

3. The computer can play efectively the role of a tutor by maintaining perfect interaction and dialogue with the individual students.

4. The computers can be used to give training to the students through simulated and gaming techniques.

5. They can be used to develop problem solving ability and creativity among the students.

6. They can supplement laboratory and other practical work specially in science subjects.

7. They can be used in providing education to the handicapped children like deaf and dumb.

Limitations or Drawbacks

The computer assisted instructions suffer from some drawbacks which are given below:

1. The use of computers in the class-rooms is very expensive and uneconomical in terms of educational returns.

2. Handling the computer is rather technical. There is always the danger of damaging the costly machine by the students.

3. Being auto-instructional, it may lead to indiscipline, truancy, carelessness and wastage of time on the part of some students.

4. The repair work or its servicing causes a serious problem to the institutions.

5. It is rather difficult to teach all subjects and all topics with the help of a computer. There is dearth of computer programmes for teaching purposes.

6. Heavy school curriculum and shortage of trained personels pose a threat to the introduction of computer assisted instruction in the educational institution.

10.13 Role of Computer in Education

In 1965, Lorence Settlor and Daniel Davis developed most complicated teaching processes in which computer was used for presenting instructions in place of teacher. They divided the teaching process of the computer in two parts:

1. Pre-tutorial phase.

2. Tutorial phase.

In the first phase, computer assisted instruction is given to the pupils to achieve the specific objectives on the basis of his entering behaviour. In the second phase, instructing material is presented accordingly. The pupil studies it. Then, the achievement of the pupil is evaluated. After presenting the instruction, computer also controls it. It also provides reinforcement to the pupils.

In the modern age, the use of computers in the field of education, made in following areas:

(i) All the researchers do all analytical tasks with the help of computers in the research work.

(ii) Computers are also used in educational guidance and counselling.

(iii) Remedial teaching of the pupils is also done by the computers.

(iv) Computers help is sought for preparing the results of the examinations.

Computer Programmes

While observing groups of students working with the computer, you would notice that students enthusiastically participate in the learning programme. The computer's novelty, the challenge involved in the programme, the wonderful display of tasks-all help in creating and sustaining their motivation. Learning with the computer is never full and monotonous. Some illustrations given below would reveal a few more qualities.

1. Codebreaker. It is a programme which keeps asking questions and the students supply the answers. In pedagogic terms this question-answer sequence provides an opportunity for useful interaction which is essential for successful learning.

2. Varietext. It is part of the text with blanks for the students to fill in. For each blank four alternative appear one after another and the student has to choose the most appropriate one. Whenever necessary, the student can get the computer to display the correct words. This instant feed-back is apart of the progaramme and no other technological instrument can be faster than the computer in providing such instant feedback.

3. Yellow River Kingdom. It is problem-solving activity. The computer displays a vast kingdom with a lot of resources. The Computer is capable of simulating such complicated situations for the purpose of teaching learning. It can be stimulated dangerous situations such as burning forest or division of atom.

Pedagogic Qualities of the Computer

1. Motives the learners
2. Interacts with the learners

3. Stimulates situations which are difficult and dangerous
4. Provides instant feedback
5. Distance Education

Such a powerful instrument has several uses in the field of distance education where technological media are a basic necessity. There is hardly any distance education institution in the world which does not make use of media such as radio and T.V. Regular, though in a small scale, radio broadcasts and TV telecasts are a part of distance education courses in India too.

Some of the major advantages of using computers in distance education are as follows:

(i) Computer brings flexibility and individuality to the study process.

(ii) Computer reduces the isolating of distance learners.

(iii) Computer-based study materials are cost-effective when produced on a large scale.

(iv) Computer stimulated students to experiment, design and create solutions to the problems.

The increasing availability of micro-computers in the developed countries offered major new opportunities for distance education. The computer has various applications for distance learning. It can be used as a teaching medium, a learning tool, a manager of learning or as an aid to educational administration.

Administrative Applications of Computers

1. Budgeting and monitoring of finances
2. Keeping students records
3. Maintaining statistics
4. Mailing of rest score

5. Student billing
6. Preparation of payroll, bills and debts ledger
7. Monitoring materials production register and so on

Instructional Situations of Computer Application

1. Pretesting of students knowledge on enrolment
2. Planning and printing individualized programmes
3. Compilling tests and scores erc. A number of such data files can be stored in the computer
4. Monitoring students progress

Other contributions of computers are word processing to aid course development and data processing to aid administration. In addition, electronic mail is also used to communicate, change and exchange materials. The course teams can also use computers for conferences, establishing a communication channel among multiple writers and other professionals.

'ON-LINE' AND 'OFF-LINE' COMPUTERS

Computers can be used in distance learning in two modes—local mode and transmitted mode—local mode or 'off-line' computer stands on its own as an independent system helping the learner to work on his own. In transmitted mode, one computer is connected to another computer which is 'on-line' and then the operation depends upon communication between these devices. By inter-connecting the computers, a complex learning Network can be created which could link all distance learners with their teacher and with a central institution.

NETWORK TECHNOLOGY (INTERNET, E-MAIL ETC.)

Information Technology broadly deals with the application of technology in the field of information. In this process, media, computer, operations related to hardware and internet play a vital role in education especially in class-room instruction. New technologies which are emerging need to be integrated in order to provide meaningful and complete information. An effort to this direction has led to constitute a NETWORK. It makes the flow of information very simple, easy, and effective on the part of transmitter (teacher) and receiver (student).

The basic structure involved in NETWORK is:

(i) Interlinkages. Defferent components involved in Information Technology are interconnected. The relevant information is passed on from one channel to another. The whole NETWORK is based on the nature and type of interlinkages (interconnectivity).

(ii) Communication. The second component in INTERNET is effective communication. Messages are passed on from one place to another. Information reaches from one point to another. Without any loss of information, complete message is commnunicated.

(iii) System. NETWORK operates through a system. There are sub-systems. Each sub-system performs its function. The integrated one whole of sub-systems leads to work as much expanded and multiple functions.

NETWORK is a vast cyberspace where one can gather, disseminate and exchange all types of information. An arrangement consisting of two or more computers is called NETWORK. It is a physical medium used to transport the data. A computer network is created when several computers are linked by data communication channels. Each computer in a network can have its own processing capabilities and can also share hardware, data files and programmes. Following are the types of Computer Network:

1. Local Area Network. A local area network is two or more computers directly linked with in a small well defined area such as a room, building or a group of closely placed buildings.

A LAN may be made up of only microcomputers or any combination of micro-computers and large systems.

A Local Area Network usually consists of the following:

(i) Two or more computers.

(ii) Peripheral devices such as printers and hard-disk drives.

(iii) Software to control the operation of the computers.

(iv) Special cables.

(v) A plug in board to handle the data transmission.

2. MAN (Metropolitan Area Network). Man is basically a bigger version of a LAN, and normally used similar technology. It might cover a group of nearby corporate offices or a city and might be either private or public. A MAN just has one or two cables and does not contain switching elements. A MAN can support both data and voice and might even be related to the local cable television network.

3. WAN (Wide Area Network). A WAN is two or more computers that are geographically dispensed, linked by communication facilities such as telephone system or microwaves relays. This type of network is usually limited to use by large corporations and government agencies because of the high costs involved in building and manitaining them.

The main difference between a WAN and LAN is that, the LAN is under the complete control of the owner, whereas the WAN needs the involvement of another authority like telecom department.

(i) LANs are successful and capable of handling very high data transfer rates at low cost because of the small area covered.

(ii) LANs have a lower error rate than WANs.

Types of WAN

There are mainly two types of WAN:

Public Networks.

Private Natworks.

Public Networks. Public Netowrks are those Networks which are installed and run by the telecommunication authorities and are made available to any organisation or individual who go for their subscription.

Private Networks. The basic technique used in all forms of Private WAN is to use private circuits to link the locations to be served by the network. Between these fixed points the owners of the network have complete freedom to use the circuits in any way they want.

10.14 Internet

Internet is a World-wide Computer Network that contains a large collection of information which could be made avaliable to you on your computer. The person having internet connection can retrieve any information of individual interest.

Internet is the abbreviation of Inter-network System. The Internet is the name for a vast, Worldwide system consisting of people, information and computers. It is also described as a network of networks because these are more than one lakh readily accessible through the Internet. Internet is the largest and most complete learning tool for a group of people with varied educational backgrounds and interests. Teachers, students, businessmen and other educators can share ideas instantly across vast distances. For scientific and research community, internet is an essential and indispensable tool.

Through Internet Scientists can gain and enjoy instant access to the world's most advanced research facilities and discuss their research problems with others, working in the same field.

It also serves as an encyclopaedia since one can get the desired information in detail on any subject of his interest.

History of Internet

ARPANET (Advanced Research Projects Agency Network) laid the foundation of today's Internet almost three decades ago. It was establised to test the security of a network.

Advantages of Internet

Internet is playing a very important role in the National Development by giving the following major benefits to the citizens world-wide:

—Education —Shopping

—Advertising —Financial Services

—Government —Careers and so on.

Using the Internet's vast resources, one can communicate with people from all over the world and about any desired subject of choice.

APPLICATION OF INTERNET

Internet being a network of networks spread world-wide is capable of offering the following major services :

(a) E-Mail

(c) WWW (World Wide Web)

Electronic-mail

E-mail is an application in which any user as a network can send/receive letters on his computer terminal to/from any person in the world who has an electronic mail address. Internet provides a world-wide electonic mail facility.

The general format of Internet e-mail address is:

< name of addressee > @ < identity of his dept. >

< Institution > < identity of Indian Network > < country code >.

Mail can be sent only to individuals but to groups, by using group identity. The Network takes care to see that the mail is delivered safely if it leaves the user's terminal.

WWW

World-wide web offers facilities to the users to share information with others. This is the fastest growing part of the internet. The web is a vast network of documents and it also gives access to every internet service. The Web server can publish text and graphics including sound and video.

10.15 Website

Website makes a user as a mode of internet. This means that if a university decides to float its own website, then all information regarding admission, scholarships, rules and regulations, courses it offers, department, staff and their profiles, workshops, conferences, seminars to be conducted etc., can be kept at university's computer centre. This computer can be accessed by any member on Internet for any particular course: it will be automatically listed with all its details. This website is important to a university or a company to offer 24 hours services and on line help to international clients.

Developing a website on Internet is a costly affair as far as hardware and other costs are concerned.

Conclusion. Learning is the result of internal cognitive processes within the learner whereas instruction is a way of organising and sequencing learning experience. A good software should not only organise learning experiences but also aim at active cognitive processes within the learner. The objectives of software and hardware are to impart knowledge, inform and entertain also. The proper handling of hardware and software contributes to the economy of time, resources and energy of teacher and students.

REFERENCES

Barker P. (1987)—Author Language for CAL. Macmillan Education Ltd., London.

Charterjee R.K. (1989)—Mass Communication NBT India.

Dean, E. & Whit Lock. Q (1988)—J. Handbook of Computer Based Technology, Kogan Page, London.

Kulkarni S.S.—Introduction to Education Teaching A System Approach to Macro Level Education, Oxford Company.

MC. Luhan (1964)—Understanding Media Routludge, London, 1964

Rahman Saulat (1976)—A Study in Educational Television Ministry of Education, Govt. of India.

❒